CAMBRIDGE

The Cambridge Guide to

OET Nursing

Student's Book

With Audio and
Resources Download

Catherine Leyshon | Gurleen Khaira | Virginia Allum

OET is owned by Cambridge Boxhill Language Assessment,
a venture between Cambridge Assessment English and
Box Hill Institute, Australia.

Cambridge University Press
www.cambridge.org/elt

Cambridge Assessment English
www.cambridgeenglish.org

Information on this title: www.cambridge.org/9781108881647

First published 2020

20 19 18 17 16 15 14 13 12 11 10 9 8 7 6 5 4 3 2 1

Printed in Italy by Rotolito S.p.A

A catalogue record for this publication is available from the British Library

ISBN 978-1-108-88164-7 Student's Book

Contents

Acknowledgements

The authors and publishers acknowledge the following sources of copyright material and are grateful for the permissions granted. While every effort has been made, it has not always been possible to identify the sources of all the material used, or to trace all copyright holders. If any omissions are brought to our notice, we will be happy to include the appropriate acknowledgements on reprinting and in the next update to the digital edition, as applicable.

Text

Listening Part A Track 2.5 and Part C Track 2.15: Cambridge Boxhill Language Assessment for the text 'Physiotherapist talking to a patient' and 'Interview with a dietician on Omega 3 supplements'. Copyright © Cambridge Boxhill Language Assessment. Reproduced with kind permission; **Reading Part A, B and C and Listening Part C**: Nursing Times for the following texts: 'Silver sulphadiazine' by NT Contributor, *Nursing Times*, 25.03.2004; 'Selecting IV fluids to manage fluid loss in critically ill patients' by NT Contributor, *Nursing Times*, 18.11.2018; 'Wound Care Fact File' by NT Contributor, *Nursing Times*, 24.06.2003; 'Improving pain management for patients in a hospital burns unit' by Steve Ford, *Nursing Times*, 26.03.2004; 'Nil by mouth: best practice and patient education' by NT Contributor, *Nursing Times*, 20.06.2014; 'Statins increase type 2 diabetes risk in susceptible individuals' by Steve Ford, *Nursing Times*, 24.08.2017; 'Major review backs benefit of statins over risk' by Steve Ford, *Nursing Times*, 09.09.2016; 'Study says there's no link between cholesterol and heart disease' by NT CONTRIBUTOR, *Nursing Times*, 20.06.2016; 'Statins linked to small increase in diabetes risk' by Steve Ford, *Nursing Times*, 24.09.2014; 'Media stories about statins cut compliance' by Steve Ford, *Nursing Times*, 30.06.2016; 'Debate: should the use of e-cigarettes be encouraged among smokers?' by Wendy Preston, *Nursing Times*, 25.03.2019; 'Evidence that smartphones help patients complete TB treatment' by Nursing Times News Desk, *Nursing Times*, 25.03.2019; 'Caesarean babies linked to obesity in later life' by The Press Association, *Nursing Times*, 27.02.2014; 'Caesareans should not be chosen for social convenience' by NT Contributor, *Nursing Times*, 21.11.2011; 'Review concludes caesarean birth 'safest' for breech delivery' by Steve Ford, *Nursing Times*, 29.07.2015; 'The high impact actions for nursing and midwifery 7: promoting normal birth' by NT Contributor, *Nursing Times*, 23.08.2010; 'Caesareans should not be chosen for social convenience' by NT Contributor, *Nursing Times*, 23.11.2011; 'Removing nine risk factors could 'prevent' third of dementia cases' by Steve Ford, *Nursing Times*, 20.07.2017. Copyright © Nursing Times. Reproduced with kind permission; **Practice Test 1 and 2:** New Scientist for the text from 'Egg Freezing', 'Circadian Rhythms' and 'Medical Cannabis'. Copyright © New Scientist Ltd. All rights reserved. Distributed by Tribune Content Agency; **Practice Test 2:** Nursing Times for the text from 'Tools and techniques to improve teamwork and avoid patient harm' by Wayne Robson, *Nursing Times*, 12.12.2016. Copyright © Nursing Times. Reproduced with kind permission; **Practice Test 1 Track PT-1.3**: Frontiers for the text 'Presentation on Myalgic Encephalomyelitis'. Comes under CC BY 4.0. **Practice Test 2 Track PT-2.3:** 'Nanopatch' by Mark Kendall. Copyright © Mark Kendall.

Photography

All the photos are sourced from Getty Images.

Intro: Sam Edwards/OJO Images; **Section I**: Jetta Productions Inc/DigitalVision; **Section II**: Caiaimage/Rafal Rodzoch; Tom Werner/DigitalVision; Morsa Images/DigitalVision; sturti/E+; Jose Luis Pelaez Inc/DigitalVision; Hero Images; Universal Images Group; skynesher/E+; izusek/E+; **Section III:** Jose Luis Pelaez Inc/DigitalVision; Hero Images; sturti/E+; Ariel Skelley/DigitalVision; SDI Productions/E+; DragonImages/iStock/Getty Images Plus; AJ_Watt/E+; **Section IV:** SDI Productions/E+; Hero Images; sturti; Manop Phimsit/EyeEm; Morsa Images/DigitalVision; Maskot; Jose Luis Pelaez Inc/DigitalVision; Cecilie_Arcurs/E+; Tinpixels/E+; **Section V:** Maskot; Jose Luis Pelaez Inc/DigitalVision; Cecilie_Arcurs/E+; Tinpixels/E+; **Section VI:** SDI Productions/E+; **Icons:** bamlou/DigitalVision Vectors; ndesign.

Cover photography by vm/E+/Getty Images.

Audio

dsound recording Ltd.

Design and Typeset

Q2A Media Services Pvt Ltd.

INTRODUCTION

CHAPTER 1

ABOUT THIS BOOK

This book has been designed to provide candidates preparing for OET Nursing with better knowledge of the test, along with the strategies and language skills required to succeed. Whether you are a candidate studying independently for the test or a teacher preparing students in a classroom setting, you will find ample test knowledge and skills practice here to help achieve the score you need.

How the book is organised

The book is divided into six sections aimed at improving relevant skills, and knowledge of test format and strategies. There are also sample practice tests that give learners the opportunity to apply what they have learned.

Section I: Introduction

'OET Fact File' covers the format of the test and essential information about OET that every test taker should know.

Sections II and III: Listening and Reading

These sections are divided into chapters that correspond to the three parts of the Listening and Reading sub-tests (Parts A, B and C). In each part, you will gain an understanding of the types of audio and text extracts that you can expect to listen to and read, and acquire strategies and skills that you can use to approach the tasks, and the extracts on which they are based. For example, 'Reading Part A' includes a complete set of 20 questions based on four extracts, just like in the test. However, instead of just having you complete the test, the questions and extracts are analysed, to help you develop strategies for approaching them on Test Day.

There are also some tasks in these sections that are not like those in the OET test. These are designed to help you acquire the skills you need to approach the test questions. Some may appear before a sample test question, while others may need to be done after completing a question. For example, you may be asked to think actively about the context of a Listening extract or reflect on how you arrived at an answer in Reading, to help you answer other questions. Most of the answers are explained either in the chapter or in the answer key. Reading these explanations is important because they help you understand the rationales behind the correct answers, and the misconceptions behind the incorrect ones.

Sections IV and V: Writing and Speaking

These sections are divided into two parts. In 'Preparing to Write the Letter' and 'Preparing for the Speaking Sub-test', the sub-skills required to meet the assessment criteria are discussed and demonstrated, and opportunities provided to practise these sub-skills in healthcare scenarios typical of OET.

In Speaking, you practise sub-skills that correspond directly to the linguistic and communication criteria. Some tasks involve listening to audio recordings of parts of role plays to help you understand the criteria better, and practise the relevant sub-skills.

In Writing, you are provided with exercises that focus on a sub-skill of writing relevant across the different assessment criteria. There are examples of various different kinds of letters, each based on specific case notes. The answer key contains additional explanations as well as sample answers.

In the Writing and Speaking sections, the practice sub-test appears at the end. This is to provide you with the opportunity to practise and develop the relevant subskills by doing a series of smaller tasks, before you undertake the complete test. It will also enable you to assess the progress you have made as a result of working through these sections. Answers for the sample practice sub-tests are provided in the answer key.

Section VI: Practice Tests

There are two practice tests, which are complete OET sub-tests for Listening, Reading, Writing and Speaking. The answer key is available online and you can check your answers there.

Features common to all sections

Here are the features that are common to all four main sections of this book (Listening, Reading, Writing and Speaking).

An introduction: Since OET is a profession-specific test, candidates need to understand the reasoning behind the format of the sub-tests and the tasks. The introduction to each sub-test section provides insights into why the format and the skills being tested are relevant, and how they are directly applicable to workplace contexts. It also explains the healthcare settings for all tasks, the distribution of marks and the allotted time. The introductions to the Writing and Speaking sections give more information on the assessment criteria, to help you understand how your performance is marked and what you can do to improve criteria-specific scores.

Tips for scoring: These will provide you with simple strategies you can use while preparing and on Test Day, to help achieve higher grades.

Frequently Asked Questions (FAQs): Candidates usually have a lot of questions about the sub-tests. These FAQs help address some common questions and misconceptions.

How to use this book

This book can be used both by candidates working independently to prepare for the test and, in a classroom situation, by teachers who are helping students prepare for the test.

If you are a candidate working independently, the tasks in each section will help build the skills you need for successful OET scores. For Listening and Reading, answers are explained thoroughly within the section or in the answer key, which may also contain additional explanations. For Writing and Speaking, sample answers to practice tests and other tasks are provided in the answer key.

If you are a teacher helping students prepare, you can use the tasks to help them build essential language skills and test-taking strategies. This book can also be used to supplement existing material you may be using.

There is no recommended order for completing the sections; you can start with any sub-test. However, it is recommended that test-takers read 'OET Fact File' before beginning their preparation, in order to understand the purpose of OET. The practice tests in Section VI can be done at intervals rather than all at once. This will help you monitor progress over a period of time.

Online resources

The online resources can be accessed using the code provided on the inside front cover of this book. The online pack contains the following:

- Audio tracks used in the Listening and Speaking sections, and in the Practice Tests
- Transcripts of all audio tracks
- Answer key for all sections (including sample answers for Speaking and Writing)

There are several ways to make the most of these online resources. Teachers using the book can play the audio tracks in class for practice, as well as when administering the sample tests. Transcripts of the Listening audio extracts can be used to analyse answers and understand the structure of the consultation, presentation, interview, etc. Teachers could also use transcripts and audio recordings to design other activities to practise the sub-skills required to meet the communication or clinical criteria in Speaking. However, when using an audio recording to administer a test task, it is recommended that it be played only once, and that students should be hearing it for the first time. After that, it can be used for other activities.

Understanding what OET is all about and how it is structured will help you perform better in the test. This section contains basic information about OET that every test taker should know.

What is OET?

OET is an internationally recognised English language proficiency test developed specifically for healthcare professionals. It tests your ability to communicate effectively in an English-speaking healthcare workplace through four skills: Listening, Reading, Writing and Speaking. The test materials and tasks reflect real-life situations you are likely to face when you enter the workplace.

OET caters to 12 healthcare professions:

- Dentistry
- Dietetics
- Medicine
- Nursing
- Occupational Therapy
- Optometry
- Pharmacy
- Physiotherapy
- Podiatry
- Radiography
- Speech Pathology
- Veterinary Science

OET comprises four components or sub-tests. The Listening and Reading sub-tests are the same for candidates from all professions, while the Writing and Speaking sub-tests have been made profession-specific in order to ensure that OET is a test of language proficiency and not of medical knowledge.

How is OET beneficial?

Successfully completing OET not only ensures recognition from healthcare organisations, but also gives you an increased sense of confidence in your own ability in English. The skills you learn while preparing for OET will be useful for the rest of your professional life. As you prepare for and then take the test, you are very likely to see your confidence increasing because you will be able to gauge how well you are communicating when performing everyday tasks at work.

How is OET different from other general and academic English tests?

While a general or academic English test assesses you on everyday English or academic skills, OET tests your ability to use English for a specific purpose in a healthcare setting. OET uses real workplace scenarios typical of those that healthcare professionals in English-speaking countries would encounter, and expects you to be proficient in the skills required to communicate successfully in those situations. That is why the Writing and Speaking sub-tests are designed differently for each of the 12 professions that OET tests.

Who marks or scores OET test papers?

OET is scored by trained Assessors and by computers. The Assessors mark Listening Part A and Reading Part A with a detailed marking guide. Answer booklets are assigned to them at random, which helps to ensure that results are fair. Answers to Reading and Listening Parts B and C are scanned and automatically scored by a computer.

OET has a strict process for scoring that ensures that test results in Speaking and Writing are objective and unbiased. In the Speaking sub-test, the test-day interlocutor (the person who plays the role of the patient in the test) does not take part in the assessment process. Each Speaking sub-test is recorded and these recorded audio files are scored by at least two trained Assessors. Similarly, Writing sub-test answer scripts are scored by at least two trained Assessors. In the event that the two Assessors assign different scores, the audio files and answer scripts will be marked by a third senior Assessor who has not previously been involved with the assessment.

What is the application process?

You can apply for OET on the website www.occupationalenglishtest.org. Ensure that you check the test dates for your chosen profession before you register for the test. If you are a candidate with health-related or any other special needs, you can make requests for requirements on the *Help and Information* section of the OET website when you apply. You will need to apply before the application closing date mentioned on the website.

Where is OET conducted?

OET is available at several locations globally. The website lists the available test dates in different locations throughout the year.

What is the best way to prepare?

Your preparation should focus on two equally important aspects:

- Improving language proficiency through regular practice: Work at your English skills daily as soon as you decide that you want to take OET. Language proficiency cannot be developed in a week or two, so practise every day, right from the start.
- Familiarising yourself with test structure and task types: Understand what skills the different sub-tests assess, and how to approach the various types of tasks/questions. Sample question papers are available for further practice, and it is valuable to do several of these to reinforce your learning and your familiarity with the format of the questions. These can be accessed from the OET website.

What happens on Test Day?

OET has a list of regulations that detail what you must and must not bring with you into the venue on Test Day. For example, MP3 players and mobile phones are not permitted, whereas you must bring the national identity document that you used in your application. It is very important to read the latest version of these regulations on the OET website well in advance of Test Day.

You'll receive information from the Test Venue prior to Test Day telling you when you should arrive at the venue for registration. Remember that the registration time is not the same as your test time, so be prepared to arrive earlier. The exact timings of sub-tests are available in the timetable that you will receive by email after you apply and pay for OET. You can also view your timetable online in your OET profile.

Where are results published?

You can view your scores and download official copies of the *Statement of Results* from your online profile on the OET website. You can also give verification institutions permission to view your results through the online portal.

Summary of OET

As stated earlier, OET tests the four language skills of Listening, Reading, Writing and Speaking. Each skill has a separate sub-test. While the Listening and Reading sub-tests are the same for all the OET professions, the Writing and Speaking sub-tests are designed to test your ability in a profession-specific context.

Let's look at an overall description of the four separate components of OET.

Sub-test	Duration	Number of tasks	Task content	Number of test items or questions
Listening	Approximately 40 mins	3	• Two consultations • Six short monologues or dialogues • Two talks/presentations/interviews	42
Reading	60 mins	3	• Four short texts • Six short extracts from the workplace • Two comprehensive texts	42
Writing	Reading time: 5 mins Writing time: 40 mins	1	• Letter writing specific to each profession	1
Speaking	20 mins	2	• Two role plays between a patient and healthcare practitioner	2

It is also important to know what each sub-test consists of and requires of you. Here is a summary of each sub-test.

Listening

The Listening sub-test consists of three parts (A, B and C), each based on topics of general medical interest that can be understood by candidates from all 12 OET professions. The total test duration is approximately 40 minutes, which includes pauses for you to check your answers.

There is a total of 42 questions and each question carries one mark, so the maximum score for the Listening sub-test is 42 marks. In order to obtain a B score, you typically need to score at least 30 marks (out of 42).

Recordings are played *only once*, and you must write your answers while listening. You have two minutes at the end of the test to check your answers.

Part A: Professional–patient consultation extracts

You will hear two consultations involving a healthcare professional and a patient. In this part, your ability to identify specific information is assessed, as you complete the healthcare professional's notes by filling in the blanks. There are headings to help you. Each extract is about five minutes long.

Part B: Short dialogues or monologues in a healthcare setting

You will hear six recordings of about a minute each. These will either be dialogues between professionals or between a professional and a patient, or monologues in which one healthcare professional talks. This part tests your ability to identify purpose or opinion, and listen for gist and detail. For each extract, there is one multiple-choice question. You need to identify the correct answer from the three options given.

Part C: Presentations, talks or interviews with healthcare professionals

You will hear two short presentations or interviews of about five minutes each. This section tests your ability to understand the kind of discussions on medical topics that you may typically hear at the workplace. There are six multiple-choice questions for each extract, each with three answer options.

Listening sub-test overview				
Part	Task	Question type	Duration	Marks
Part A	Two consultations involving a healthcare professional and patient	Fill in the blanks guided by headings	15 mins	24
Part B	Six short dialogues or monologues in workplace contexts	Multiple choice	15 mins	6
Part C	Talk/presentation by a healthcare professional	Multiple choice	15 mins	12

Reading

The Reading sub-test has three parts: A, B and C. You can expect a variety of text types, from policy documents to dosage charts. The whole Reading test is 60 minutes; this includes time for reading the questions, answering them, and checking your answers. The test carries a total of 42 marks with Part A accounting for 20 marks, Part B for 6 marks and Part C for 16 marks. If you want a grade B, you typically need to score a minimum of 30 marks in this section.

Part A: Fast reading

Part A tests your ability to skim different types of texts and extract key information. So you will read four short texts of a type that you would typically encounter while treating patients, such as dosage charts, instructions on how to administer medication, or advice to give patients. One of these texts will include visual or numerical information. There is a total of 20 questions to answer in 15 minutes. These can be in the form of matching exercises, sentence completion tasks or short answer (one-word or short phrase) questions. You need to write your answers in a separate answer booklet for Part A, which is collected at the end of the 15 minutes. So you need to use this allocated time for Part A efficiently, as you won't get an opportunity to check your answers for this part later in the test.

Part B: Careful reading based on workplace extracts

Part B tests your ability to identify the gist, main point or details of these texts. So you will read six short texts (100–150 words each) based on different workplace documents such as guidelines, manuals, policy documents, emails and memos. There is one multiple-choice question per text, each with three options to choose from.

Part C: Careful reading based on longer, comprehensive texts

Part C tests your ability to comprehend slightly more dense sources of information, identify opinions and infer meaning. So you will read two texts (800 words each) based on healthcare topics similar to those found in academic or professional journals. For each text there are eight multiple-choice questions, each with four possible answers.

You will record your answers to the questions for Parts B and C in the same answer booklet, by shading the circle next to the correct option.

Reading sub-test overview				
Part	Task	Question type	Duration	Marks
Part A	Fast reading of four texts	Short answer, matching, sentence completion, etc.	15 mins	20
Part B	Six workplace extracts	Three-option multiple choice	45 mins	6
Part C	Two comprehensive extracts from medical/professional journals	Four-option multiple choice		16

Writing

There is a specific Writing sub-test for each of the 12 professions covered by OET. In the case of OET Nursing, the task involves writing a letter (of discharge, referral, transfer or advice) to another health professional or client after reading the 'stimulus material', which is typically a set of patient case notes and/or other related documentation. The letter should be approximately 180–200 words in length.

The total duration of the sub-test is 45 minutes: five minutes at the beginning to read the material and the remaining 40 minutes to compose the letter. You won't be allowed to write anything on the question paper during the initial five minutes, so use this time to read the case notes carefully.

In order to succeed at the task, you need to select relevant parts of the stimulus material and construct a logical, structured letter keeping in mind the target reader. You will be assigned a band score for each of the following criteria:

- Purpose
- Content
- Conciseness and clarity
- Genre and style
- Organisation and layout
- Language

Each criterion is assigned a band score from 0–7, except *Purpose*, which has a band score of 0–3. If you want to achieve a higher grade such as a B, you should aim for higher band scores. It is very important to study the assessment criteria and level descriptors for the sub-test thoroughly so that you know what the Assessors are looking for in your answer, and what might cause you to lose marks. On the following pages you will find summaries of these criteria and level descriptors, as well as glossaries that explain the terminology used in them. These are also available at www.occupationalenglishtest.org.

WRITING Assessment Criteria and Level Descriptors

Band	Purpose	Content	Conciseness & Clarity	Genre & Style	Organisation & Layout	Language
7	Purpose of document is immediately apparent and sufficiently expanded as required	Content is appropriate to intended reader and addresses what is needed to continue care (key information is included; no important details missing); content from case notes is accurately represented	Length of document is appropriate to case and reader (no irrelevant information included); information is summarised effectively and presented clearly	Writing is clinical/factual and appropriate to genre and reader (discipline and knowledge); technical language, abbreviations and polite language are used appropriately for document and recipient	Organisation and paragraphing are appropriate, logical and clear; key information is highlighted and sub-sections are well organised; document is well laid out	Language features (spelling/punctuation/vocabulary/grammar/sentence structure) are accurate and do not interfere with meaning
6			Performance shares features of bands 5 and 7			
5	Purpose of document is apparent but not sufficiently highlighted or expanded	Content is appropriate to intended reader and mostly addresses what is needed to continue care; content from case notes is generally accurately represented	Length of document is mostly appropriate to case and reader; information is mostly summarised effectively and presented clearly	Writing is clinical/factual and appropriate to genre and reader with occasional, minor inappropriacies; technical language, abbreviations and polite language are used appropriately with minor inconsistencies	Organisation and paragraphing are generally appropriate, logical and clear; occasional lapses of organisation in sub-sections and/or highlighting of key information; layout is generally good	Minor slips in language generally do not interfere with meaning
4			Performance shares features of bands 3 and 5			
3	Purpose of document is not immediately apparent and may show very limited expansion	Content is mostly appropriate to intended reader; some key information (about case care) may be missing; there may be some inaccuracies in content	Inclusion of some irrelevant information distracts from overall clarity of document; attempt to summarise only partially successful	Writing is at times inappropriate to the document or target reader; over-reliance on technical language and abbreviations may distract reader	Organisation and paragraphing are not always logical, creating strain for the reader; key information may not be highlighted; layout is mostly appropriate with some lapses	Inaccuracies in language, in particular in complex structures, cause minor strain for the reader but do not interfere with meaning
2			Performance shares features of bands 1 and 3			
1	Purpose of document is partially obscured/unclear and/or misunderstood	Content does not provide intended reader sufficient information about the case and what is needed to continue care; key information is missing or inaccurate	Clarity of document is obscured by the inclusion of many unnecessary details; attempt to summarise not successful	The writing shows inadequate understanding of the genre and target reader; mis- or over-use of technical language and abbreviations cause strain for the reader	Organisation not logical, putting strain on the reader or heavy reliance on case note structure; key information is not well highlighted and the layout may not be appropriate	Inaccuracies in language cause considerable strain for the reader and may interfere with meaning
0			Performance below Band 1			

Source: www.occupationalenglishtest.org

WRITING Assessment Criteria and Level Descriptors

Criterion	Description
Purpose • Helps the reader get a **quick and precise sense** of what is asked of them	Due to time constraints, health professionals want to understand the purpose behind a written handover document (e.g. referral letter) very quickly and efficiently. This criterion therefore examines how clearly the writing communicates the purpose of the document to the reader. The purpose for writing should be introduced early in the document and then clearly expanded on later (often near the end of the document). The purpose should be easily and immediately identifiable to the reader, so there is no need to search for it. For example, a writer might at the beginning of the letter write, "I'm writing to you today to refer patient X who is now being discharged from hospital into your care'. Later in the letter, specific instructions for the health care professional on continuing care should be listed.
Content • Considers **necessary information** (audience awareness: what does the reader need to know?) • Considers **accuracy** of information	The content criterion examines a number of aspects of the content: • all key information is included • information is accurately represented Audience awareness is key here. The writing needs to be appropriate to the reader (and their knowledge of the case) and what they need to know to continue care.
Conciseness & Clarity • Considers **irrelevant information** (audience awareness: what doesn't the reader need to know?) • Considers how **effectively** the case is **summarised** (audience awareness: no time is wasted)	Health professionals value concise and clear communication. This criterion, therefore also considers: • whether unnecessary information from the notes is included and how distracting this may be to the reader, i.e. Does this affect clarity? Is there any information that could be left out? • how well the information (the case) is summarised and how clearly this summary is presented to the reader.
Genre & Style • Considers the **appropriateness** of features such as **register and tone** to the document's purpose and audience	Referral letters and similar written handover documents need to show awareness of genre by being written in a clinical/ factual manner (e.g. not including personal feelings and judgements) and awareness of the target reader through using professional register and tone. The use of abbreviations should not be overdone thereby assuming common prior knowledge. If written to a medical colleague in a similar discipline, then judicious use of abbreviations and technical terms would be entirely appropriate, but if the medical colleague was in a totally different discipline, or a letter was from a specialist to a GP, more explanation and less shorthand would be desirable. If the target readership includes the patient, the information must be worded appropriately, e.g. minimising medical jargon.
Organisation & Layout • Considers **organisational features** of the document	Health professionals value documents that are clearly structured so it is easy for them to efficiently retrieve relevant information. This criterion examines how well the document is organised and laid out. It examines whether the paragraphing is appropriate, whether sub-sections within the document are logically organised, and whether key information is clearly highlighted to the reader so that it is not easily missed. The criterion also considers whether the layout of the document is appropriate.
Language • Considers aspects of language proficiency such as **vocabulary, grammar, spelling, punctuation**	Health professionals are concerned with linguistic features only to the extent that they facilitate or obstruct retrieval of information. This criterion examines whether the language is accurate, used appropriately and whether it interferes with reading comprehension or speed.

You will write your answer in pen or pencil in the space given in the answer booklet. There is space at the back of the booklet which you may use to make notes and plan your answer.

Writing sub-test overview				
Part	Task	Question type	Duration	Marks
Only one task	Letter of discharge/ referral or advice based on a specific workplace requirement	Write your answer in the booklet	Reading time: 5 mins Writing time: 40 mins	Band scores based on six criteria

Speaking

Like Writing, the Speaking sub-test is also specific to each profession. It tests your ability to communicate effectively in a consultation typical of your profession. There are two role plays between a patient and a health professional. The interviewer plays the role of the patient, relative or caregiver, while you play the role of the health professional.

Before the role plays begin, the interlocutor checks your identity and profession and engages in a short warm-up conversation about your professional background. This part is not assessed. You are then given your role play card, which states the setting, and provides a brief background and a set of instructions about your role in the consultation. You have three minutes to prepare for each role play, during which you may make notes on your card. If you have any questions about the content or the format of a role play, you can ask the interlocutor.

It is important to remember that the Speaking sub-test does not test your medical knowledge. Instead, an audio recording of your role plays is made, and assigned a band score from 0–6 based on the following linguistic criteria:

- Intelligibility
- Fluency
- Appropriateness of language
- Resources of grammar and expression

There are also five clinical communication criteria on which you are assessed. Your performance on these is given a band score from 0–3. These criteria are:

- Relationship building
- Understanding and incorporating the patient's perspective
- Providing structure
- Information gathering
- Information giving

If you want a grade B, you need to achieve the highest score in all the descriptors for each criterion. Candidates who get a grade B mostly achieve scores of 5 out of 6 in each linguistic criterion, and 2 out of 3 in each clinical communication criterion.

Here is a closer look at the Speaking assessment criteria and level descriptors.

SPEAKING Assessment Criteria and Level Descriptors (from September 2018)

I. Linguistic Criteria

Band	Intelligibility	Fluency	Appropriateness of Language	Resources of Grammar and Expression
6	• Pronunciation is easily understood and prosodic features (stress, intonation, rhythm) are used effectively. • L1 accent has no effect on intelligibility.	• Completely fluent speech at normal speed. • Any hesitation is appropriate and not a sign of searching for words or structures.	• Entirely appropriate register, tone and lexis for the context. • No difficulty at all in explaining technical matters in lay terms.	• Rich and flexible. • Wide range of grammar and vocabulary used accurately and flexibly. • Confident use of idiomatic speech.
5	• Easily understood. • Communication is not impeded by a few pronunciation or prosodic errors and/or noticeable L1 accent. • Minimal strain for the listener.	• Fluent speech at normal speed, with only occasional repetition or self-correction. • Hesitation may occasionally indicate searching for words or structures, but is generally appropriate.	• Mostly appropriate register, tone and lexis for the context. • Occasional lapses are not intrusive.	• Wide range of grammar and vocabulary generally used accurately and flexibly. • Occasional errors in grammar or vocabulary are not intrusive.
4	• Easily understood most of the time. • Pronunciation or prosodic errors and/or L1 accent at times cause strain for the listener.	• Uneven flow, with some repetition, especially in longer utterances. • Some evidence of searching for words, which does not cause serious strain. • Delivery may be staccato or too fast/slow.	• Generally appropriate register, tone and lexis for the context, but somewhat restricted and lacking in complexity. • Lapses are noticeable and at times reflect limited resources of grammar and expression.	• Sufficient resources to maintain the interaction. • Inaccuracies in vocabulary and grammar, particularly in more complex sentences, are sometimes intrusive. • Meaning is generally clear.
3	• Produces some acceptable features of spoken English. • Difficult to understand because errors in pronunciation/stress/intonation and/or L1 accent cause serious strain for the listener.	• Very uneven. • Frequent pauses and repetitions indicate searching for words or structures. • Excessive use of fillers and difficulty sustaining longer utterances cause serious strain for the listener.	• Some evidence of appropriate register, tone and lexis, but lapses are frequent and intrusive, reflecting inadequate resources of grammar and expression.	• Limited vocabulary and control of grammatical structures, except very simple sentences. • Persistent inaccuracies are intrusive.
2	• Often unintelligible. • Frequent errors in pronunciation/stress/intonation and/or L1 accent cause severe strain for the listener.	• Extremely uneven. • Long pauses, numerous repetitions and self-corrections make speech difficult to follow.	• Mostly inappropriate register, tone and lexis for the context.	• Very limited resources of vocabulary and grammar, even in simple sentences. • Numerous errors in word choice.
1	• Almost entirely unintelligible.	• Impossible to follow, consisting of isolated words and phrases and self-corrections, separated by long pauses.	• Entirely inappropriate register, tone and lexis for the context.	• Limited in all respects.
0	• Candidate does not provide any response.			

II. Clinical Communication Criteria

In the role play, there is evidence of the test taker ...

A. Indicators of relationship building

A1	initiating the interaction appropriately (greeting, introductions, nature of interview)
A2	demonstrating an attentive and respectful attitude
A3	adopting a non-judgemental approach
A4	showing empathy for feelings/predicament/emotional state

A. Relationship building

- 3 – Adept use
- 2 – Competent use
- 1 – Partially effective use
- 0 – Ineffective use

B. Indicators of understanding & incorporating the patient's perspective

B1	eliciting and exploring the patient's ideas/concerns/expectations
B2	picking up the patient's cues
B3	relating explanations to elicited ideas/concerns/expectations

B. Understanding & incorporating the patient's perspective

- 3 – Adept use
- 2 – Competent use
- 1 – Partially effective use
- 0 – Ineffective use

C. Indicators of providing structure

C1	sequencing the interview purposefully and logically
C2	signposting changes in topic
C3	using organising techniques in explanations

C. Providing structure

- 3 – Adept use
- 2 – Competent use
- 1 – Partially effective use
- 0 – Ineffective use

D. Indicators for information gathering

D1	facilitating the patient's narrative with active listening techniques, minimising interruption
D2	using initially open questions, appropriately moving to closed questions
D3	NOT using compound questions/leading questions
D4	clarifying statements which are vague or need amplification
D5	summarising information to encourage correction/invite further information

D. Information gathering

- 3 – Adept use
- 2 – Competent use
- 1 – Partially effective use
- 0 – Ineffective use

E. Indicators for information giving

E1	establishing initially what the patient already knows
E2	pausing periodically when giving information, using the response to guide next steps
E3	encouraging the patient to contribute reactions/feelings
E4	checking whether the patient has understood information
E5	discovering what further information the patient needs

E. Information giving

- 3 – Adept use
- 2 – Competent use
- 1 – Partially effective use
- 0 – Ineffective use

Source: www.occupationalenglishtest.org

You can prepare better if you understand what each criterion means and what Assessors will look out for when marking you on the linguistic and clinical communication criteria.

Speaking assessment criteria glossary

SPEAKING Assessment Criteria Glossary (from September 2018)

I. Linguistic Criteria

Intelligibility

This criterion refers to the ability to produce comprehensible speech. It includes such features as pronunciation, intonation, stress, rhythm and accent. Assessors consider whether the candidate

- pronounces words/sounds clearly (especially final consonants, recognisable vowels, correct word stress)
- projects/pitches the voice appropriately, without mumbling or slurred speech
- uses intonation and selective stress effectively/appropriately (to enhance meaning)
- produces a natural English sentence rhythm.

NB While an L1 accent is to be expected in even the most able candidate, the main point to consider is the extent to which this causes strain for the listener. In many cases, accent poses no impediment to communication.

Fluency

This criterion refers to the rate and flow of speech. Assessors consider whether the candidate speaks

- at a normal rate (not too fast or too slow) that can be easily understood
- continuously and smoothly, with pauses or hesitations that are situationally appropriate, rather than a sign of searching for words or structures (indicated by disruptive false starts, excessive use of fillers, or unnecessary repetition of words or phrases).

Appropriateness of Language

This criterion refers to the ability to use language, register and tone that are suitable for the situation and the patient. In particular, assessors consider whether the candidate

- uses expressions comprehensible to a lay person in explaining technical procedures or medical conditions (are inappropriate choices a barrier to communication?)
- adopts a tone of voice suitable to the situation, with the flexibility to adapt as necessary.

Resources of Grammar and Expression

This criterion refers to the range and accuracy of the candidate's linguistic repertoire. Assessors consider whether

- the candidate's vocabulary and control of grammatical expression are adequate to express necessary ideas clearly and unambiguously, and whether any deficits form a barrier to communication
- the candidate can paraphrase when required
- the candidate has the capacity to maintain longer utterances rather than single sentences, with appropriate use of cohesive devices
- can use idiomatic expressions accurately.

II. Clinical Communication Criteria

A. Indicators of relationship building

A1	Initiating the interaction appropriately (greeting, introductions, nature of interview)	Initiating the interview appropriately helps establish rapport and a supportive environment. Initiation involves greeting the patient, introducing yourself, clarifying the patient's name and clarifying your role in their care. The nature of the interview can be explained and, if necessary, negotiated.
A2	Demonstrating an attentive and respectful attitude	Throughout the interview, demonstrating attentiveness and respect establishes trust with the patient, lays down the foundation for a collaborative relationship and ensures that the patient understands your motivation to help. Examples of such behaviour would include attending to the patient's comfort, asking permission and consent to proceed, and being sensitive to potentially embarrassing or distressing matters.
A3	Demonstrating a non-judgemental approach	Accepting the patient's perspective and views reassuringly and non-judgementally without initial rebuttal is a key component of relationship building. A judgemental response to patients' ideas and concerns devalues their contributions. A non-judgemental response would include accepting the patient's perspective and acknowledging the legitimacy of the patient to hold their own views and feelings.
A4	Showing empathy for feelings/ predicament/emotional state	Empathy is one of the key skills of building the relationship. Empathy involves the understanding and sensitive appreciation of another person's predicament or feelings and the communication of that understanding back to the patient in a supportive way. This can be achieved through both non-verbal and verbal behaviours. Even with audio alone, some non-verbal behaviours such as the use of silence and appropriate voice tone in response to a patient's expression of feelings can be observed. Verbal empathy makes this more explicit by specifically naming and appreciating the patient's emotions or predicament.

B. Indicators of understanding & incorporating the patient's perspective

B1	Eliciting and exploring patient's ideas/concerns/expectations	Understanding the patient's perspective is a key component of patient-centred health care. Each patient has a unique experience of sickness that includes the feelings, thoughts, concerns and effect on life that any episode of sickness induces. Patients may either volunteer this spontaneously (as direct statements or cues) or in response to health professionals' enquiries.
B2	Picking up the patient's cues	Patients are generally eager to tell us about their own thoughts and feelings but often do so indirectly through verbal hints, or changes in non-verbal behaviour (such as vocal cues including hesitation or change in volume). Picking up these cues is essential for exploring both the biomedical and the patient's perspectives.

	Some of the techniques for picking up cues would include echoing, i.e. repeating back what has just been said and either adding emphasis where appropriate or turning the echoed statement into a question, e.g. *'Something could be done….?'*. Another possibility is more overtly checking out statements or hints, e.g. *'I sense that you are not happy with the explanations you've been given in the past'*.
B3	**Relating explanations to elicited ideas/ concerns/expectations**	One of the key reasons for discovering the patient's perspective is to incorporate this into explanations often in the later aspects of the interview. If the explanation does not address the patient's individual ideas, concerns and expectations, then recall, understanding and satisfaction suffer as the patient is worrying about their still unaddressed concerns.

C. Indicators of **providing structure**

C1	**Sequencing the interview purposefully and logically**	It is the responsibility of the health professional to maintain a logical sequence apparent to the patient as the interview unfolds. An ordered approach to organisation helps both professional and patient in efficient and accurate data gathering and information giving. This needs to be balanced with the need to be patient-centred and follow the patient's needs. Flexibility and logical sequencing need to be thoughtfully combined. It is more obvious when sequencing is inadequate: the health professional will meander aimlessly or jump around between segments of the interview, making the patient unclear as to the point of specific lines of enquiry.
C2	**Signposting changes in topic**	Signposting is a key skill in enabling patients to understand the structure of the interview by making the organisation overt: not only the health professional but also the patient needs to understand where the interview is going and why. A signposting statement introduces and draws attention to what we are about to say. For instance, it is helpful to use a signposting statement to introduce a summary. Signposting can also be used to make the progression from one section to another and explain the rationale for the next section.
C3	**Using organising techniques in explanations**	A variety of skills help to organise explanations in a way that leads particularly to increased patient recall and understanding. Skills include: categorisation in which the health professional informs the patient about which categories of information are to be provided labelling in which important points are explicitly labelled by the health professional; this can be achieved by using emphatic phrases or adverb intensifiers chunking in which information is delivered in chunks with clear gaps in between sections before proceeding repetition and summary of important points.

D1	Facilitating the patient's narrative with active listening techniques, minimising interruption	Listening to the patient's narrative, particularly at the beginning of an interview, enables the health professional to more efficiently discover the story, hear the patient's perspective, appear supportive and interested and pick up cues to the patient's feelings. Interruption of the narrative has the opposite effect and, in particular, generally leads to a predominantly biomedical history, omitting the patient's perspective. Observable skills of active listening techniques include: the use of silence and pausing verbal encouragement such as *um, uh-huh, I see* echoing and repetition such as *'chest pain?'* or *'not coping?'* paraphrasing and interpretation such as *'Are you thinking that when John gets even more ill, you won't be strong enough to nurse him at home by yourself?'*
D2	Using initially open questions, appropriately moving to closed questions	Understanding how to choose between open and closed questioning styles at different points in the interview is of key importance. An effective health professional uses open questioning techniques first to obtain a picture of the problem from the patient's perspective. Later, the approach becomes more focused with increasingly specific, though still open, questions and eventually, closed questions to elicit additional details that the patient may have omitted. The use of open questioning techniques is critical at the beginning of the exploration of any problem, and the most common mistake is to move to closed questioning too quickly. Closed questions are questions for which a specific and often one-word answer is elicited. These responses are often *'yes/no'*. Open questioning techniques in contrast are designed to introduce an area of enquiry without unduly shaping or focusing the content of the response. They still direct the patient to a specific area but allow the patient more discretion in their answer, suggesting to the patient that elaboration is both appropriate and welcome.
D3	NOT using compound questions/leading questions	A compound question is when more than one question is asked without allowing time to answer. It confuses the patient about what information is wanted and introduces uncertainty about which of the questions asked the eventual reply relates to. An example would be *'have you ever had chest pain or felt short of breath?'*. A leading question includes an assumption in the question, which makes it more difficult for the respondent to contradict the assumption, e.g. *'You've lost weight, haven't you?'* or *'You haven't had any ankle swelling?'*.
D4	Clarifying statements which are vague or need amplification	Clarifying statements which are vague or need further amplification is a vital information gathering skill. After an initial response to an open-ended question, health professionals may need to prompt patients for more precision, clarity or completeness. Often patients' statements can have two (or more) possible meanings: it is important to ascertain which one is intended.

D5	Summarising information to encourage correction/invite further information	Summarising is the deliberate step of making an explicit verbal summary to the patient of the information gathered so far, and is one of the most important of all information gathering skills. Used periodically throughout the interview, it helps with two significant tasks – ensuring accuracy, and facilitating the patient's further responses.

E. Indicators for information giving

E1	Establishing initially what the patient already knows	One key interactive approach to giving information to the patient involves assessing their prior knowledge. This allows you to determine at what level to pitch information, how much and what information the patient needs, and the degree to which your view of the problem differs from that of the patient.
E2	Pausing periodically when giving information, using the response to guide next steps	This approach, often called chunking and checking, is a vital skill throughout the information-giving phase of the interview. Here, the health professional gives information in small pieces, pausing and checking for understanding before proceeding and being guided by the patient's reactions to see what information is required next. This technique is a vital component of assessing the patient's overall information needs: if you give information in small chunks and give the patient ample opportunity to contribute, they will respond with clear signals about both the amount and type of information they still require.
E3	Encouraging the patient to contribute reactions/feelings	A further element of effective information giving is providing opportunities to the patient to ask questions, seek clarification or express doubts. Health professionals must be very explicit here: many patients are reluctant to express what is on the tip of their tongue and are extremely hesitant to ask the doctor questions. Unless positively invited to do so, they may leave the consultation with their questions unanswered and a reduced understanding of and commitment to plans.
E4	Checking whether the patient has understood information	Checking that the patient has understood the information given is an important step in ensuring accuracy of information transfer. This can be done by asking 'does that make sense?', although many patients will say 'yes' even though they are still unsure, because they don't want to admit that they didn't understand. A more effective method is to use patient restatement, i.e. asking the patient to repeat back to the doctor what has been discussed to ensure that their understanding is the same as that of the health professional.
E5	Discovering what further information the patient needs	Deliberately asking the patient what other information would be helpful enables the health professional to directly discover areas to address which the health professional might not have considered. It is difficult to guess each patient's individual needs, and asking directly is an obvious way to prevent the omission of important information.

Source: www.occupationalenglishtest.org

The whole Speaking sub-test takes about 20 minutes, with each role play taking about five minutes.

Speaking sub-test overview				
Part	**Task**	**Question type**	**Duration**	**Marks**
• Warm up conversation (not assessed) • Two role plays	Two role plays between patient/caregiver/relative and healthcare professional	Role cards containing information on role play given	20 mins	• Band score of 0–6 based on linguistic criteria • Band score of 0–3 based on clinical communication criteria

Scoring in OET

Your *Statement of Results* shows your score for each of the four sub-tests. There is a numerical score on a 0–500 scale, as well as a grade from A to E.

Grade	Numerical score	OET band descriptors	IELTS equivalent band score
A	500 490 480 470 460 450	Can communicate very fluently and effectively with patients and health professionals using appropriate register, tone and lexis. Shows complete understanding of any kind of written or spoken language.	8.0–9.0
B	440 430 420 410 400 390 380 370 360 350	Can communicate effectively with patients and health professionals using appropriate register, tone and lexis, with only occasional inaccuracies and hesitations. Shows good understanding in a range of clinical contexts.	7.0–7.5
C+	340 330 320 310 300	Can maintain the interaction in a relevant healthcare environment despite occasional errors and lapses, and follow standard spoken language normally encountered in his/her field of specialisation.	6.5

Grade	Numerical score	OET band descriptors	IELTS equivalent band score
C	290		5.5–6.0
	280		
	270		
	260		
	250		
	240		
	230		
	220		
	210		
	200		
D	190	Can maintain some interaction and understand straightforward factual information in his/her field of specialisation, but may ask for clarification. Frequent errors, inaccuracies and mis- or overuse of technical language can cause a strain in communication.	Less than 5.5
	180		
	170		
	160		
	150		
	140		
	130		
	120		
	110		
	100		
E	90	Can manage simple interaction on familiar topics and understand the main point in short, simple messages, provided he/she can ask for clarification. High density of errors and mis- or overuse of technical language can cause significant strain and breakdowns in communication.	
	80		
	70		
	60		
	50		
	40		
	30		
	20		
	10		
	0		

Source: www.occupationalenglishtest.org

There is no overall grade for OET. Do not worry if you are unable to obtain the same score on all four sub-tests. For example, you may do better at the Writing sub-test and not so well in the Listening sub-test. This is because everyone has different strengths and areas of weakness, even when it comes to language proficiency.

In fact, some candidates who take the test on different test dates find that their scores are not the same because their performance may differ due to specific Test Day factors. A candidate on the borderline score between two bands is more likely to experience this.

What is the passing grade?

The boards, councils or government departments that regulate the various medical professions have their own benchmarks for OET grades. You can find out about their requirements on their websites or by emailing them, so that you know what score you should aim to achieve.

How long are test results valid?

Similarly, the boards, councils, universities or government departments that recognise OET determine the duration of validity. This kind of information is usually available on the authority's website, so check there to understand their particular requirements.

Finally, remember that hard work and preparation along with appropriate knowledge of OET will help you achieve your target score. We hope this book will help you improve specific language sub-skills required for OET and add to your knowledge of the test, so that you are fully equipped for Test Day.

LISTENING IN OET

INTRODUCTION
TO THE LISTENING SUB-TEST

The Listening sub-test assesses your ability to understand a variety of spoken interactions typical of the healthcare environment. Some examples of these are:

- a patient speaks to a healthcare professional
- two healthcare professionals speak during a consultation about a health issue
- a healthcare professional speaks with a colleague about the care of a patient
- a healthcare professional passes on information to a colleague
- a healthcare professional gives a short presentation about a topic relating to patient care
- a healthcare professional gives a short interview about a topic relating to their work

The Listening sub-test contains three parts. Each part assesses different skills, such as listening for gist (the general meaning), listening for specific information, and listening for the speaker's point of view or attitude to the topic. All of the listening extracts are set in a healthcare environment (for instance, a hospital ward, GP surgery or operating theatre), and each extract you hear has a different context.

General description of OET Listening

Paper format	3 parts
Number of items	42 in total
Task types	Structured note completion, 3-option multiple choice
Text types	Medical consultations, workplace interactions, interviews and presentations

Sources	All texts are based on real-life situations and source material
Instructions	Candidates hear instructions and also read them on the question paper
Time allowed	45 minutes (approx)
Recording	All parts are heard once only
Level	B2/C1

Summary of the Listening sub-test

The Listening sub-test consists of three parts, and a total of 42 question items. The topics are of generic healthcare interest and accessible to candidates across all professions. The total length of the Listening audio is about 40 minutes, including recorded speech and pauses to allow you time to write your answers. You will hear each recording once, and are expected to write your answers while listening.

The Listening sub-test structure

Part A – Consultation extracts (about five minutes each)

Part A assesses your ability to identify specific information during a consultation. You will listen to two recorded health professional–patient consultations, and you will complete the health professional's notes using the information you hear.

Note: the health professionals may be from any one of the 12 OET professions.

Part B – Short workplace extracts (about one minute each)

Part B assesses your ability to identify the detail, gist, opinion or purpose of short extracts from typical healthcare workplace interactions. You will listen to six recorded extracts (e.g. team briefings, handovers or health professional–patient dialogues) and answer one multiple-choice question for each extract.

Part C – Presentation extracts (about five minutes each)

Part C assesses your ability to follow a recorded presentation or interview about a range of accessible healthcare topics. You will listen to two different extracts and answer six multiple-choice questions for each extract.

How is listening ability assessed in OET?

The Listening sub-test is designed to assess a range of listening skills, such as identifying specific information, detail, gist, opinion or the speaker's purpose. These skills are assessed through note-completion tasks and multiple-choice questions. Assessors who mark the Listening sub-test are qualified and highly trained. Candidate responses are assessed against an established marking guide. During the marking session, any problematic or unforeseen answers are referred to a sub-group of senior Assessors for guidance, and all papers are double-marked to ensure fairness and consistency.

How is the listening test scored?

Your answers for Part A are double-marked by trained OET Assessors. These answers are randomly assigned to Assessors to avoid any potential for conflict of interest. Your answers for Part B and Part C are computer scanned and automatically scored. For Part A, Assessors use a detailed marking guide that sets out which answers receive marks, and to decide whether you have provided enough correct information to be given the mark. Assessors are monitored for accuracy and consistency.

Listening Part A

During Part A, you will hear part of a consultation between a healthcare professional and a patient about the patient's experience of a health issue. There are two such extracts in Part A, each between 4.5 and 5 minutes in length, and each featuring a different condition. The extract can be taken from any point in the consultation where you hear the patient talking for extended periods. This means that you won't hear the consultation from the beginning to the end. You'll mainly hear the patient talking during Part A. The healthcare professional, a specialist doctor or specialist nurse, might ask questions or perhaps prompt the patient to continue with their story.

Listening Part B

In Listening Part B, you will hear six short extracts from typical workplace interactions. These will feature a variety of healthcare professionals talking to their colleagues, patients and others about something that is happening in the workplace.

As there are six different extracts in Part B, you can expect to hear about six different healthcare contexts. You will not be expected to understand very specialised language from any one profession, but you will need to listen carefully to what is actually said. These short extracts are not linked in any way.

Many of the extracts are dialogues between healthcare professionals or between a healthcare professional and a patient or carer. Some extracts are monologues, although, you may hear *listening noises* from the people listening to the monologue, such as *Mm, Uh huh, Okay*.

The extracts in Part B are interactive workplace communications. If the workplace setting is one you are not familiar with, don't worry: you are not expected to have specialised knowledge.

Listening Part C

In Listening Part C, you will hear two extracts about two different topics, taken from workplace presentations or interviews similar to those you are likely to encounter in the course of your work.

Here are some examples of the types of extracts you may listen to in Part C:

- A CPD (Continuing Professional Development) presentation to healthcare professionals in a hospital. The speaker may describe his or her experience of changes in policy, and give examples of changes they have made in their work area.
- A healthcare professional may talk about his/her job. For example, a physiotherapist talks about his/her work in a fracture clinic where a new treatment has been offered to patients for the management of serious fractures. During the presentation or interview, the physiotherapist presents a short description of one patient's experience of the treatment used in the unit. The physiotherapist goes on to describe how his/her perspective on the treatment has been affected by the patient's experience.
- A description of some *action research* undertaken by a group of healthcare professionals who identified a particular problem in their work area. For example, a group of nurses may have read an article about an intervention to help optimise patient nutrition, such as implementing a *red tray* scheme to identify patients who need additional help to eat their meals. The nurses set up a trial of the scheme on their ward, and are now giving feedback on the progress of the action research. During the presentation or interview, the nurses may express the opinion that they had thought the intervention might not be very successful, but were surprised by its effectiveness at the end of the trial period.

Imagine that you are listening to a presentation at work. You will probably be thinking about your own practice as you do so. You might also be thinking about ways in which you could alter your practice to implement some of the ideas you are hearing about.

The topics of Listening Part C are of general interest. Therefore, the presentations or interviews don't contain a lot of detailed factual information that could only be understood by specialist healthcare professionals. Instead, you'll hear about the speaker's attitude towards an aspect of the overall topic.

Listening Part C is the final part of the Listening test, and you will get a chance to check all your answers at the end of it.

Listening Part A starts with and focuses on what the patient says, so the healthcare professional says very little. Listening Part B focuses on what healthcare professionals say to each other or to a patient. Listening Part C focuses on a group of healthcare professionals listening to a colleague speaking about a topic of general interest.

What does the test look like?

What can you expect to hear during Listening Part A?

Part A tests your ability to understand what a patient is telling you and make notes about what you hear. So you will hear part of a consultation, but not necessarily the beginning or the end. In a consultation, the healthcare professional often speaks a lot and the patient mainly answers questions. In Part A, however, you often hear a healthcare professional seeing a patient with a long-standing condition for the first time, such as a patient referral. In these types of first-time consultations, the patient is likely to speak quite a lot, giving the background to their condition or explaining changes they have recently experienced.

Time to read before you start the test

Before you start Listening Part A, you have 30 seconds to look at the notes and get an idea of the type of information you need to listen for. These notes give you a general idea of what the patient is going to talk about, for example, recent gastrointestinal symptoms. In this case, you would need to listen particularly closely to the patient describing his or her experience of these symptoms.

Imagine that you are in the room with the patient and the healthcare professional, and are observing the consultation. You listen to the patient describing recent changes in symptoms or the worsening of a new complaint. The patient may have been referred by their GP to a specialist and may need to explain what has been happening to them since their last GP visit; or a patient may present to the Emergency Room, and need to give some background to the reason for their visit.

How to use the preparation time

- Underline the words in the notes that tell you what you are listening for (e.g. type of pain).
- Think about the type of information that is missing in each gap.
- Think about the sequence of the conversation (look at the headings).

What do the notes look like?

As the healthcare professional listens to the patient during the consultation, he or she makes notes about what the patient is saying. In the Part A task, you will see a set of notes. Twelve pieces of information have been taken out of the notes. You will listen to the audio to find the information needed to fill each of the gaps. The notes are set out in the form of bullet points under headings. The headings help to guide you through the general stages of the consultation, for example, *Recent symptoms*, *Past medical history*, *Current treatment*.

In a real scenario, when healthcare professionals make notes of a consultation they are likely to use abbreviations or note form. In OET, the notes are always written out in full. In general, the notes will use the correct medical terms, although the patient may use different words. For example, the patient might say that they have *difficulty sleeping* and the healthcare professional's notes will refer to *insomnia*. Sometimes, however, the healthcare professional may quote the patient's actual words. For example, they might write, *describes pain as 'like a knife in my side'*. The quotation marks here make it clear that this is the patient's own description of the pain. Following the notes as you listen will help you keep track of what stage the consultation is at. There will be gaps in some places in the notes, and you need to write your answers in these gaps. The notes may also include information that will not be tested.

What do you write down?

The words you write in the gaps are words that you hear the patient saying. You don't have to change the patient's words into medical language. You also don't need to change the form of the words (adjectives to nouns, singular to plural).

For example:

The patient says: I've noticed that the pain in my stomach gets more intense in the evening.

The notes say: notices pain in stomach (1) _____ in the evening.

You fill the gap with: (1) <u>more intense</u>.

There is no word limit for your answers, but all answers will only require a word or short phrase.

What can you expect to hear during the consultation?

Firstly, think about the reasons a patient may be referred to a specialist and what they might talk about. Perhaps they may talk about:

- Recent symptoms
  They may talk about changes in symptoms that have prompted them to see their GP in the first place, for example, a deterioration in or exacerbation of the symptoms. They may have noticed something that triggers their symptoms now.
- Past family history
  The specialist may ask for some additional information about the patient's family medical history, especially if a family member suffers from the same or a similar condition, for example, heart disease.
- Past medical history
  The patient may talk about other conditions they suffer from. The patient may wonder if one of the conditions was having an effect on the current complaint.
- Past surgical history
  The patient might have had recent surgery, which the specialist needs to know about.

- Regular medication
The specialist may want to know about the patient's current medications. The patient may need to explain how effective the treatment has been so far. Note that you won't need to write down complicated drug names. Any references to medication will be about common drugs such as steroids, NSAIDs or paracetamol.
- Tests and investigations
Sometimes patients tell specialists about tests they might have already had, for example, blood tests or CT scans.

How do patients talk about their symptoms?

Vocabulary development: Talking about chest pain

When patients describe their pain, it is a subjective description, because it is from the patient's point of view. They'll describe the level or severity of pain in their own words, and may describe it as being 'like something', for example, *It's like a red hot poker in my eye* or *It feels like a bee sting when you take off the dressing*. They may also use a simile to describe the pain, saying that it feels as if something was happening to them: for example, *It feels as if a knife is being twisted in my side*.

Task 1

2.1 **Listen to the audio and complete the summary of what the patient says about her chest pain.**

The patient said that the chest pain had become more severe lately. The pain felt like a _____ on her chest and was a constant pain. The patient thought at first that she had _____, until the pain worsened and felt like a _____ pain. When the pain was severe, the patient used to sit down and try to _____ through the pain. She has noticed that the pain has begun to go up the left side of her neck and has started to radiate along her _____ as well.

Pain collocations

We often use a variety of pain collocations to describe the quality of pain. The descriptive terms often relate to the type of pain, for example, neuropathic or nerve pain is often described as a *burning pain*. Some collocations are fixed expressions. For example, we say a *dull ache* (a sort of persistent low-grade pain) and a *sharp pain* (an acute or short-term pain that is quite severe).

Task 2

Complete the pain descriptions using the words given below.

griping	wrenching	stinging	throbbing	shooting
scalding	pounding	nagging	crushing	cramping

1. Menstrual or period pain is described as _____.

2. The pain caused by a burn is described as _____.

3. Pain caused by a cold sore or shingles is described as _____.

4. Pain which moves down your legs is often described as _____ pain.

5. A severe headache or migraine is described as a _____ headache.

6. Toothache is described as _____ pain.

7. Muscle spasms, e.g. with a muscle sprain, are often described as _____ pain.

8. Angina or chest pain is described as a _____ pain.

9. Stomach pain caused by gastroenteritis is described as a _____ pain.

10. A dull ache tends to be a type of chronic pain described as a _____ pain.

Task 3

Listen to a dialogue in which a patient describes his pain symptoms. Circle the correct answer.

1. What kind of pain does the patient describe?
   knife pain and twisting pain / stabbing and griping pains / spasms after eating

2. How does the patient describe the stabbing pain?
   The pain is … linked to digestion. / a type of stomach pain. / like a knife in his side.

3. How does the patient describe the spasms?
   It's as if his stomach is twisting around. / like a sharp twist in his stomach. / as if he is gripped with pain.

Vocabulary development: Talking about changes in symptoms

During a consultation, patients may talk about how their symptoms have changed recently. Healthcare professionals may ask patients if there is anything that triggers the symptoms, or makes them better or worse. They may use the following expressions:

The healthcare professional asks ...	The patient says ...
Trigger symptoms What sets it off? Is there anything that triggers the headaches?	It flares up when I ... It starts when I ...
Alleviate symptoms Is there anything you do that seems to make it better?	The pain eases if I ... It feels better if I ... It settles down if I ...
Aggravate symptoms Is there anything you do that seems to make it worse?	It gets worse if I ... Eating bread seems to aggravate the symptoms.

Task 4

🎧 2.3 **Listen to a dialogue between a doctor and a patient, and answer the questions.**

1. What does the doctor ask the patient about first?

   _____

2. Why did the patient keep a food diary?

   _____

3. Which foods cause the patient the most problems?

   _____

4. What does the patient say she has to do to alleviate the symptoms?

   _____

Doing Listening Part A

Now, let's look at an example of a Listening Part A consultation and its note-completion task. In this part of the book, you're going to go through each section of the Listening Part A task to understand how to approach it successfully.

Listening Part A example

You hear a dermatologist talking to a patient called Nigel MacNess. For questions 1 to 12, complete the notes with a word or phrase. You have 30 seconds to look at the notes.

Patient: Nigel MacNess

Current symptoms

- initially thought he had dermatitis or a **(1)** _____
- describes skin patches as thick, **(2)** _____ and slightly elevated
- patches on elbows, kneecaps and **(3)** _____ (concerned they're visible)
- pain described as a **(4)** _____ sensation on the skin
- itchiness worse at night – reports insomnia
  - feels **(5)** _____ most of the time
  - affects his work as a **(6)** _____

Treatment

- topical medication from pharmacy – ineffective
- tried **(7)** _____ – also ineffective

Medical history

- reports mild problems with **(8)** _____ (teenage years)
- infestation with **(9)** _____ on holiday (2 years ago)
- single episode of **(10)** _____ (last year)
  - no abnormalities detected in recent urine test

General mood

- reports **(11)** _____ affected by condition
- has affected his social life – reports feeling depressed
- concerned not to have commenced treatment yet

Recommended tests

- has appointment for a **(12)** _____ next week

Understanding the setting of the consultation

Look at the example above. Take note of the context sentence, headings and 12 questions. Look at the context sentence, 'You hear a dermatologist talking to a patient called Nigel MacNess'. What kind of diseases and conditions does a dermatologist deal with? (answer: skin) Why might the patient have been referred to the dermatologist? (answer: to get a definite diagnosis / confirm a suspected diagnosis / for further treatment)

Preparing to Listen

First, look at the five headings used to organise the notes. Think about what you might expect to read under them.

Current symptoms: As the patient is talking to a dermatologist, it is likely that the symptoms relate to a skin condition. You may hear the patient talk about the appearance of his skin, e.g. red, inflamed, dry, pale, or the way the condition makes his skin feel, e.g. itchy, sore, uncomfortable.

Treatment: You would expect to hear about the sort of treatment used for skin conditions, e.g. creams, ointment or lotions.

Medical history: Some patients have more than one condition that affects their health. In this section, you may hear about conditions which are unrelated to the current skin complaint, so you need to listen carefully to find out if past conditions continue to be a problem or have been successfully treated.

General mood: Skin disorders can be embarrassing, especially those that affect the face. You could imagine that the skin condition might have a negative effect on the patient. The patient may use words such as 'depressed' to explain how the skin condition makes him feel.

Recommended tests: Tests and investigations are often used to make sure that a correct diagnosis is made. In this section you may hear about blood tests and scans, but you may also hear about tests which are used specifically by dermatologists, e.g. a skin biopsy or allergy testing.

Now, look at the notes above and underline any words which will give you clues about what you need to listen for. Remember that you may not hear the same words as you find in the notes, for example, you read _initially_, but you hear _at first_.

Then, look at the gaps and think about what will 'fit'.

For example, the first note is: _initially thought he had dermatitis or a (1)_ _____

The dermatologist explains that the patient first thought the condition was dermatitis or another skin condition. Question (1) is therefore likely to be the name of that other skin condition.

The note for question (2) is *describes skin patches as thick, (2) _____ and slightly elevated.* The dermatologist writes 'describes' to indicate that these are the patient's words about his skin condition. Question (2) will be another word about their appearance, perhaps their colour or texture.

Question (3) is about the location of the skin patches:

patches on elbows, kneecaps and (3) _____ (concerned they're visible)

Two locations are mentioned (elbows and kneecaps). Question (3) must be a third body part that can be seen easily.

Question (4) is another example of the dermatologist reporting what the patient says:

- pain described as a (4) _____ sensation on the skin

The patient describes their pain as a type of sensation. Some terms used to describe skin sensations are *burning, stinging* or *tingling.*

In between the questions, you read other notes written by the dermatologist, for example,

itchiness worse at night – reports insomnia

These notes are not tested, but help you keep track of where the consultation is up to. The dermatologist has used a medical term 'insomnia' for the patient's expression, 'Sometimes it's so bad that I find it hard to get comfortable and I can't sleep'.

Questions (5) and (6) both relate to the patient's sleep difficulties. Try to imagine how sleeplessness might affect the patient, e.g. *feels (5) _____ most of the time.*

Task 5

Write down four words the patient might say that are related to lack of sleep.

_____

Question (6) is based on a note of the work the patient does:

affects his work as a (6) _____

This will be an occupation the patient has, for example, teacher, accountant, manager.

Now, read the notes under the heading *Treatment:*

- *topical medication from pharmacy – ineffective*
- *tried (7) _____ – also ineffective*

The dermatologist writes down a medical term – *topical,* but it is likely that the patient uses an everyday term instead. Think about what types of medication are topical (i.e that go on the surface of the skin).

Task 6

Write down four everyday terms related to skin treatment that the patient might say.

_____

You can also expect to hear the patient telling you that the treatment he tried didn't work well. Remember to use this note to help you keep on track with your listening.

It appears that the patient tried another treatment [question (7)] which was also ineffective. For question (7), you need to listen for another possible skin treatment the patient may have tried.

Now, look at the notes under the heading *Medical history*.

Question (8) is an example of another way the dermatologist makes notes about the patient's actual words, using the word 'reports':

reports mild problems with (8) _____ (teenage years)

The patient is going to talk about a medical problem he had as a teenager. You will need to listen for the name of a disease or description of a medical condition.

In question (9), the term *infestation* gives you a clue about the health problem the patient contracted two years before, while he was on holiday. Think about the difference between an *infection*, which is caused by a pathogen, e.g. a virus, and an *infestation*, which is caused by a parasite on the skin, e.g. an insect, mite or worm.

infestation with (9) _____ on holiday (2 years ago)

Task 7

Write down four everyday terms related to skin infestations that the patient might say.

_____

_____

The patient also describes another health problem which he had last year. The dermatologist's (untested) note tells you that the patient has recently had a urine test, so you need to listen for a condition that affects the urinary system (kidneys, bladder, urine).

single episode of (10) _____ (last year)

- no abnormalities detected in recent urine test

Task 8

What does the doctor mean by 'no abnormalities detected'? What words do you think the doctor might use to explain this to the patient?

_____

_____

Now, look at the notes under the heading *General mood*.

Although most of the notes under this heading are untested, you may want to underline the terms <u>affected his social life</u>, <u>depressed</u> and <u>concerned</u>. These notes suggest that the patient's mood is quite low and that the medical condition has had a significant impact on his life.

To complete question (11), you need to listen for an aspect of his life that has been affected by his current condition. The next note tells you that the patient's social life has been affected, so question (11) must be about a different aspect of his life.

- *reports (11) _____ affected by condition*
- *has affected his social life – reports feeling depressed*
- *concerned not to have commenced treatment yet*

Finally, look at the notes under the heading *Recommended tests*.

There is only one question under this heading. The dermatologist makes a note of the type of test the patient will have the following week. You might expect to hear about a test used in dermatology. *Has appointment for a (12) _____ next week*

Task 9

Write down the kinds of tests a patient with a skin disorder might have.

_____

Listening to the consultation

Task 10

 Listen to the audio of the consultation and answer the questions. After you listen, look at the transcript of the audio and check your answers with the answer key.

You hear a dermatologist talking to a patient called Nigel MacNess. For questions 1–12, complete the notes with a word or short phrase. You now have 30 seconds to look at the notes.

Patient: Nigel MacNess

Current symptoms

- initially thought he had dermatitis or a **(1)** _____
- describes skin patches as thick, **(2)** _____ and slightly elevated
- patches on elbows, kneecaps and **(3)** _____ (concerned they're visible)
- pain described as a **(4)** _____ sensation on the skin
- itchiness worse at night – reports insomnia

    - feels **(5)** _____ most of the time
    - affects his work as a **(6)** _____

Treatment

- topical medication from pharmacy – ineffective
- tried **(7)** _____ – also ineffective

Medical history

- reports mild problems with **(8)** _____ (teenage years)
- infestation with **(9)** _____ on holiday (2 years ago)
- single episode of **(10)** _____ (last year)
    - no abnormalities detected in recent urine test

General mood

- reports **(11)** _____ affected by condition
- has affected his social life – reports feeling depressed
- concerned not to have commenced treatment yet

Recommended tests

- has appointment for a **(12)** _____ next week

Medical terms and everyday terms

Task 11

Look at the transcript and underline the words the patient says that match the dermatologist's notes below.

1. itchiness worse at night – reports insomnia
2. topical medication from pharmacy – ineffective
3. no abnormalities detected in recent urine test
4. has affected his social life – reports feeling depressed
5. concerned not to have commenced treatment yet

Task 12

Listen to the following Part A extract as if you were doing a real test. Allow yourself time to read the questions and think about what you might expect to hear. Then, listen to the audio once only. Answer the questions as you listen. Check your answers.

You hear a physiotherapist talking to a patient called Greg Freeman, who has been referred to her by a sports medicine clinic.

For questions **1–12**, complete the notes with a word or short phrase. You now have 30 seconds to look at the notes.

Patient: Greg Freeman (student)

History of condition

- right lateral wrist injury – fall sustained while **(1)** _____ (two years ago)
- **(2)** _____ was negative, given exercises to do
- injured following a fall from a **(3)** _____ (one year ago)
    - ongoing pain to right lateral shoulder
- has visited clinic ten times reporting joint injuries

Current symptoms

- pain in shoulder and wrist aggravated by pull-ups, **(4)** _____ and free weights
- constant pain throughout the day
- some **(5)** _____ disturbance when on right side
- generally in good health
- reports that right wrist and **(6)** _____ sometimes feel cold (no apparent reason)
- no decreased blood flow or **(7)** _____

General medical history

- acne on face and back (mid-teens)
- little effect from

    - initial treatment with **(8)** _____
    - antibiotics
    - avoiding **(9)** _____
    - prescribed stronger medication by **(10)** _____
    - some improvement but caused cracked **(11)** _____

- reports episodes **(12)** _____
- condition now resolved with no further treatment

What does the test look like?

Let us look at Listening Part B in detail and understand how it works.

What can you expect to hear during Listening Part B?

Part B extracts are all examples of interaction between healthcare professionals, each focusing on a different workplace situation. You will either hear two people talking to each other or just one speaker briefing colleagues, patients or others (for example carers, hospital managers, healthcare professionals in training).

Below are some examples of situations you may find in Listening Part B.

Healthcare professionals speaking to colleagues during:

- *handovers* providing information or giving an opinion about patient care
- *safety briefings* about potential safety concerns in a particular area
- *staff briefings* giving new staff information about the workplace
- *feedback on training sessions or staff observations* pointing out what went well, and which areas need improvement
- *adverse incident reporting* highlighting areas of concern for staff members, for example, a medication error

Healthcare professionals speaking to a patient or carer about:

- a concern
- their admission
- their discharge

What are the extracts like?

Part B extracts are much shorter than those in Parts A and C. Each one lasts approximately 45 seconds and features a different healthcare professional speaking. For instance, you may hear extracts where a community nurse, specialist doctor, physiotherapist, dentist or pharmacist talks to a colleague or a patient. Think of each extract as if it were a 'snapshot' of a longer interaction. Before each extract, there is a context sentence to give you guidance on what you are about to hear. A single question is asked about each extract, with answer options for you to choose from.

Time to prepare before each extract

Before you listen to each extract, you will hear the context sentence, which gives you some background information. It tells you who is speaking (the type of healthcare professional), and the setting (e.g. hospital, community health centre). The context sentence also gives you a general idea of what the extract is about. After the context sentence, you will have time to read the question, which tells you the type of information you need to listen for. You should read the question with the context sentence in mind. For example:

(Context sentence) You hear two physiotherapists talking about a patient with a knee injury.

(Question) What are they concerned about?

In this case, the question asks what the physiotherapists are worried about regarding the patient. Consider what the problem with the knee might be, and what they might need to discuss. For instance, they may need to try a different sort of therapy, or use a new piece of equipment.

The question that you hear before the extract may be in the form of a direct question (beginning 'who/ what/where'), or it could be in a 'complete a sentence' form.

For example:

What does the customer tell the pharmacist? (direct question)

The customer wants to know whether herbal remedies … (complete a sentence)

Look at an example of a Listening Part B question.

---

1. You hear a pharmacist talking to a customer.

What concerns the customer about herbal remedies?

(A) possible or harmful side effects

(B) effectiveness for short-term use

(C) interactions with regular medications

The context sentence is, 'You hear a pharmacist talking to a customer'. This tells you that the setting of the conversation is a pharmacy in the community, and that the conversation is between a pharmacist and a customer.

The question is, 'What concerns the customer about herbal remedies?'.

This suggests that the customer has asked the pharmacist about using herbal remedies.

The three answer options are:

(A) possible or harmful side effects

(B) effectiveness for short-term use

(C) interactions with regular medications

First, underline the words in the question that tell you what to listen for:

What <u>concerns</u> the customer about <u>herbal remedies</u>?

Next, underline the words that help you to listen for the correct answer:

(A) possible or harmful <u>side effects</u>

(B) effectiveness for <u>short-term use</u>

(C) <u>interactions</u> with regular medications

Something that you might notice about the options is that all three are plausible answers to questions customers might ask, as they all relate to medication. Some of the terms you might hear when talking about medication include:

- *side effects*, e.g. may cause drowsiness
- *contraindication*, e.g. don't take if you have a kidney problem
- *interaction*, e.g. don't take at the same time as aspirin
- *precautions*, e.g. don't take with alcohol
- *for short-term use*, e.g. don't take for longer than a week
- *dosage*, e.g. don't take more than 6 tablets a day

 Now, listen to the audio to find out which aspect(s) of taking the medication the customer is concerned about. Look at the options to work out which is correct.

Option A asks whether you hear anything about <u>side effects</u>. This might distract you, as you might imagine that pharmacists who talk to customers about concerns with medications often discuss side effects that customers need to be aware of. This means that the option sounds reasonable, but in this case, side effects are not mentioned by the pharmacist.

Option B asks if the customer wants to know if herbal remedies are effective for <u>short-term use</u>. The pharmacist tells the customer that herbal remedies are not for a 'chronic problem'. Therefore, they are for short-term use. So, the option is correct in itself, but it wasn't a concern raised by the customer, so it doesn't answer the question.

Option C asks if the customer is concerned about <u>interactions</u> with other medication he is taking. He asks the pharmacist if he can 'take these tablets with' his 'other medication', meaning that he is asking about the interaction of herbal remedies with other medications. This means that Option C is the correct answer.

Listening to a handover

Clinical handovers are undertaken by all healthcare professionals at various times during shifts or patient transfer times. Handovers are important opportunities for staff to convey information about patients. They are typically undertaken in the following situations:

- between colleagues at shift changeover times
- as a patient is transferred to another part of the hospital or to a different healthcare environment, for example, from hospital to care home
- as a patient is transferred for a test or specialist appointment
- to a colleague before taking a break or leaving the ward

Handovers from colleague to colleague at shift changeover inform the person taking over of the patient's clinical condition. Healthcare professionals ensure that incoming staff are aware of any changes in the patient's status, especially deteriorations in their general health. The patient's vital signs may be discussed, as well as medications of note, e.g. IV (intravenous) fluids.

Handovers between different healthcare professionals may differ in content. For example, a physiotherapist giving a handover to a colleague may discuss a patient's mobility issues, whilst a speech pathologist may discuss a patient's progress with speech rehabilitation after a stroke.

Handovers usually take around five minutes to complete. In Listening Part B, you may hear only a small part of the handover, rather than the whole handover.

The information passed on in a handover differs depending on the purpose of the handover. For instance, in a handover to transfer a patient to a care home you might hear about:

- the patient's current health status, e.g. their recovery from an infection/surgery, their reduced mobility, or their need for supervision with personal care
- instructions about ongoing care for the patient when he or she is discharged from hospital, e.g. they may have a dressing which needs to continue after discharge, or they may need to continue physiotherapy/occupational therapy exercises
- issues that may need addressing, e.g. the patient may require a pain management/dementia assessment

Look at an example of a Listening Part B question about a nursing handover.

---

2. You hear a ward nurse giving a handover to a care home manager.

What is the nurse explaining?

(A) the patient's personal details

(B) the patient's discharge needs

(C) the patient's medical background

The context sentence is, 'You hear a ward nurse giving a handover to a care home manager'. This tells you that the setting of the conversation is a hospital, and that the conversation is about a transfer of a patient from a hospital to a care home.

The question is, 'What is the nurse explaining?'. This suggests that some information may be more important than other information in the handover.

First, underline the words in the question which tell you what to listen for.

What is the nurse <u>explaining</u>?

As you are given three options from which to select your answer, you can assume that the audio will include vocabulary from all three options. What you're listening for here is the main idea, or the most important piece of information, that the nurse is speaking about.

Next, underline the words that help you to listen for the correct option.

(A) the patient's <u>personal details</u>

(B) the patient's <u>discharge needs</u>

(C) the patient's <u>medical background</u>

Think about what you might hear if the nurse talks about:

- personal details: full name, date of birth, age, male or female
- discharge needs: medications, personal care assistance, mobility needs, wound care (dressings), psychological/emotional support
- medical background: recent procedures, medical treatment, tests or investigations

🎧 2.7 **Now, listen to the audio to find out what aspects of the patient's care are the most important for the nurse to hand over to the care home manager.**

Option A asks whether the patient's <u>personal details</u> are the most important. However, the only information given was the patient's full name (Mrs Nora Eastman).

Option B asks whether the nurse talks about the patient's <u>discharge needs</u>. The nurse talks about three areas the patient needs help in: her personal care; her mobility; and emotional support, as the patient gets upset about not being able to manage at home. Therefore, Option B is the correct answer.

Option C asks if the nurse talks about the patient's <u>medical background</u>. Short-term memory loss and the patient's recent stroke are the only aspects of the patient's medical background that are mentioned. Whilst they relate to the patient's current needs, they're not the focus of the nurse's handover.

Listening to a safety brief

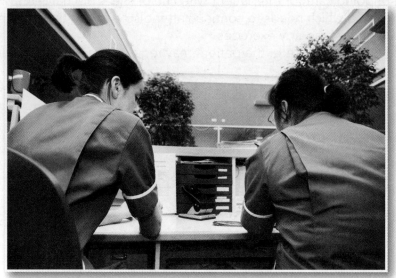

Safety briefings are short staff meetings usually held at the beginning of each shift to make sure that all staff are aware of any patient safety issues in their workplace. During the briefing, concerns can be raised about individual patients who may be at risk of adverse safety incidents.

Task 1

🎧 2.8 **A Senior Nurse is giving a safety briefing to a group of nurses before the commencement of a shift. Listen to the briefing and select the option you think is correct.**

What is the Senior Nurse talking about?

Ⓐ bed changes relating to the ward

Ⓑ a patient who is a high infection-control risk

Ⓒ how to monitor patients with gastrointestinal problems

Managing Listening Part B extracts

Here is an example of a question based on a Listening Part B extract. Let's look at how to approach such a question.

Extract 1: You hear a Diabetes Nurse talking to a patient during a home visit.

Why has the nurse come to see the patient?

Ⓐ to fit a new piece of equipment for him

Ⓑ to encourage him to use some new equipment

Ⓒ to check how he's managing with some new equipment

Look at the context sentence first: 'You hear a Diabetes Nurse talking to a patient during a home visit.'. This tells you that the extract is set in the community during a home visit, and that a Diabetes Nurse is talking to a patient, possibly about something related to the treatment of the patient's diabetes.

The question then asks about the purpose of the visit: 'Why has the nurse come to see the patient?'. Looking at the three options, you see that all of them relate to 'new equipment'.

The question has given you a clue about what the content of the extract will be. The interaction has been narrowed down from 'Diabetes Nurse talks to patient at home' to 'Diabetes Nurse talks to patient at home about new equipment'.

Task 2a

Look at the three options and underline the parts of the options that make them different from each other.

(A) to fit a new piece of equipment for him

(B) to encourage him to use some new equipment

(C) to check how he's managing with some new equipment

Option A suggests that the purpose of the nurse's visit is to get the new piece of equipment set up. It also tells us that the patient has agreed to use it.

Option B suggests that the nurse is going to give the patient some information about the benefits of the new equipment.

Option C suggests that the patient has already started using the equipment, and the nurse wants to see how the patient is managing with it.

Task 2b

Now listen to Extract 1 and select the option you think is correct.

Write the correct option here: _____

Look at the answer key to check the answer. Why do think that was the correct option and the other two options were wrong?

> **Extract 2:** You hear a radiographer talking to a patient about a PET scan.
>
> What is the radiographer mainly doing?
>
> (A) dealing with the patient's anxiety
>
> (B) checking the patient's understanding
>
> (C) obtaining the patient's consent for the procedure

Look at the context sentence first: 'You hear a radiographer talking to a patient about a PET scan.'. This interaction takes place in the radiography department, as a radiographer is talking to a patient who is about to have a PET scan.

Now look at the question, 'What is the radiographer mainly doing?'. Think about what the radiographer might talk to the patient about. For example:

- asking if the patient understands what's going to happen during the scan
- asking if the patient has given consent to have the scan
- explaining what will happen during the scan
- telling the patient what to expect after the scan, for example, the patient might feel tired, thirsty or dizzy
- warning the patient about activities that should not be done after the scan, for example, driving a car, operating heavy machinery or drinking alcohol

Now, look at the options. Notice that there are two parts to each option, a verb and a noun.

(A) dealing with the patient's anxiety

(B) checking the patient's understanding

(C) obtaining the patient's consent for the procedure

Underline both parts of each option and think about the two things you need to listen for in order to decide which option is correct.

(A) <u>dealing with</u> the patient's <u>anxiety</u>

(B) <u>checking</u> the patient's <u>understanding</u>

(C) <u>obtaining</u> the patient's <u>consent</u> for the procedure

Notice that all three options relate to the patient having the scan, not to the scan itself.

Option A suggests that the patient might be feeling anxious about the scan. Some of the expressions you might hear are:

- I'm feeling apprehensive.
- I'm feeling anxious.
- I'm a bit worried about …

Option B suggests that the radiographer might need to check whether the patient understands the process of the scan. Radiographers often make sure that patients know what to expect when they have a scan, especially if patients have to remain still during the procedure.

Option C suggests that the radiographer is asking the patient to give consent or permission to have the scan. Some of the expressions you might hear the radiographer say are:

- give permission to have the scan
- give consent to have the scan
- agree to have the scan

Task 3

 Now listen to Extract 2 and select the option you think is correct.

Write the correct option here: _____

Look at the answer key to check the answer. Why do think that was the correct option and the other two options were wrong?

> **Extract 3:** You hear a hospital pharmacist instructing a ward nurse about a new dressing technique.
>
> The pharmacist is telling him
>
> (A) why the new technique is effective.
>
> (B) how to use the new technique correctly.
>
> (C) who can benefit from the new technique.

Look at the context sentence first: 'You hear a hospital pharmacist instructing a ward nurse about a new dressing technique'. This interaction takes place in the hospital setting, where the pharmacist is talking to a ward nurse about a new dressing technique.

Now look at the question. This time, the question is in the form of a sentence completion: 'The pharmacist is telling him …'.

You know that the dressing technique is new, so you could imagine that the pharmacist might:

- explain why the dressings should be used in place of older dressing types
- describe the types of wounds that the dressings are suitable for
- talk about precautions – store them in the fridge, don't let them dry out, don't clean the wound with saline before using them (use sterile water)
- explain how to dispose of used dressings – in a clinical waste bin, in a sharps bin, in a hazardous waste bin
- talk about the cost of the new dressings

Now, look at the options again.

(A) why the new technique is effective

(B) how to use the new technique correctly

(C) who can benefit from the new technique

Task 4

Underline the parts of each option under Extract 3 that will help you decide which answer is correct.

(A) why the new technique is effective

(B) how to use the new technique correctly

(C) who can benefit from the new technique

Check the answers in the answer key. Notice that the options all relate to new techniques.

Option A suggests that the pharmacist is going to explain why the new dressings work well. There may be a comparison with older dressings to highlight the benefits of using the new dressings.

Option B suggests that the pharmacist is going to explain the procedure for using the dressings, for example, how to prepare the wound, prepare the dressings, and place them on the wound correctly.

Option C suggests that the pharmacist is going to explain the types of wounds that the new dressings can be used for, for example, wounds that don't heal easily.

Task 5

 Now listen to Extract 3 and select the option you think is correct.

Write the correct option here: _____

Look at the answer key to check the answer. Why do think that was the correct option and the other two options were wrong?

Extract 4: You hear a hospital pharmacist talking to a patient about discharge medication.

What is she explaining about pain relief patches?

(A) how to dispose of them safely

(B) how long they're going to last

(C) what the side effects might be

Look at the context sentence first: 'You hear a hospital pharmacist talking to a patient about discharge medication.'. This interaction takes place in the hospital, as a pharmacist is talking to a patient about medication that needs to be taken after the patient returns home.

Now look at the question, 'What is she explaining about pain-relief patches?'.

Think about what pharmacists might explain about medication. For example:

- how to store the medication, e.g. in a cool place
- when to replace the patches, e.g. three times a day / once a day in the morning
- where to put topical medication, e.g. on the skin of the upper arm

Now, look at the options again.

(A) how to dispose of them safely

(B) how long they're going to last

(C) what the side effects might be

Task 6

Underline the parts of each option in Extract 4 that will help you decide which option is correct.

(A) how to dispose of them safely

(B) how long they're going to last

(C) what the side effects might be

Check your answer. Notice that the options all relate to pain relief patches.

Option A suggests that the pharmacist is going to give instruction about what to do with a used patch. Some of the expressions you might hear are:

- You should …
- You must be sure to …
- It's important to …
- It's important that you …

Option B suggests that the pharmacist needs to explain how long the medication in the patch will be effective. You might hear the pharmacist using time phrases, for example:

- The patches last 48 hours.
- You should use the patches for two days.
- The patches are effective for two days.

Option C suggests that the pharmacist is going to give the patient some information about possible side effects of the patches. Some of the expressions you might hear the pharmacist say are:

- The patches might make you feel …
- The patches can cause / result in …
- Look out for signs of …

Task 7

Now listen to Extract 4 and select the option you think is correct.

Write the correct option here: _____

Look at the answer key to check the answer. Why do think that was the correct option and the other two options were wrong?

Extract 5: You hear a physiotherapist briefing ward staff about an elderly patient.

What should be done today to improve the patient's mobility?

(A) A new assessment should be made.

(B) A short activity should be supervised.

(C) A mobility aid should be provided for him.

Look at the context sentence for Extract 5 first: 'You hear a physiotherapist briefing ward staff about an elderly patient.'. What does this tell you about the extract?

_____

_____

Task 9

Think about the things a physiotherapist might talk about. Add two more examples of your own.

Examples:

* whether the patient has started an exercise programme
* how well the patient does his exercises

* _____

* _____

Task 10

Now look at the question, 'What should be done today to improve the patient's mobility?'. The physiotherapist is briefing the ward staff about something that needs to be done for the patient. What might the physiotherapist brief ward staff about? Add two examples of your own.

The physiotherapist might:

* give instructions about a task that needs to be done later that day, for example, an assessment of the patient's mobility
* make a request for something to be done later that day, for example, supervision of the patient doing mobility exercises

* _____

* _____

Now, look at the options again and see whether there are examples of the things you anticipated that you might hear.

(A) A new assessment should be made.

(B) A short activity should be supervised.

(C) A mobility aid should be provided for him.

Option A suggests that the patient has already had one kind of assessment, and the physio therapist is requesting that another one be done. As the physiotherapist is talking about mobility, you could imagine that the assessment might relate to the patient's ability to mobilise with or without aids.

Task 11

What do Options B and C in Extract 5 suggest?

Option B

_____

_____

Option C

_____

_____

Task 12

 Now listen to Extract 5 and select the option you think is correct.

Write the correct option here: _____

Look at the answer key to check the answer. Why do think that was the correct option and the other two options were wrong?

> **Extract 6:** You hear a Senior Nurse talking to a Student Nurse about an incident with a patient.
>
> What is the Senior Nurse doing?
>
> (A) advising him on how to avoid problems in future
>
> (B) trying to find out exactly where he went wrong
>
> (C) reassuring him about the way he handled things

Look at the context sentence first: 'You hear a Senior Nurse talking to a Student Nurse about an incident with a patient.'. This tells you that the extract is set in the hospital environment during a feedback session between a Senior Nurse and a Student Nurse. The Senior Nurse is talking about a recent incident that occurred between the Student Nurse and a patient.

Task 13

Now look at the options under Extract 6. What kind of feedback do you think the Senior Nurse might be giving? Underline the verbs in the options that describe what the Senior Nurse is doing.

(A) advising him on how to avoid problems in future

(B) trying to find out exactly where he went wrong

(C) reassuring him about the way he handled things

In **Option A** the relevant verb is *advise*, so you might expect to hear the Senior Nurse using expressions such as:

- It would be a good idea to ….
- You should …
- Why don't you try …?

In **Option B** the verb phrase is *try to find out*, so you might expect the Senior Nurse to ask about the Student Nurse's part in the incident. For example:

- What …?
- How …?
- Why …?

In **Option C** the verb is *reassure*, so you might expect to hear expressions such as:

- You did the right thing.
- You managed well.

Task 14

 Now listen to Extract 6 and select the option you think is correct.

Write the correct option here: _____

Look at the answer key to check the answer. Why do think that was the correct option and the other two options were wrong?

What does the test look like?

Listening Part C contains two extracts. Each extract is either a presentation or an interview, and is based on a different health-related topic.

Here are some examples of Listening Part C extracts:

- an interview with a healthcare professional about a health-related topic of general interest
- a workplace presentation relating to the speaker's field of work, perhaps as an example of CPD (Continuing Professional Development)
- a presentation about a healthcare professional's experience caring for a patient with a particular disease or condition (similar to a case review presentation)
- a presentation about recent research a healthcare professional may have undertaken, e.g. action research around an issue of concern in their area of practice

What type of language do you listen for in Listening Part C?

During Listening Part C, you hear examples of the speaker's attitude or opinion about something they know about. The speaker may also tell you about someone else's point of view about an issue. For example, a presentation may be about an action research project undertaken by a group of healthcare professionals in response to a need they've identified in their work area. The speaker describes the research and how it was set up, and expresses an opinion about how successful he or she thought the project would be. The speaker may express some initial hesitation about the project, for example,

'I thought it would be difficult to set up, as the project needed a lot of co-operation from staff members.'. Perhaps the speaker expected the project to be successful and was disappointed when the project appeared to fail initially. Other staff members or patients who took part in the project may have a different viewpoint from the speaker. This might have been surprising for the speaker.

Here are some examples of expressions a speaker may use to describe their point of view.

- My guess is that there are lots of good things in oily fish.
- As a physio, I am convinced that targeted exercise programmes are essential for elite athletes.
- I had some concerns, but I was keen to explore how it might be of help to my patient.

Time to read before you start the test

Before you start each Listening Part C extract, you have 90 seconds to read the context sentence and look at the questions. This will help you to get an idea of the type of information you need to listen for. You may also underline important words or phrases in the questions during this time.

The context sentence will make it clear who is talking in the interview or presentation.

For example:

- 'You hear an interview with a **geriatrician** called **Dr Bryan Munro** who specialises in pain management for people with dementia.' The speaker in the interview is Dr Bryan Munro, a doctor who specialises in the care of elderly patients.
- 'You hear a **Diabetes Nurse Specialist** called **Tim Cox** giving a presentation about some research he's done on teenagers with type 1 diabetes.' The speaker in the presentation is Tim Cox, a nurse who is a specialist in the management of diabetes.

The context sentence also tells you what the interview or presentation is about. This will help you to narrow the topic down and think about the language you might hear during the interview or presentation. For example:

- 'You hear an interview with a geriatrician called Dr Bryan Munro who specialises **in pain management for people with dementia**.' This narrows the topic down from the 'care of the elderly' in general to 'caring for people with dementia who have pain'.
- 'You hear a Diabetes Nurse Specialist called Tim Cox giving a presentation about some **research he's done on teenagers with type 1 diabetes**.' This narrows the topic down from 'diabetes' to 'research into teenagers who have type 1 diabetes'.

The questions may be in the form of a direct question with three answers options to choose from, or you may be asked to complete a sentence using the multiple-choice options.

For example:

What was Tim surprised to hear about from teenagers with a recent diabetes diagnosis? (direct question)

Dr Munro was disappointed to find that many healthcare professionals were … (complete a sentence)

When you read the options for each question, you'll notice that the words in the question are not repeated in any of the options. For example:

Why does Kate suggest that the new **dressings** are preferable?

(A) **They** are more cost-effective.

(B) **They** cause less pain when removed.

(C) **They** get better feedback from patients.

Notice that the key term in the question is *dressings*, but the term is not used in the options. Instead, each option uses *they*. This is useful because it means you don't have too much to read, but make sure you understand what *they* refers to.

What is an interview like?

During a Listening Part C interview, an interviewer provides the structure of what you hear. At the beginning, the interviewer will introduce the topic and the speaker. After that, the interviewer asks six questions, each on a different aspect of the topic. This means that there are six sections to the interview. The interviewer's six questions are similar to the questions you have to answer.

The questions asked by the interviewer give you cues about the next thing the speaker will talk about. There is usually a *key word* or *idea* in the question which the interviewee picks up on. You need to listen to everything the interviewee says in answer to the interviewer's question.

The wording of the interviewer's question in the extract will also be reflected in the corresponding question on the test paper. It might include some of the same vocabulary, or synonyms, or it might paraphrase the test question. For example, the question could say, 'When Dr Simms first heard about social prescribing, she was worried that...' and the audio that follows may begin with, 'When I first heard about social prescribing...'. The speaker may also use signposting language to let everyone know that he or she is going to move on to the next aspect of the topic, for example, 'Now, let's look at what the studies show...'.

Example of a Listening Part C interview

First, look at the context sentence to find out who is talking and what the topic of the interview is. For example:

'You hear an interview with a **dietician** called **Megan Fowler**, who's talking about a **study of trials on the effects of omega-3 supplements**.' You now know that a dietician called Megan Fowler is being interviewed. As dieticians are concerned with nutrition and people's eating habits, you can assume that you will hear information around this topic. Look at the rest of the context sentence and you read that Megan will talk about omega-3 supplements.

Now look at the six questions, so that you can see what you think the interview might be about.

1. How does Megan feel about the overall findings of the omega-3 study?

2. What surprised the researchers about the effect of the omega-3 supplements in reducing triglycerides?

3. What does Megan say about early studies of the diet of the Inuit people?

4. What is Megan's attitude towards the eating of oily fish?

5. Megan suggests that the manufacturers' complaints about the doses used in the study …

6. Variations in the rate of absorbency of omega-3 were taken into account by only considering trials …

Notice that there are four direct questions and two sentence completions for this extract. Look at the words in the questions which tell you how the paragraphs are organised: omega-3 study, reducing triglycerides, diet of the Inuit people, the eating of oily fish, doses used in the study, rate of absorbency of omega-3. This helps you prepare to listen to each section and answer the relevant question. Some of the questions seek Megan's point of view about the topic. For example:

How does Megan **feel**?

What **surprised** the researchers about …

Megan **suggests** that …

Question 1 asks about Megan's feelings about the findings of the study. The answer to this question may be about her reaction to the findings. Her reaction may range between being negative to being positive about the study, e.g. *uncertain, optimistic, encouraged*.

Task 1

Look at the options for Question 1 and underline the words which describe a person's feelings towards something.

1. How does Megan feel about the overall findings of the omega-3 study?

   Ⓐ She's confident that they're reliable.

   Ⓑ She's convinced of their positive implications.

   Ⓒ She's concerned they're based on inaccurate data.

Question 2, 'What surprised the researchers about the effect of the omega-3 supplements in reducing triglycerides?', asks you for the reaction to a specific finding. You are asked what surprised the researchers about the effect of reducing triglycerides.

Task 2

Look at the options for Question 2, above, and write down the area(s) each option focuses on.

   Ⓐ the variation between the cardiac and the vascular effects

   Ⓑ the difference they made to levels of the fat itself

   Ⓒ the lack of any impact on related conditions

Question 3 asks what Megan says about early studies of the diet of the Inuit people. Read the question and underline the word 'early' in the question. This helps to focus your listening on what Megan says about the initial or first studies that were undertaken.

Task 3

Now look at the options for Question 3 and underline the words that will help focus your listening.

   Ⓐ Their claims don't apply to fish oil supplements.

   Ⓑ Their findings weren't confirmed by later research.

   Ⓒ Those involved selected the wrong information to analyse.

Question 4 is, 'What is Megan's attitude towards the eating of oily fish?'. This section of the interview comes after Megan has talked about fish oil supplements. She is now going to compare taking fish oil supplements with the eating of oily fish.

Task 4

Now look at the options for Question 4, and consider what you should listen for based on the wording of the question. Which words will you underline?

- (A) It may have a range of benefits for the body.
- (B) It's probably better for the heart than supplements.
- (C) It lacks certain elements essential for a balanced diet.

Question 5, 'Megan suggests that the manufacturers' complaints about the doses used in the study…' is a multiple-choice question for which you have to complete a sentence. Underline 'complaints about the doses' in the question. This will help to focus your listening on the specific complaints that were made.

Task 5

Now, underline the words in the options for Question 5 that help you to focus on the ideas you need to listen for.

- (A) were unjustified in a few cases.
- (B) were based on a misunderstanding.
- (C) were a misrepresentation of the truth.

Question 6, 'Variations in the rate of absorbency of omega-3 were taken into account by only considering trials…" is another multiple-choice question where you have to complete the sentence. Underline 'Variations in the rate of absorbency' to help you focus on the correct option. The word 'rate' is very important, as all the options are likely to be about time.

Task 6

Which words will you underline in the options for Question 6 below?

Variations in the rate of absorbency of omega-3 were taken into account by only considering trials

- (A) that were carried out over a year or longer.
- (B) on patients who showed rapid adaptation to the drug.
- (C) by researchers able to commit to an eight-year study.

It's important to note that underlining the words which you feel are important in the options is a good way to keep pace with the audio and be confident that the question you're attempting matches that of the segment of audio you're listening to. This, however, is not something you should rely heavily on when selecting your answer, as such words or their synonyms will generally be mentioned at some stage. Your primary focus should be on the question and the words that will help you identify and anticipate what you need to listen for. You should try to answer the question as you listen.

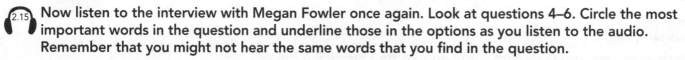

🎧 2.15 **Now listen to the first part of an extract. Look at the questions below. We've circled the important words in the questions, and underlined those in the options that help you identify what you need to listen for.**

You hear an interview with a dietician called Megan Fowler, who's talking about a study of trials on the effects of omega-3 supplements.

1. How does Megan ⟨feel⟩ about the ⟨overall findings⟩ of the omega-3 study?

    Ⓐ She's <u>confident</u> that they're <u>reliable</u>.

    Ⓑ She's <u>convinced</u> of their <u>positive implications</u>.

    Ⓒ She's <u>concerned</u> they're based on <u>inaccurate data</u>.

2. What ⟨surprised⟩ the ⟨researchers⟩ about the ⟨effect⟩ of the omega-3 supplements in ⟨reducing⟩ ⟨triglycerides⟩?

    Ⓐ the <u>variation</u> between the <u>cardiac</u> and the <u>vascular effects</u>

    Ⓑ the <u>difference</u> they made to <u>levels</u> of the <u>fat</u> itself

    Ⓒ the <u>lack</u> of any <u>impact</u> on <u>related conditions</u>

3. What does Megan ⟨say⟩ about ⟨early studies⟩ of the ⟨diet⟩ of the Inuit people?

    Ⓐ Their <u>claims</u> <u>don't apply</u> to fish oil <u>supplements</u>.

    Ⓑ Their <u>findings</u> <u>weren't confirmed</u> by <u>later research</u>.

    Ⓒ <u>Those involved</u> selected the <u>wrong information</u> to analyse.

Task 7

🎧 2.15 **Now listen to the interview with Megan Fowler once again. Look at questions 4–6. Circle the most important words in the question and underline those in the options as you listen to the audio. Remember that you might not hear the same words that you find in the question.**

4. What is Megan's attitude towards the eating of oily fish?

    Ⓐ It may have a range of benefits for the body.

    Ⓑ It's probably better for the heart than supplements.

    Ⓒ It lacks certain elements essential for a balanced diet.

5. Megan suggests that the manufacturers' complaints about the doses used in the study

    Ⓐ were unjustified in a few cases.

    Ⓑ were based on a misunderstanding.

    Ⓒ were a misrepresentation of the truth.

6. Variations in the rate of absorbency of omega-3 were taken into account by only considering trials

    Ⓐ which were carried out over a year or longer.

    Ⓑ on patients who showed rapid adaptation to the drug.

    Ⓒ by researchers able to commit to an eight-year study.

What is a presentation like?

During a Listening Part C presentation, the speaker provides the structure of what you hear. The speaker introduces himself or herself and the topic at the beginning of the presentation, then talks about six different aspects of the topic. This means that there are six sections to the presentation. The speaker will pause before the beginning of each section, and will introduce the new aspect of the topic they're going to talk about. Sometimes, this may take the form of a question. For example:

So, what does this mean in terms of treatment?

What happened when this was put into practice?

What research has been done into this?

At other times, they will use the same or similar vocabulary as that of the question on your test paper.

Task 8

Can you identify the question cue in this introductory segment of an audio? Underline the words that show that the speaker is moving to the next question.

'When I first heard about social prescribing, I had some concerns, but I was still keen to explore how it might be of help to my patients who suffer from moderate levels of depression and anxiety.'

Task 9

Given below are three questions based on an audio extract. Can you identify which question relates to this introductory segment of the audio?

'Looking back, I realised that I'd been unnecessarily sceptical about prescribing activities that were already available in the community.'

1. Initially, Dr Simms was concerned that her patients on the gardening project might

    (A) be put off by the demanding nature of the work.

    (B) injure themselves whilst working in the garden.

    (C) feel frustrated by the scale of the project.

2. Dr Simms was pleased that, in their feedback, all three of her patients mentioned

    Ⓐ how much they enjoyed spending time outdoors.

    Ⓑ feeling satisfaction on the completion of tasks.

    Ⓒ a willingness to take part in future projects.

3. Looking back at the project, Dr Simms now understands that the success of social prescribing depends upon

    Ⓐ the type of activity that is selected.

    Ⓑ the attitude of individual patients.

    Ⓒ the central role played by the GP.

During a presentation, the speaker might focus on a disease or condition which has affected one of their patients. There may be some discussion about interventions that were put in place, and whether they were effective or not. This type of presentation may resemble a case review, in which healthcare professionals talk about interesting or difficult patient cases with their colleagues. Or it may be a review of recent research into a topic and how it has affected the speaker's practice.

Task 10

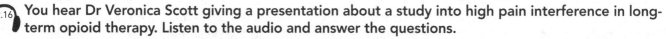 **You hear Dr Veronica Scott giving a presentation about a study into high pain interference in long-term opioid therapy. Listen to the audio and answer the questions.**

1. Why did Dr Scott read about the study?

    Ⓐ Her patients have musculoskeletal pain.

    Ⓑ Her patients reported the same pain levels.

    Ⓒ Her patients take the same type of painkiller.

2. Why was Dr Scott interested in one patient's comment?

    Ⓐ He described his pain in his own words.

    Ⓑ He scored his pain as greater than 70.

    Ⓒ He couldn't use the scores to describe his pain.

Continuing Professional Development

Some presentations are used for staff training, which is known as Continuing Professional Development (CPD). CPD sessions are often provided for all healthcare professionals in a hospital about a topic of general interest, and also cover mandatory (compulsory) training which must be provided every year on topics such as Infection Control, Moving and Handling, Data Confidentiality and CPR (Cardiopulmonary Resuscitation).

During the presentations, you hear healthcare professionals giving their view about a topic. For example, a healthcare professional may describe an initiative in patient care that they have been involved with. They may talk about their expectations of how successful they thought an initiative might be, or express surprise at the positive outcome of an initiative.

Imagine that you're listening to a presentation at work. You might hear about a project that a colleague has undertaken, and think about how you could make use of the information in your own practice. In Listening Part C, you will be assessed on your ability to understand the speaker's point of view or opinion about concrete facts relating to the topic.

You will hear a physiotherapist called David Browne giving a presentation about managing shin splint injuries. Listen to the audio and answer the questions.

1. What does David agree with his department about?

   (A) the importance of non-weight-bearing exercise

   (B) a steady return to high-impact exercise programmes

   (C) evidence about the effectiveness of yoga or swimming

2. What expression did you hear that told you about the physiotherapist's attitude?

_____

Example of a Listening Part C presentation

First, look at this context sentence to find out who is talking and what the topic of the presentation is:

'You hear a GP called Dr Georgia Simms giving a presentation on the subject of social prescribing.' You now know that a GP called Georgia Simms is the speaker, and that she's talking about social prescribing.

Now, look at these six questions to see what you think the interview might be about.

1. What does Dr Simms point out about the idea of social prescribing by GPs?

2. When Dr Simms first heard about social prescribing, she was worried that …

3. Why did Dr Simms choose a gardening project for her patients?

4. Initially, Dr Simms was concerned that her patients on the gardening project might …

5. Dr Simms was pleased that, in their feedback, all three of her patients mentioned …

6. Looking back at the project, Dr Simms now understands that the success of social prescribing depends upon …

Look for the words in the questions that tell you what you'll hear in each paragraph.

Question 1: asking about her attitude

Question 2: her reaction to the idea of social prescribing

Question 3: the reasons she chose that particular project for her patients

Question 4: her concerns about her patients doing the gardening project

Question 5: the results of the project

Question 6: what she's understood about social prescribing as a result of the project

The questions ask about Dr Simms' experience of being involved in the project and how her attitude towards social prescribing was influenced by it.

Some questions ask about Dr Simms' feelings about the project she was involved with, for example,

- (2) When Dr Simms first heard about social prescribing, she was **worried** that …
- (4) Initially, Dr Simms was **concerned** that her patients on the gardening project might …
- (5) Simms was **pleased** that, in their feedback, all three of her patients mentioned …

For question 2, you need to listen for what it was regarding social prescribing that Dr Simms was worried about. Perhaps she was worried about how to use social prescribing in her practice, or about how much time it would take to implement. Reading the questions will help you to find out what to listen for.

Some questions ask about the speaker's opinion after being involved in action research or reading about a study. The speaker may have changed their opinion, or have had it confirmed. Question 6, 'Looking back at the project, Dr Simms *now understands* that the success of social prescribing depends upon...', is an example of one of these questions. It asks about Dr Simms' opinion of social prescribing after setting up a gardening project for her patients.

Now, start the practice test. Allow yourself 90 seconds to read the context sentence and questions. Then listen to the audio **once** only.

Task 12

 You hear a GP called Dr Georgia Simms giving a presentation on the subject of social prescribing. You now have 90 seconds to read questions 1–6.

1. What does Dr Simms point out about the idea of social prescribing by GPs?

    (A) It has been promoted as part of their practice.

    (B) It was initially developed in her own local area.

    (C) It hasn't been well received by them all.

2. When Dr Simms first heard about social prescribing, she was worried that

    (A) she would no longer have a say in her patients' treatment.

    (B) some of her patients wouldn't want to see her any more.

    (C) she would be allocated less time with her patients.

3. Why did Dr Simms choose a gardening project for her patients?

    (A) Previous patients of hers had done it.

    (B) It offered them a range of health benefits.

    (C) The emphasis on physical fitness appealed to them.

4. Initially, Dr Simms was concerned that her patients on the gardening project might

    (A) be put off by the demanding nature of the work.

    (B) injure themselves whilst working in the garden.

    (C) feel frustrated by the scale of the project.

5. Dr Simms was pleased that, in their feedback, all three of her patients mentioned

    (A) how much they enjoyed spending time outdoors.

    (B) feeling satisfaction on the completion of tasks.

    (C) a willingness to take part in future projects.

6. Looking back at the project, Dr Simms now understands that the success of social prescribing depends upon

    (A) the type of activity that is selected.

    (B) the attitude of the individual patients.

    (C) the central role played by the GP.

READING
IN OET

CHAPTER 1

INTRODUCTION
TO THE READING SUB-TEST

The Reading sub-test is the same for all candidates taking OET. It is designed to assess the Reading skills you need in a medical workplace, so all of the topics relate to healthcare and can be understood by candidates from all professions. The questions test not only your comprehension, but also how well you can read to fulfil a particular function as a healthcare professional.

The reading texts will be extracts from reference materials used in the workplace, healthcare documents such as guidelines and policies, and articles on medical topics. Each part of the test focuses on specific skills; for example, reading to locate specific information, reading to understand main ideas, and reading to understand opinions and attitude. Understanding the purpose of each part will help you prepare for the test and apply these skills in the workplace, too.

A general medical background is enough to understand the texts in all three parts of the Reading sub-test. This makes the test accessible to candidates from all of the OET professions. There's no need to worry if you haven't read anything about the topics before. In fact, in all three parts of the Reading sub-test, you need to read the texts even if the topic seems familiar. OET tests the reading skills required in healthcare, and not knowledge of specific healthcare topics.

The Reading sub-test consists of 42 test questions, and takes a total of 60 minutes to complete. You get 15 minutes to do Part A, then 45 minutes to do Parts B and C together.

Reading Part A

As a healthcare professional, you probably refer to various sources of information in the course of your work. These can include presenting factors, dosage charts, discharge advice and procedures manuals, for example. The specific reasons for which healthcare professionals consult these reference materials vary according to their fields, but the general aim is usually to locate information needed in a healthcare situation. In Reading Part A, you will read extracts from four such reference materials, one of which will contain visual information.

The questions focus on finding information from these reference materials. The question types in Part A are matching, short answer, and sentence/note completion. The matching questions focus on testing whether you know where to find information from the sources provided in the test, such as extracts from presenting factors, medical guidelines, treatment pathways, drug information, medication tables, warnings, patient advice, etc. For example, you could be asked which extract contains:

- procedures for delivering pain relief for a fracture
- symptoms of an antidepressant overdose
- information about medication containing opioids
- nutrition advice for patients with anaemia

The short answer and sentence/note completion questions focus on locating specific pieces of information. For example, you could be asked to find:

- from a dosage chart, the maximum dose of morphine to give a patient
- from a medication table, recommended medication for patients over 16 years old with a severe urinary tract infection
- from a procedure document, a precaution you must take when deflating a Foley catheter balloon
- from a patient information leaflet, a condition that might develop in patients after a paracetamol overdose
- from a hospital protocol, a recommended course of action when administering IV fluids

To do well in Part A, you must understand how reference materials make information more accessible through layout features such as headings, tables, flow diagrams, bullet points and short paragraphs. Using these features to locate and read information is part of the key to success in Part A.

Reading Part B

Policy documents, institutional guidelines, manuals and other official workplace communications play an important role in guiding you during the course of your work in a healthcare setting. In Reading Part B, you read extracts from different types of workplace communication used by an organisation to convey information to its employees. Each question in Part B has a different focus, such as understanding the purpose, the main message or important details of a workplace communication.

The questions in Part B are in a multiple-choice format with three answer options and one correct answer.

Part B questions could ask you to identify, for example:

- what a notice on feeding tubes says about staff authorised to change these tubes
- what an administrative guideline on blood administration says about staff training
- the purpose of an email about the safe use of opioids
- what to do when seeking consent for a post-mortem examination
- what a memo reminds staff to do when using bed rails

The key to doing well in Part B is to understand what kind of information you can expect from these types of workplace communications. You also need to understand what the questions are asking you to do. They are usually related to how you would read in real life; for example, if there's an email about a change in pre-operative procedure, you would read it quickly to see what it is about and whether it applies to you. It's important to practise reading such documents so you're familiar with their purpose and language.

Reading Part C

In addition to reading materials directly related to their work, healthcare professionals also read to keep themselves updated on the latest developments in healthcare as part of their continuing professional development. Reading Part C focuses on this kind of reading. The texts are typically extracts from articles, and often contain several opinions from different researchers. They may also contain a discussion about the experiences of a professional or a patient, from different points of view. Questions for Part C are also in a multiple-choice format, but in this part there are four answer options to choose from, with one correct answer.

Reading Part C questions could ask you to recognise:

- how a writer feels about an expert's views on something; for example, a common thyroid therapy
- the writer's purpose in quoting different opinions on the latest research; for example, a new surgical method for joint replacements
- what a writer is suggesting through the use of a particular word or phrase
- the main message of a paragraph that explains an example or quotes a study

Part C requires a different set of skills from Parts A and B. Reading review articles on research will help you to develop the ability to recognise opinion, attitudes and main ideas. The kind of articles you'll read in Part C relate to how research affects the treatment and management of medical conditions. You may even read about the experience of professionals and patients in the context of practice. Rather than presenting a lot of detailed facts, statistics and data, however, these kinds of articles focus on discussing a topic from different points of view. To do well in Part C, it's helpful to read articles commenting on research rather than the original research papers themselves.

The Reading sub-test covers three core types of reading that healthcare professionals need to do at work. Part A deals with reading reference materials consulted in specific medical situations; Part B moves to reading *background* documents that guide the work of healthcare professionals; and Part C deals with reading about wider medical issues, to stay well informed in the workplace. If you approach the test in this way, you will be well placed to understand the requirements of each part, and how to maximise your score.

CHAPTER 2

READING
PART A

Format of Reading Part A

At work, you often use reference materials to find information that assists you in performing everyday tasks. For example, you may need to verify dosage amounts from a chart, or consult presenting factors to diagnose a problem. To find specific information, you generally read sections of these reference materials rather than reading every word from start to finish, as you would a book or an article. Reading Part A tests your ability to find the information you're looking for quickly and accurately.

Reading Part A has four short texts that a health professional may refer to in the workplace. To understand this better, imagine a specific healthcare situation in which you would need to consult different reference materials to find relevant information for completing a task. For example, if a patient is presenting with burns, you may need to check the appropriate treatment pathway to understand what to do next; or you may need to consult some medical guidelines to find out what discharge advice to give a patient after a joint replacement. At least one of the extracts in Part A will have visual or numerical information, but you won't need to make calculations.

You will have 15 minutes to answer 20 questions, writing directly in the spaces provided in the question paper. At the end of this time, both the question paper and text booklet containing the texts will be collected.

The questions assess your ability to locate information for a purpose, just as you would do as a healthcare professional. These are the question types in Part A:

• matching questions
• short answer questions
• sentence completion or note completion

Part A is structured to mimic your professional practice. So it starts with questions that require you to determine where the information is located, before reading more carefully to locate the specific information you require: for example, finding the correct dosage. As there is a natural progression to the test, it is crucial that you start from the beginning with the matching questions, and not in the middle of the test or working your way backwards. The content and nature of the four texts in this first section helps to orientate you. This then assists you in speed and accuracy as the test progresses to include more detailed reading in later questions. You go from reading quickly in order to understand where to find information, to reading carefully to locate specific information.

Each question carries one mark and there is no negative marking, so there's a total of 20 marks for this section.

Preparing for Reading Part A

The key to preparing for Reading Part A lies in understanding its purpose. As mentioned earlier, you probably refer to texts like this all the time at work, and therefore will have already developed some reading skills to locate information from different sources. You may be using these skills subconsciously, but using them actively during the test will help you to perform better.

Matching questions

When you read something, you do not necessarily read every single word. This may be because you are looking for something specific in the text to help you complete a task, and therefore don't need to read the whole document to get this information.

If you want to find a piece of information, the first thing you probably ask yourself is, *What reference materials will contain this information?* Then, when you access the relevant reference materials, you look at them quickly to see which one contains the information you need.

The matching questions test whether you can identify where to look if you need to find some specific information. These questions are always at the beginning of Reading Part A because they can help you in answering the later questions.

Reference materials such as dosage charts, treatment pathways and so on, are also written in a way that makes it easy for readers to get the information they want efficiently. For example, they may have bullet points, tables, graphs, short paragraphs, or pictures. Use these features to locate the information required. You can get an idea of what the reference materials are about by glancing quickly through:

- titles of the texts
- headings and sub-headings within the text
- picture labels or diagrams
- words formatted in bold or italics

You should also scan the texts for any words that stand out to you. When you're searching for answers to the matching task questions, you don't need to read every word because the matching questions aren't focused on details. Instead, they assess whether you're able to identify *where* you can find the information you're looking for. For example, if you will need to make an assessment of a burn wound, you need to refer to a table like the one in Text C of the sample task on page 72, which describes the features of the wound at each depth.

Use this approach to do the sample matching tasks that follow.

Task 1

For each question, 1–6, decide which text (A, B, C or D) the information comes from. You may use any letter more than once.

In which text can you find information about:

1. the time frame for healing of burn wounds? _____
2. pain management for burns? _____
3. the procedure for replacing fluids lost by the body? _____
4. degrees of burns? _____
5. progression of analgesic medication for burns? _____
6. possible adverse reactions to a dressing? _____

Treatment of burns: Texts

Text A Silver sulphadiazine; Flamazine

Cautions

- hepatic and renal impairment
- Glucose-6-PD deficiency
- may inactivate enzymatic debriding agents

Contraindications

- pregnancy
- breastfeeding
- sensitivity to sulphonamides
- not recommended for neonates

Side effects

- allergic reactions including burning, itching, rashes, urticaria, scaling and redness
- Argyria has been reported after prolonged use.

- Leucopenia has been reported so blood levels should be monitored if a large area is being treated.

Administration

- Silver sulphadiazine should be applied with a sterile applicator.
- Apply in a layer 3–5 mm thick.
- Dressings should be changed daily for burns and three times a week for ulcers.
- In burns, silver sulphadiazine should be applied daily (more frequently if there is heavy exudate).
- It should be applied daily or on alternate days in leg ulcers and pressure ulcers (not recommended if there is heavy exudate).
- It should be applied every two or three days to fingertip injuries.

Fluid resuscitation algorithm in adults

Step 1: Using the ABCDE (Airway, Breathing, Circulation, Disability, Exposure) approach, assess whether the patient is hypovolaemic and needs fluid resuscitation

Assess fluid volume considering clinical examination, trends, context and indicators that a patient may need fluid resuscitation (see text).

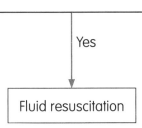

Yes

Fluid resuscitation

Step 2: Initiate treatment

- Identify cause of fluid deficit, and respond.
- Give a fluid bolus of 500 ml of crystalloid (containing sodium in the range of 130–154 mmol/L) over less than 15 minutes.

Step 3: Reassess the patient using the ABCDE approach

Does the patient still need fluid resuscitation? Seek expert help if unsure.

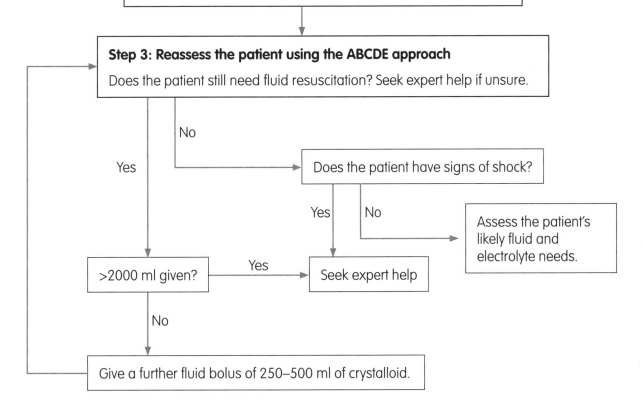

No

Yes

Does the patient have signs of shock?

Yes   No

Assess the patient's likely fluid and electrolyte needs.

>2000 ml given?   Yes   Seek expert help

No

Give a further fluid bolus of 250–500 ml of crystalloid.

Adapted from NICE (2013)

Characteristics of a burn wound

Depth of burn	Skin structures involved	Key characteristics	Scar formation
Superficial	Epidermis	• skin is dry and intact, red and very painful • blanches under pressure • minimal tissue damage • usually no blisters but may form blisters up to 48 hours following initial injury	• heals well within three to seven days with minimal or no treatment • no obvious scarring
Superficial – partial thickness	Epidermis and superficial dermis	• blisters immediately (pink/red wound bed under blister) • red in areas, moist and exuding • brisk capillary refill (blanches under pressure) • painful and sensitive to temperature changes	• should heal spontaneously within 10–21 days if no infection within or pressure on the wound • minimal scarring but difficult to predict • scar may appear very red for the first six weeks then hypo-pigmented or hyper-pigmented
Deep partial thickness (deep dermal)	Epidermis and dermis; hair follicles and sebaceous glands	• pale, white/creamy in colour; may have large, easily 'liftable' blisters less moist initially • difficult to assess capillary refill • slightly painful with areas that are insensate – sensitive to deep pressure but not pin prick	• will take >30 days to heal and therefore it is preferable to skin graft early to maximise healing • will have scar of the graft and donor site
Full thickness	Epidermis and dermis; subcutaneous tissue – possibly deeper structures if chemical or electrical injury	• may appear waxy white, cherry red, grey or leathery • minimal or no pain in actual wound – no response to pressure or temperature • wound may have less deep and very painful peripheries	• skin graft required to heal as too few regenerative elements remain in skin structure to allow for spontaneous healing • scar will be influenced by genetic predisposition and grafting techniques used

Text D Recommended standards for analgesics for burn patients

All patients should be prescribed the following:

- regular paracetamol (1g every six hours)
- regular non-steroidal anti-inflammatory drugs (unless contraindicated)
- opioid analgesia in a dose – the route and frequency appropriate to the individual
- antiemetic medication to be given as needed
- laxative to be given if opioids are administered

The analgesic ladder has three steps, which are to be followed in sequence until the patient is free of pain. It involves prompt oral administration of drugs as follows:

- Step 1 – non-opioids (paracetamol and NSAIDS)
- Step 2 – mild opioids such as codeine
- Step 3 – strong opioids such as morphine

Drugs from the previous step of the ladder can be continued or not as appropriate. Additional adjuvant drugs can be used to calm fear and anxiety. WHO recommends that drugs be given *by the clock* every three to six hours to prevent breakthrough pain, rather than on demand when the patient is already experiencing pain.

Task 2

Tick the layout features that helped you answer the matching questions for the task you just did.

Text	Headings and sub-headings	Bullet points	Numbered list	Short paragraphs	Words in bold or italics	Pictures/ labels of pictures	Table row and column headings
A							
B							
C							
D							

Short answer and sentence/note completion questions

Once you've identified the correct source of information, the next step is to look for the specific details you need, in the correct section. For example, let's assume that you want to know whether you can prescribe stronger painkilling medication like an opioid for someone with a burn wound. After finishing the matching questions, you know that this sort of information is in *Recommended standards for analgesics for burn patients* (Text D), so you can search for the information there. Rather than starting at the beginning and reading the information in order, you can look across the section to find something about opioids. Opioids are mentioned in three places in the second section of the text, but the bullet points in Steps 2 and 3 tell you exactly what kind of opioids you can use, and how they should be administered.

Extract from Text D

The analgesic ladder has three steps, which are to be followed in sequence until the patient is free of pain. It involves prompt oral administration of drugs as follows:

- Step 1 – non-opioids (paracetamol and NSAIDS)
- Step 2 – mild opioids such as codeine
- Step 3 – strong opioids such as morphine

> Information about opioids is given in these bullet points.

It is important to rely on the texts, not on your medical knowledge, to answer the questions. You shouldn't worry if the topic seems unfamiliar. The focus is still on finding information, but you may need to read more carefully to answer short answer and sentence/note completion questions. However, by the time you begin answering these questions, you will have become more familiar with the four sources of information.

Follow these steps to answer short answer and sentence/note completion questions.

- Read the question carefully. You may choose to underline a word or phrase from the question if you feel this helps you, but always make sure you understand the meaning of the question.
- Understand what kind of information the question is asking you to find. For example, you may need to look for a particular type of medication or possible adverse reaction to the medication.
- Find the relevant section where the information is likely to be.
- Read the surrounding text to see if it answers the question.
- Finally, copy the relevant information as your answer without changing it in any way.

Let's look at short answer question examples based on the texts you just skimmed. Key words in each question are in bold.

Question	What kind of information do I look for?	Answer
How often should an **antibiotic** be applied to a burn if there isn't a great amount of **exudate**?	a time reference	daily
At what depth of burn is it essential to have a **skin graft as quickly as possible**?	name of layer of skin	full thickness

In the first example, you know that you need to look for a time reference that tells you when an antibiotic should be applied. The answer is under the *Administration* sub-heading of Text A on Silver sulphadiazine.

Extract from Text A

Administration

- Silver sulphadiazine should be applied with a sterile applicator.
- Apply in a layer 3–5 mm thick.
- Dressings should be changed daily for burns and three times a week for ulcers.
- In burns, silver sulphadiazine should be applied daily (more frequently if there is heavy exudate).
- It should be applied daily or on alternate days in leg ulcers and pressure ulcers (not recommended if there is heavy exudate).
- It should be applied every two or three days to fingertip injuries.

> There are time references in both bullet points. If you read carefully, you can understand that one refers to burns while the other refers to ulcers.

In the second example, you need to identify which depth of burn requires a graft. However, there are two places in Text C that refer to skin grafts (*Deep partial thickness* and *Full thickness*). If you read the question carefully, you will see that it is asking when it is essential to have a skin graft. Using this information, you can narrow the answer down to *Full thickness* because it is at that depth that skin grafts are required, and not at *Deep partial thickness* where they are preferable or optional.

Extract from Text C

Deep partial thickness (deep dermal)	Epidermis and dermis; hair follicles and sebaceous glands	• pale, white/creamy in colour; may have large, easily 'liftable' blisters less moist initially • difficult to assess capillary refill • slightly painful with areas that are insensate – sensitive to deep pressure but not pin prick	• will take >30 days to heal and therefore it is preferable to skin graft early to maximise healing • will have scar of the graft and donor site
Full thickness	Epidermis and dermis; subcutaneous tissue – possibly deeper structures if chemical or electrical injury	• may appear waxy white, cherry red, grey or leathery • minimal or no pain in actual wound – no response to pressure or temperature • wound may have less deep and very painful peripheries	• skin graft required to heal as too few regenerative elements remain in skin structure to allow for spontaneous healing • scar will be influenced by genetic predisposition and grafting techniques used

Copy the answer directly from the text, paying special attention to spelling, to ensure that you record the answer correctly.

> Grafts are mentioned in these two rows. Since they're mentioned in all these bullet points, you need to read carefully to find the answer.

Task 3

Using the table below, find answers to the questions from the texts on burns on pages 70–73. Make sure you:

- **identify the sort of information you will need to find**
- **underline any keywords that might help you find your answer.**

Question	What kind of information do I look for?
What medication should accompany the use of opioids?	
What should be done if the patient exhibits signs of shock?	
What condition may develop after long-term use of sulphadiazine?	

Check your answers before moving on to Task 4.

Task 4

Answer each of the questions with a word or short phrase from one of the texts. Each answer may include words, numbers or both.

1. What medication should accompany the use of opioids?

   _____

2. What should be done if the patient exhibits signs of shock?

   _____

3. What condition may develop after long-term use of sulphadiazine?

   _____

The questions later in the test require more careful reading. Let's look at a couple of examples of sentence completion questions that need careful reading.

> The wound will not respond to _____ if it is waxy white or leathery.

Since you're familiar with what kind of information the texts contain, you should be able to locate the section that will give you this information. In this case it is in the table (Text C). You probably also know that the appearance of the wound is described in the *Key characteristics* column of the table, so this would be the first place to look for the answer.

Extract from Text C

Key characteristics
• skin is dry and intact, red and very painful • blanches under pressure • minimal tissue damage • usually no blisters but may form blisters up to 48 hours following initial injury
• blisters immediately (pink/red wound bed under blister) • red in areas, moist and exuding • brisk capillary refill (blanches under pressure) • painful and sensitive to temperature changes
• pale, white/creamy in colour; may have large, easily 'liftable' blisters less moist initially • difficult to assess capillary refill • slightly painful with areas that are insensate – sensitive to deep pressure but not pin prick
• may appear waxy white, cherry red, grey or leathery • minimal or no pain in actual wound – no response to pressure or temperature • wound may have less deep and very painful peripheries

> Using the words *waxy white* and *leathery* you can locate the information in the table. However, you need to read the bullet points carefully to complete the sentence.

After you find the information, be sure to record it correctly. In this case, you only need to write *pressure or temperature* and nothing more. Don't write *no response to temperature or pressure* because it doesn't make grammatical sense in the sentence.

The wound will not respond to **no response to pressure or temperature** if it is waxy white or leathery. ✗

The wound will not respond to **pressure or temperature** if it is waxy white or leathery. ✓

Here is another sentence completion question:

> Analgesics should be administered _____ rather than when the patient is already experiencing pain.

The answer is in Text D which is about pain management. The sentence completion question indicates that you need to look for what to do to prevent a patient from experiencing pain. The answer is in the last paragraph of Text D.

Extract from Text D

…Drugs from the previous step of the ladder can be continued or not as appropriate. Additional adjuvant drugs can be used to calm fear and anxiety. WHO recommends that drugs are given 'by the clock', every three to six hours to prevent breakthrough pain rather than on demand when the patient is already experiencing pain.

> You can see that the answer is in the last sentence, but you still need to read carefully because 'by the clock' could easily be mistaken for the answer. *By the clock* refers to the method of recording or keeping time, but doesn't tell you how often you should administer medication to prevent pain.

Now, the information you found needs to be recorded carefully. In this example, you need to include the word *every* because the sentence won't make grammatical sense without it.

Analgesics should be administered **three to six hours** rather than when the patient is already experiencing pain. ✗

Analgesics should be administered **every three to six hours** rather than when the patient is already experiencing pain. ✓

Task 5

Complete each of the sentences with a word or short phrase from one of the texts on pages 70–73. Each answer may include words, numbers or both.

1. If _____ formed soon after injury, the wound has affected the dermis and epidermis of the skin.

2. Fear and anxiety in burns patients should be treated with _____.

3. The fluid bolus must be administered within a period of _____.

4. NSAIDs can be administered in _____ of the analgesic ladder.

5. Patients can expect red scars of partially thick superficial burn wounds to become pigmented after _____.

Tips for scoring

- Since this is a timed task, remember that the challenge comes from being able to find the information quickly. The questions themselves won't require you to do more than finding a specific piece of information, so don't worry if you see complicated tables, charts and graphs.

- When you're doing the matching task, pay special attention to the titles of the texts because they will give you clues about the purpose of the texts which, in turn, will help you answer the questions in the later sections.
- Don't spend too much time on one question if you can't find the answer to it. You may come across it later, when scanning for other answers. Note that the questions don't follow the order of the texts.
- Take care to record your answers correctly. You should use the same form of the word or short phrase as given in the four texts and check that you've spelled it correctly. Once you've added the answer to the sentence completion question, re-read the whole sentence to ensure it makes grammatical sense.
- Don't rely on any previous medical knowledge you may have on the topic. The sub-task is focused on language and not knowledge, so the answer will always be given in the text. If you rely on your own knowledge to answer the question, you may get it wrong and lose marks in the test.

FAQs

1. **What does 'You may use any letter more than once' in the matching question mean?**

   Each of the reference materials in Reading Part A is identified with a letter (Texts A, B, C and D). You need to use these letters when writing the answers for the matching question. One text will be the answer for more than one question, so don't worry if you use a letter more than once.

2. **What does 'letters, numbers or both' mean in the short answer questions?**

   'Both' here refers to a combination of words and numbers. For example, an answer like '15 minutes' is a combination of a number and a word. You don't need to change the words in any way; for example, if the answer is a verb in the present tense, you don't need to change it into the past tense. Therefore, it is important to copy the word or phrase exactly as it appears in the text.

3. **What if I spell a word wrong?**

   An answer that is incorrectly spelled won't receive marks. You can use either British or American spelling variations (for example, litre or liter), but ensure that you spell them correctly. As all answers are taken from the text, you can always check the spelling of the word in the text to ensure that you have not made any spelling errors.

4. **Can I use abbreviations or short forms?**

   Abbreviations should only be used if that is how the word appears in the reference materials themselves. Don't use short forms of words such as those used in SMS or chat communications.

5. **How do I prepare for Reading Part A?**

   You can practise using all kinds of reading materials, even non-medical ones. For example, you can read a restaurant menu to find the price of a dish, or check the contents of a textbook to see if it contains a chapter on a specific topic. Get into the habit of looking at the headings, titles, pictures and differently formatted words. When trying to find information, look for unusual features of words rather than just for the beginning of the word. For example, notice what makes the word stand out from the others. It might contain unusual letters (for example x, z or j) or double letters (for example ss, mm or cc): look for these features when searching for the word. Setting your devices to English and using an English-only dictionary also helps in improving the skills needed to complete this part of the test successfully.

CHAPTER 3

READING
PART B

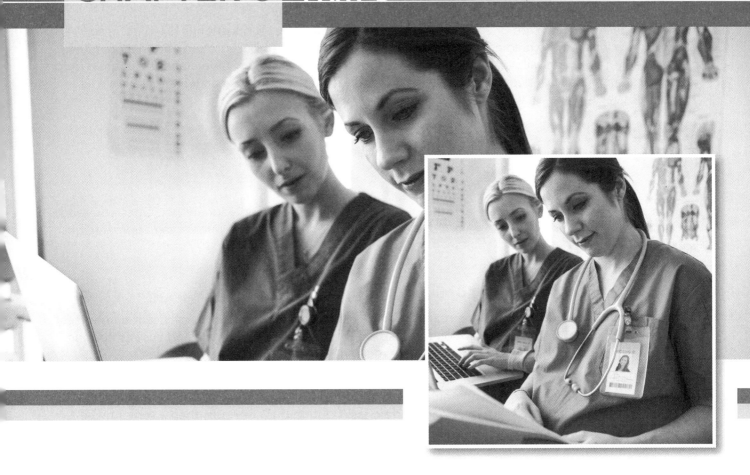

Format of Reading Part B

In your work as a healthcare professional, you often need to read a lot of workplace communications such as guidelines, manuals, emails, memos and policy documents. The purpose of these communications is to help you work according to the standards of an organisation, and to understand changes and updates to existing workplace requirements. Part B focuses on workplace communications and assesses a range of reading skills, particularly your ability to recognise their main message, purpose and details.

There are six extracts, each about 100–140 words. These may be complete, for example, an email on a change in policy, or a part of a longer text, such as a policy on patient safety.

Part B contains only six questions, all in a three-option multiple choice format. There is a total of six marks, each question carring one mark. To answer, you need to shade the circle next to the option you believe is correct, in a separate answer booklet that will be given to you with your question paper. The total time available for both Parts B and C is 45 minutes, so you need to manage your time effectively. Part C has more questions than Part B, so you need to leave more time for Part C.

Preparing for Reading Part B

You can expect to read a variety of workplace communications in the test, so a good way to approach these questions is to think about what kind of information the communication contains, and what your purpose for reading it might be in a healthcare setting. Just like any other part of the Reading sub-test, questions in Part B reflect the real-life purpose of reading, so approaching it from that point of view will help you prepare. For example, if a patient refuses to allow marking of the surgical site before an operation, you would check the pre-operative guidelines to see what you should do. A Part B question on pre-operative guidelines may ask you to identify what the guidelines say about what to do if patients refuse pre-operative surgical site marking.

You are always told what type of communication the extract in a Part B question is taken from, so you will know what you're reading about. You will also be given some background information in the context sentence, which will help you understand its setting. Take time to understand the context before reading the extract and answering the question. A good strategy is to focus on what the extract as a whole is conveying, and on what the question is asking you to do.

To do this, ask yourself:

- What kind of extract is this and who are the intended readers?
- Why would the readers need to read this sort of communication?
- What is the question asking me to do?

Use the context given in the extract and the question before deciding on your answer. Once you read the extract with the context in mind, you'll be able to focus on its meaning, rather than approach it in isolation.

Reading questions and answer options

Workplace communications typically contain specific verbs that carry subtle but significant differences in meaning. It's important to pay attention to these words when reading extracts and answer options, because they can help you better understand the meaning of the text or the question.

For example, the words 'supervise' and 'delegate' are typically used in the context of communications for staff in charge of a department, and although related, they mean different things. For example, if a notice instructs senior nurses to *delegate* certain tasks during busy periods, then a senior nurse would need to decide which tasks are suitable for *delegating* (giving) to other members of staff, and would then need to *supervise* (oversee) these staff to ensure they were carrying out the delegated tasks properly. Understanding the difference in meaning between these two words is crucial.

Similarly, answer options in Part B questions may also contain verbs that could help you understand what the question is asking. Look at the following short extract from an email to nurses in charge of operating rooms, and a sample question.

Charge nurses are instructed to assign responsibility of assessing availability of rooms and room allocation to another nurse in the Operating Room (OR) team. However, please continue to oversee patient flow from other units into the OR. It is imperative to continue all other work related to scheduling of patients with the attending anaesthesiologist.

The email asks charge nurses to

Ⓐ *delegate* distribution of rooms.

Ⓑ *supervise* the anaesthesiologist.

Ⓒ *authorise* OR team members to perform surgery.

If you understand the meaning of the three verbs in italics, you'll be able to answer the question since you can connect the meaning in the answer options to the meaning of the extract. In this example, the answer is Option A since the only responsibility charge nurses can 'delegate', or give away, to another team member is assessing the availability and distribution of rooms.

Match the verbs with their meanings.

	Verb		Meaning	Answer
1.	install	a.	watch regularly to find out what's happening	1 – b
2.	set up	b.	fix or connect equipment, usually for the first time	
3.	supervise	c.	give part of your work or duties to someone else	
4.	delegate	d.	use a tool to find the exact size or amount of something	
5.	authorise	e.	make something ready to use	
6.	adjust	f.	examine something to find out if it's working properly	
7.	measure	g.	approve or give permission to something	
8.	monitor	h.	check that someone is doing something correctly	
9.	check	i.	begin	
10.	initiate	j.	change something to make it more accurate	

Reading details in workplace communication

Every organisation communicates to its employees through emails, memos, guidelines or policies. The way you read them depends on your purpose for doing so. For example, you usually consult guidelines or policies when faced with a problem or unusual situation and want to know what to do. When looking for advice in a guideline or policy, you read one or two details carefully. Some Part B questions test your ability to read for detail. This means you read some pieces of information very carefully, paying attention to the meaning of a particular part of the text.

Guidelines

Guideline extracts in Part B typically deal with work practices related to the administration and implementation of safety procedures. In Part B, you may read a small part of a set of such guidelines on a subject. This guideline extract has a heading, and is usually numbered to show that it's part of a bigger set of guidelines.

When you read these kinds of guidelines, you probably look for what they say on a particular issue, so it's often the case that in these types of questions you need to read certain sentences of the extract more carefully than others. For example, you may be asked to read a detail relating to

- when to do something
- how to do something
- why it is important to do something

When answering these questions, focus on a part of the extract rather than the whole text, and read the question carefully to understand exactly what you need to look for.

Read these sentences from Part B extracts from guidelines that will be used in the tasks in this Chapter. Identify whether the sentence tells you when to do something, how to do something, or why it's important to do something.

What the guideline says ...	When, how or why?
a. Patients must be referred to a doctor and evaluated immediately should their oxygen saturation levels fall suddenly.	When it is necessary to refer a patient to a doctor
b. A patient's oxygen saturation levels must be recorded at the same time as their vital signs, as frequently as their condition requires.	
c. Deterioration in a patient's condition can be assessed by observing their skin colour and respiratory rate.	
d. 'Standing' is offered to patients post-discharge after first introducing the procedure during their hospital admission.	
e. Chlorhexidine mouthwashes can reduce the level of plaque and bacteria, but should not be used more than twice a day because of their alcohol content.	

Look at an example of a question about guideline extract 4.2.3 on the next page.

Part B Question 1

1. The extract from the guidelines reminds nurses to monitor oxygen saturation levels

   (A) when a patient's condition changes unexpectedly.

   (B) less frequently in patients with certain conditions.

   (C) with other observations to assess a patient's condition.

If you think about the wording of question 1 and its implications, this kind of guideline extract would probably be consulted by nurses when they want to check whether they're doing something correctly. The question asks what the guidelines 'remind' nurses to do. Their purpose for reading is to look for the reminder about what they must do. In the question, the word 'monitor' means observing or checking over a period of time, so they're looking for guidance on *when* to do something. In this case, they need to look for guidance on when to monitor oxygen saturation levels.

The extract explains that patients should be referred to a doctor if their saturation levels drop. It also describes how to tell if a patient's condition has deteriorated. However, there is only one sentence that explains when to record their oxygen saturation levels.

Now, read the extract with this context in mind and then answer the question.

4.2.3 Oxygen saturation levels

Patients must be referred to a doctor and evaluated immediately should their oxygen saturation levels fall suddenly. The Early Warning Score (EWS) protocol gives medical and nursing staff guidance about which oxygen saturation levels should be reported (< 90%). A patient's oxygen saturation levels must be recorded at the same time as their vital signs as frequently as their condition requires. Deterioration in a patient's condition can be assessed by observing a patient's skin colour and respiratory rate. A bluish tinge to the skin can indicate peripheral cyanosis whilst a respiratory rate of less than 8, or more than 25, is outside the normal respiratory rate range.

Now that you've understood how to read guidelines with a context and purpose, try and answer a Part B question based on a notice using the same approach. To help you understand how to do this, the context and purpose have been described in the table below with the help of three questions.

a. What kind of extract is this, and who are the intended readers?	It is a notice for care home staff.
b. Why would the readers need to read this sort of communication?	The notice may be announcing a new update, informing them of changes, or reminding them to do something.
c. What is the question asking me to do?	It is asking me to find out what care home staff need to do regarding residents who manage their own medication.

Now answer Part B Question 2, referring to the notice below for context and purpose.

Part B Question 2

2. The notice is informing care home staff of the need to

   Ⓐ supervise residents closely if they're managing their own medication.

   Ⓑ encourage residents who would like to manage their own medication.

   Ⓒ monitor residents to ensure that they are able to manage their own medication.

Self-administration of medications

Care home staff should assume that residents can manage their own medicines, unless a risk assessment indicates otherwise. An individual risk assessment should always be undertaken to determine how much support is needed by a resident to continue their self-administration of medications. Risk assessments take a resident's wishes into consideration as well as deciding whether residents may be harmed, should they continue managing their own medications. Mental capacity plays a part in whether the correct dose and time of administration can be followed, so regular reviews of the risk assessment must be performed. The frequency of the risk assessment will be based on the individual needs of each resident, and must involve both the resident and their family in the decision-making.

Reading for main ideas in workplace communications

You may also be asked to identify the main idea in a workplace communication. This requires reading for the overall message of the extract rather than for one or two details.

In order to recognise the main idea, identify what each sentence is about. The sentences may be instructions, reasons, examples or descriptions of the main idea. One or two details in the extract may not be related to the main idea, so focus on the overall meaning rather than worrying about one or two details.

Guidelines

You may consult guidelines when you want to know what to do in a particular situation or when faced with a specific issue.

Look at the following extract from some guidelines on oral hygiene. Think about the key phrases in each sentence. Some words have been highlighted to help you.

4.2.1 Oral hygiene

Mouthwash should be available for patients; they may prefer to use their own but those that contain alcohol can have <u>a drying effect on the mouth</u>. Chlorhexidine mouthwashes can reduce the level of plaque and bacteria but should not be used more than twice a day because of their alcohol content. Using 0.9% saline is advised as this <u>does not affect the pH of saliva</u> and is flavourless. Lemon and glycerine swabs are discouraged – the lemon's acidity damages tooth enamel and <u>glycerine draws fluid away from the tissues, reducing saliva production</u>. Glycerol or petroleum jelly can be applied to the lips but can feel sticky; patients' own lip balm or a water-soluble gel can be used.

> Most of the sentences in this extract talk about appropriate ways to maintain oral hygiene without affecting saliva.

The main idea of this guideline extract is how to maintain moisture balance in the mouth when using oral hygiene products. Most of the sentences in the extract are about products to use or avoid in order to maintain moisture balance in the mouth.

Task 3

Look at the following guideline extracts and select the main idea that fits each one best. As you read, pay attention to what the reasons, examples, descriptions or instructions are about.

Extract 1

5.1.3 Pre-operative ECG

ECG is recommended for patients who are known to have coronary heart disease, significant arrhythmia, peripheral arterial disease, cerebrovascular disease or any other significant structural heart disease – except when undergoing low risk surgery.

ECG is reasonable for patients who are undergoing vascular surgery but have no clinical risk factors, or for patients with one or more clinical risk factors who are scheduled for intermediate risk surgery.

Low risk patients who are undergoing low risk surgeries do not need any ECG; nor do patients undergoing cataract surgery.

1. Which of the following is the best main idea for the extract?

   (A) classification of patients for testing

   (B) exceptions to testing

   (C) precautions to take when testing

Extract 2

3.2.3 Preparation for surgery: Hand scrub

All staff working on the surgical team must use an antiseptic solution to scrub arms and hands for a minimum of two minutes before the first procedure of the day. For subsequent procedures, a shorter period is acceptable. A thorough cleaning under fingernails is necessary for the first scrub of the day. After the surgical scrub, members of the surgical team are advised to keep their hands up and away from the body to allow water to drip away from the tips of the fingers towards the elbows.

2. Which of the following is the best main idea for the extract?

   (A) instructions on how to clean hands

   (B) instructions on how to maintain hygiene during surgery

   (C) instructions on what to use when cleaning hands

Extract 3

4.3.3 Gloves

Good quality sterile gloves must be worn for all procedures. The use of two pairs of gloves is recommended in orthopaedic surgeries where studies show that as much as 50% of gloves are punctured, especially during cemented total joint arthroplasties. Another advantage of wearing double gloves is that they prevent viral transmissions to other surgical team members. In the event of an accidental puncture, gloves must be changed immediately. Routine changing of outer gloves after the draping procedure is also advised because draping could cause contamination.

3. Which of the following is the best main idea for the extract?

   (A) reasons why gloves are delicate

   (B) reasons why extra gloves prevent infections

   (C) reasons why extra gloves are optional

Task 4

Answer Part B Question 3 below, which is based on a guideline extract. As you read, use these questions to help you think about the context and purpose:

- What kind of extract is this and who are the intended readers?
- Why would the readers need to read this sort of communication?
- What is the question asking me to do?

Part B Question 3

3. The extract from the guidelines for physiotherapists dealing with spinal injuries

   (A) explains how to implement a standing procedure.

   (B) suggests alternative ways of initiating a standing procedure.

   (C) outlines possible problems arising from a standing procedure.

3.4.5 Standing adults following Spinal Cord Injury

Because Spinal Cord Injury (SCI) is a long-term condition, it is important that patients, health professionals and caregivers recognise their key role in SCI management. 'Standing' is offered to patients post discharge after first introducing the procedure during their hospital admission. Physiotherapists initiate a standing programme with patients after advising about the potential benefits of standing, explaining the barriers to standing and listing the equipment that will be needed for the process. The equipment used compensates for the loss of muscle control following a spinal cord injury, and relies on support from the splinting of lower limbs and the use of a tilt-table to enable patients to remain upright.

Main message questions can be based on other types of communication, such as manuals, memos, emails, memos or notices.

Manuals

You refer to manuals at work when you want to know how to handle medical equipment, so Reading Part B questions may ask you what to do when something goes wrong with a piece of equipment, how to find out what the problem is (troubleshooting), or how to use the equipment in a particular situation.

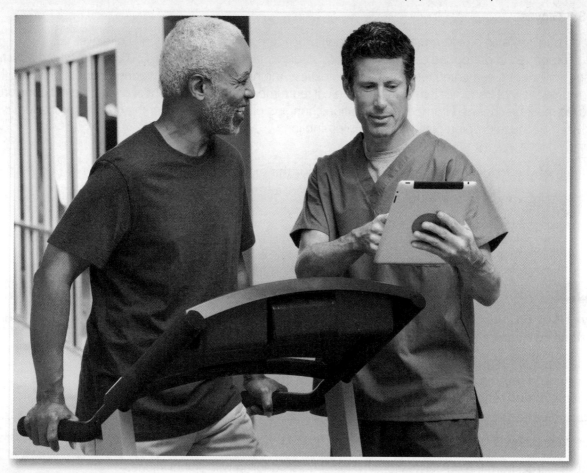

Task 5

Answer Part B Question 4, which is based on an extract from a manual. As you read, use the questions below to help you think about context and purpose.

- What kind of extract is this and who are the intended readers?
- Why would the readers need to read this sort of communication?
- What is the question asking me to do?

Part B Question 4

4. The extract from the manual explains how to

  (A) install a CPM machine in the physiotherapy department.

  (B) set up a CPM machine for an individual patient.

  (C) use a CPM machine for particular exercises.

Continuous Passive Motion (CPM) Machine

- Before using the CPM Machine, calibrate the machine to fit the patient. Measure the length of the patient's femur from the greater trochanter to the joint line of the knee.
- Adjust the thigh cradle to match this measurement by loosening the thigh adjustment knobs and sliding the thigh cradle to the proper length.
- Loosen the calf cradle adjustment knobs and extend the foot assembly to accommodate placement of the patient's foot.
- Position the patient's leg in the unit.
- Slide the foot assembly towards the patient leaving a 15 cm gap between the patient's foot and the footplate. Tighten the calf cradle adjustment knobs securely.
- To adjust the foot assembly in plantar flex or dorsi flex positions, loosen the adjustment knobs on the foot assembly and adjust the foot plate to the desired positioning. Tighten the adjustment knobs securely.

Policies

Some Reading Part B extracts are from policy documents. Part B questions may focus on aspects of policies such as what you must or mustn't do, what is allowed under certain conditions, or exceptions to the policy.

Look at an example of a Reading Part B question based on an extract from a policy document. Remember to ask yourself the following questions.

- What kind of extract is this and who are the intended readers?
- Why would the readers need to read this sort of communication?
- What is the question asking me to do?

Part B Question 5

5. The policy document establishes that latex gloves

   (A) should only be used by nominated members of staff.

   (B) may need to be used by staff during certain procedures.

   (C) can be used as long as all staff are given advance warning.

Latex Allergy Policy

If a latex allergy has been identified in healthcare workers, non-latex gloves should be offered as an alternative. Where there may be a clinical requirement to use latex gloves, a risk assessment must justify their use and must also assess the risk of contracting dermatitis. Staff who are at risk of latex-related contact dermatitis must be identified and remain under health surveillance.

Non-latex gloves can offer a suitable alternative to latex gloves in most situations. However, latex gloves may be required for precision and dexterity in certain procedures. In such cases, a risk assessment confirms this need and ensures that a process is put in place, so that healthcare workers are monitored whilst using latex gloves and receive appropriate health screening each year.

Now, reflect on how you answered Part B Question 5, and fill in the table below.

What is the policy about?	What does it say about latex gloves?	What is the recommended action?	Are there any special conditions or exceptions mentioned?

Emails, memos and notices

Generally, when you receive an email or memo at work, you read it quickly first to see what it's about. Notices are similar. If it's relevant to you, then you read carefully, especially if there are one or two details that are new or important. Therefore, questions based on these three forms of workplace communication may ask you to identify main ideas, the purpose of communication or a detail.

For example, emails, memos or notices in Reading Part B extracts may ask you

- what an update on a change in procedure or policy is all about.
- the purpose of the email/memo about an update in procedure or policy.
- what the email/memo is reminding or informing staff to do.
- why there is a change in procedure or policy.

Answer Part B Question 6, which is based on an extract from a memo. As you read, use the questions below to help you think about context and purpose.

- What kind of extract is this and who are the intended readers?
- Why would the readers need to read this sort of communication?
- What is the question asking me to do?

Part B Question 6

6. The memo reminds nursing staff handling slide sheets how to

  (A) assess the correct size for each patient.

  (B) ensure that they are always used safely.

  (C) decide whether their use is appropriate.

Memo: To all Nursing Staff

Subject: Correct moving and handling of slide sheets

A recent injury to a staff member when using a slide sheet to change a patient's position has highlighted the need to reinforce correct moving and handling procedures. Before using a slide sheet, ensure that the material is clean and in good condition. Discard the slide sheet if any edges are frayed or if holes are noted. Before repositioning patients, check that bed brakes are on and bed rails are lowered. Never try to move a patient by reaching over bed rails, as this will place excessive stress on the lower back. It is important to ensure that slide sheets are handled using flat, open hands, not by grasping the slide sheet with opposing thumb and fingers.

Reading workplace communications to understand purpose

Some Reading Part B questions assess your ability to understand the purpose of a piece of communication such as an email, memo or notice. In other words, you're tested on whether you can understand why the communication was written, and what readers are supposed to do as a result of it. For example, nurses in the paediatric department of a hospital get an email that describes an incident surrounding a recent adverse event. It then goes on to tell them that they must perform an additional step in the standard operating procedure to prevent this from happening again. The purpose of the communication is to explain the background for an update in procedure.

Task 8

Match the examples of communications with their possible purposes.

Communication	Purpose	Answer
1. Nurses working in the surgical team get a memo about a proposed change in the consent taking guidelines, and where they can access the information.	a. Requesting use of alternatives	1 – b
2. Surgeons get an email summarising the main points of a recent meeting on guidelines about reducing surgical site infection. The email ends with an action point everyone needs to note.	b. Preparing for a future update	
3. Nurses see a notice about the troubleshooting procedure for a defibrillator following recent problems with a few defibrillators.	c. Reducing the rate of complications after surgery	
4. Physiotherapists get an email informing them about low stock of night splints and suggesting what they can do until they get new stock.	d. Reminding staff to follow a guideline	
5. Nurses get a memo about a large number of postoperative cases of hyperglycaemia, which asks them to follow stringent glucose control intra-operatively as well as postoperatively.	e. Giving information about what to do when equipment isn't functioning	

Task 9

Read this email and answer the question that follows.

To: All surgical team members

Sub: Refusal of marking

A recent incident involving a patient who refused surgical site marking has prompted an addition to the standard operating procedure for such incidents. While a patient has the right to refuse marking, the response of healthcare staff on duty should be no different than any other situation where patients refuse care, treatment or services. In such cases, the first step should be to inform the patient why site marking is required and advise of the consequences of refusing site marking. Refusal of site marking by the patient does not warrant a cancellation of the procedure. There is already a provision in the pre-operative verification checklist to document such incidents. Now, in addition, such cases must be further documented in the patient's file, with a detailed description of the incident including reasons given for refusal, if any.

The purpose of the email is to

(A) explain the need for a change in practice.

(B) remind staff to record instances of non-compliance.

(C) inform staff of the need to complete an extra step in the process.

Tips for Scoring

- Think about the type of document you're reading and its purpose so you can understand the context of the extract. Further context is given in the question, so this should also help you. By doing this, you set yourself up to read what comes next.
- When reading the question, think about whether it's asking you to find the main idea, a detail or the purpose. Once you do this, you'll be able to approach the extract better.
- Underline any words or phrases in the question and the text that you think are important. The words/phrases you underline could help you see evidence that the answer option you've chosen is the right one.
- Focus on the meaning of the extract rather than looking for words from the answer options to help you find the answers.

FAQs

1. **How much time should I take to answer Reading Part B?**

   You have 45 minutes to answer both Parts B and C together. Since Part B has only six questions, you should try and finish it in 10–15 minutes so that you leave 30–35 minutes to answer Part C, which is longer. You'll get better at time management if you use a timer when you practise sample tests.

2. **How should I prepare for Reading Part B?**

   Reading a variety of different documents such as policies and guidelines will help you prepare for Part B. If you're working in healthcare, you probably already have access to these documents. They could also be found online. Most of these documents are divided into sections, so when reading, focus on trying to understand the main idea or important points in each section.

Format of Reading Part C

As a healthcare professional, you read review articles or medical journals for your continuing professional development, to keep yourself up to date on opinions in the medical field, recent research, advice from professional regulatory bodies, and other developments in care and medicine. Part C of the Reading sub-test assesses your ability to recognise attitude and opinion in these longer, more complex pieces of writing.

Reading Part C contains two articles that are about 800 words long and not related to a specific medical profession. The questions test a range of reading skills, including recognising opinion, identifying the writer's attitude and understanding the main points of a text.

For each article, you need to answer eight multiple-choice questions with four options to choose from. Each question carries one mark, and there is a total of 16 marks for Part C. The questions may be in the form of 'direct questions' with three possible answers, or they might be incomplete sentences, with three answer options that provide the missing words. The questions follow the sequence of the paragraphs in the article, and there is typically one question per paragraph.

You will have a total of 45 minutes to answer both Parts B and C, so you must use your time efficiently. How long you spend on Part C depends on your abilities, and you can improve your reading time if you practise. To indicate your chosen answer to a question, you shade the circle next to the option you believe is correct, in the answer booklet provided for Parts B and C.

As a medical professional, you need to read articles about developments in healthcare relating to new treatments, technologies and medicine. These articles are usually based on research or reviews, and feature differing ideas and opinions on a medical topic. They could also contain differing views on how research affects treatment or on the management of medical conditions, or focus on a discussion about the experience of a patient or healthcare professional.

If you've paid close attention, you will have noticed that the writers don't try to convince readers about a single opinion, but present different points of view on the topic. For example, in an article on e-cigarettes, a writer may explain why some experts support their use, while other experts think they aren't appropriate for certain age groups. A writer may also refer to different studies showing actual benefits and disadvantages of e-cigarettes. In articles like this, writers keep their paragraphs very focused, and each paragraph carries an important message or opinion that they want to communicate. This is why Reading Part C focuses on your ability to recognise opinion, attitude and main points. Therefore, reading opinion-based articles will help you more than looking up actual medical research papers, which tend to be fact-based.

Let's look at a sample article for Reading Part C. Take a minute to understand the topic of the article.

Statin therapy and cholesterol

Statins have been used to lower cholesterol and help reduce the risk of cardiovascular diseases. However, researchers argue that the benefits of statin therapy have been repeatedly underestimated and the harms exaggerated due to misinterpretation of the evidence. A major review of the available evidence on the safety and efficacy of statin therapy, published in *The Lancet*, said there had previously been a failure to acknowledge properly both the wealth of evidence from randomised trials and the limitations of other types of studies. The authors said they hoped their review would help both clinicians and patients to make informed decisions about the use of the drugs. The authors noted that, although further research may identify small additional beneficial or adverse effects, it probably won't materially alter the balance of benefits and harms for patients because of the quantity of evidence generated so far.

Review author Professor Rory Collins, from the clinical trial service unit at Oxford University, says, 'Our review shows that the numbers of people who avoid heart attacks and strokes by taking statin therapy are very much larger than the numbers who have side effects with it. In addition, whereas most of the side effects can be reversed with no residual effects by stopping the statin, the effects of a heart attack or stroke not being prevented are irreversible and can be devastating.' Dr Maureen Baker, chair of the Royal College of General Practitioners, says, 'This study cuts through a lot of the controversy surrounding statins – it recognises the benefits that these drugs have for many patients, but also the potential side effects that any prescribing healthcare professional should be aware of. A decision to prescribe statins will never be *taken lightly* and should always be the result of a discussion. It remains essential that patients who are prescribed statins undertake regular medication reviews.'

Dr Alessandro Ble, Senior Research Fellow at the University of Exeter's medical school, described the review as a 'great contribution to clinical practice,' but also called for more studies into the impact of statins in those over 80, noting that 'few very old patients were included in the statin clinical trials. As large numbers of the oldest patients are prescribed statins, I would welcome more evidence for very elderly patients. The oldest patients often have several diseases and can be more susceptible to adverse effects.'

It has long been thought that cholesterol is a key cause of the fatty build-up in arteries (atherosclerosis) that causes heart disease. A controversial study now claims that total cholesterol becomes less of a risk factor for all-cause or cardiovascular mortality the older people get. The authors of this study found that as LDL cholesterol went down, all-cause mortality went up – higher LDL was apparently linked to lower all-cause mortality. *These findings* contradict the popular 'cholesterol hypothesis' and some of the authors of this study are members of THINCS – The International Network of Cholesterol Skeptics – a group of scientists who 'oppose […] that animal fat and high cholesterol play a role [in heart disease].' One could argue that this represents a preconceived view of the authors regarding the role of cholesterol, rather than the open, unbiased mind you would hope for in the spirit of scientific enquiry. That said, many important scientific breakthroughs happened due to the efforts of individuals who challenged a prevailing orthodoxy of thinking.

Nonetheless, there appears to be only limited evidence for concerns over the use of statins. Statin use was associated with a heightened risk of a diagnosis of diabetes. Being prescribed statins was associated with a 36% heightened risk of going on to be diagnosed with type 2 diabetes. However, one of the researchers studying this explains, 'The modest increases in weight and diabetes risk could easily be mitigated by adopting healthier diets and lifestyles. Reinforcing the importance of lifestyle changes when discussing these issues with patients would further enhance the benefit of statin treatment in preventing heart attacks and strokes.'

Meanwhile, the controversy surrounding statin therapy has been intensely debated in the media. It may come as no surprise that patients already taking statins were more likely to stop taking them for both primary and secondary prevention, following the high media coverage period. This is particularly true of older patients and those with a longer continuous prescription, say researchers from the London School of Hygiene and Tropical Medicine. Professor Liam Smeeth says, 'Our findings suggest that widespread coverage of health stories in the mainstream media can have an important, real world impact on the behaviour of patients and doctors. This may have significant consequences for people's health.' Although he acknowledged it was 'undoubtedly important' for such debates to be 'reflected in the media,' he believes that in the case of statins widespread reporting of the debate may have 'given disproportionate weight to a minority view about possible side effects.'

Now that you have an idea of the overall topic, let's look at some strategies and skills that can help you answer questions on these kinds of articles.

Opinion and attitude questions

Review articles give readers different opinions on previously reported facts about a medical issue. These articles contain opinions based on research, analysis and critical thinking, so they may not be as strongly expressed as opinions you would read in the editorial section of a newspaper. In fact, reporting different views gives readers the impression that the article is an objective one.

For example, in the article you just read, the writer presents different views from experts on research related to statins. The writer agrees with some of these views, while others are included in order to present further information, or to make the reader aware of other points of view.

Difference between facts and opinions

A very important first step in reading Part C articles is to learn to recognise the difference between facts and opinions.

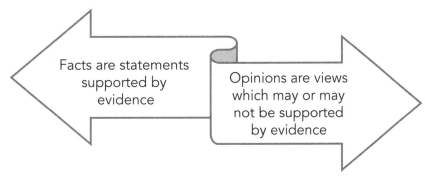

Facts are statements supported by evidence

Opinions are views which may or may not be supported by evidence

Facts are based on research, can be verified, and are not open to debate, whereas opinions are an individual's point of view on a topic.

One way to tell the difference between fact and opinion is to pay close attention to the language used by the author. Look at the examples below to see how verbs can be used to introduce facts and opinions.

Facts	Opinions
The review *confirms* …	The hospital *claims* that …
The study *found* …	Professor Collins *believes* …
Scientists *discovered* …	Researchers *think* it could be …

Remember that some views quoted by writers may even be neutral (they don't favour one idea over another), but these views are still not facts.

Task 1

The phrases below have been taken from the article you just read. Look at the verb in each phrase and decide whether it is introducing fact or opinion, then write it under the appropriate column. Two of the phrases have already been done for you.

our review shows that …	a study now claims …	the authors found that …
he believes that …	one could argue that …	the findings suggest …

Facts	Opinions
our review shows that ...	he believes that ...
_____	_____
_____	_____
_____	_____

Recognising the difference between facts and opinions helps you move on to understanding opinions better. When you read an opinion, ask yourself these four questions to understand more about it.

Is it the writer's own point of view?	Is it neutral or in favour of an idea?
Opinion = Point of view	
Is it someone else's point of view being reported by the writer for a reason?	Is it against an idea in the article?

For example, the writer of the article reports several opinions on statins. Some opinions are in favour of the benefits of statin therapy, such as Professor Rory Collins' opinion in the second paragraph.

Review author Professor Rory Collins, from the clinical trial service unit at Oxford University, says, 'Our review shows that the numbers of people who avoid heart attacks and strokes by taking statin therapy are very much larger than the numbers who have side effects with it. In addition, whereas most of the side effects can be reversed with no residual effects by stopping the statin, the effects of a heart attack or stroke not being prevented are irreversible and can be devastating.'

Other opinions – like Dr Maureen Baker's in the same paragraph – give us a more neutral view, advising caution.

'This study cuts through a lot of the controversy surrounding statins – it recognises the benefits that these drugs have for many patients, but also the potential side effects that any prescribing healthcare professional should be aware of. A decision to prescribe statins will never be *taken lightly* and should always be the result of a discussion. It remains essential that patients who are prescribed statins undertake regular medication reviews.'

In the third paragraph, the writer explores the opinion of an expert who says that there isn't enough research being done.

Dr Alessandro Ble, Senior Research Fellow at the University of Exeter's medical school, described the review as a 'great contribution to clinical practice', but also called for more studies into the impact of statins in those over 80 …

The opinions of experts and scientists are directly stated in this article, but writers often reveal their feelings about a subject in an indirect way. This is called 'attitude'. In a review article, for example, attitude may be slightly difficult to spot because the writer is trying to give readers different points of view rather than present just one argument. However, if you read carefully, the text gives you some hints about the writer's attitude. You can understand what a writer's attitude is by looking at the language used, and at the details that the writer has selected for inclusion in the article. There are three major language points that can help you understand more about attitude and opinion. Let's look at some sentences from the article to see how these language points can help you identify the writer's opinion.

Adjectives	Adverbs of degree	Tentative language
• Nonetheless, there appears to be only **limited** evidence for concerns over the use of statins. • A **controversial** study now claims that total cholesterol becomes less of a risk factor for all-cause or cardiovascular mortality the older people get.	• The authors of this study found that as LDL cholesterol went down, all-cause mortality went up – higher LDL was **apparently** linked to lower all-cause mortality. • The authors noted that, although further research may identify small additional beneficial or adverse effects, it **probably** won't materially alter the balance of benefits ...	• ... he believes that in the case of statins widespread reporting of the debate **may** have ... • Nonetheless, there **appears** to be only limited evidence for concerns over the use of statins.

Adjectives

In the sample text, notice the words in bold to see how the writer comments about the available evidence.

> Nonetheless, there appears to be only **limited** evidence for concerns over the use of statins.

The word *limited* is used to describe the evidence, telling us that the writer thinks there is not enough evidence against the use of statins.

Adverbs of degree

The word *apparently* means *it seems that*. Notice how the writer uses it when referring to the results of the *controversial* study that showed that lower cholesterol was actually related to higher rates of mortality.

> The authors of this study found that as LDL cholesterol went down, all-cause mortality went up – higher LDL was **apparently** linked to lower all-cause mortality.

This shows that the writer isn't convinced about the results of the study.

Tentative language

Modals like *may*, *might* or *could* help present views as more reasoned and less emotional than *must* and *should*. The writer uses *may* when referring to the impact of the statin debate.

> ... he believes that in the case of statins widespread reporting of the debate **may** have ...

Rather than suggesting certainty, the writer uses *may* before introducing a very strong opinion by an expert. This tells us that the writer probably wants to appear as objective as possible. However, there are several other clues about the attitude of the writer, who seems to largely agree with the results of the review on the benefits of statins.

Task 2

Look at these adjectives about evidence and decide what they tell us about the writer's attitude.

inadequate   speculative   substantial   comprehensive

overwhelming   insufficient   extensive   reliable

Writer thinks there is strong evidence	Writer thinks there is weak evidence
extensive	insufficient

Task 3

Read the following statements taken from the sample article for Reading Part C and decide if each one is a fact (F) or an opinion (O).

- Underline any expressions of opinion and attitude in the statements.
- If you think a statement is an opinion, explain why, and why you think the writer uses it. Write your explanation in the 'Reasons why' column.

Statement	Fact or opinion?	Reasons why
1. 'In addition, whereas most of the side effects can be reversed with no residual effects by stopping the statin, the effects of a heart attack or stroke not being prevented are <u>irreversible</u> and can be <u>devastating</u>.'	O	The adjectives *irreversible* and *devastating* to describe the effects of stopping statin medication show the expert is in favour of statins. By quoting this expert, the writer uses someone else's opinion to support the view that statins are beneficial.
2. The authors of this study found that as LDL cholesterol went down, all-cause mortality went up.		
3. Being prescribed statins was associated with a 36% heightened risk of going on to be diagnosed with type 2 diabetes.		
4. … he believes that in the case of statins, widespread reporting of the debate may have 'given disproportionate weight to a minority view about possible side effects'.		
5. 'This study cuts through a lot of the controversy surrounding statins – it recognises the benefits that these drugs have for many patients, but also the potential side effects that any prescribing healthcare professional should be aware of.'		

6. 'Reinforcing the importance of lifestyle changes when discussing these issues with patients would further enhance the benefit of statin treatment in preventing heart attacks and strokes.'		

Using what you've just learnt, try the following test question based on opinion and attitude.

Task 4a

Choose the answer (A, B, C or D) that you think fits best according to the text below.

Extract

Review author Professor Rory Collins, from the clinical trial service unit at Oxford University, says, 'Our review shows that the numbers of people who avoid heart attacks and strokes by taking statin therapy are very much larger than the numbers who have side effects with it. In addition, whereas most of the side effects can be reversed with no residual effects by stopping the statin, the effects of a heart attack or stroke not being prevented are irreversible and can be devastating.' Dr Maureen Baker, chair of the Royal College of General Practitioners, says, 'This study cuts through a lot of the controversy surrounding statins – it recognises the benefits that these drugs have for many patients, but also the potential side effects that any prescribing healthcare professional should be aware of. A decision to prescribe statins will never be taken lightly and should always be the result of a discussion. It remains essential that patients who are prescribed statins undertake regular medication reviews.'

1. Professor Rory Collins' opinion of the side effects of statins differs from Dr Maureen Baker's because he

   (A) advises caution and patient-doctor consultation.

   (B) downplays the importance of possible adverse reactions.

   (C) discourages medication appraisals for patients under treatment.

   (D) emphasises the importance of recognising the negative outcomes of treatment.

Note: If you're unsure of the correct answer, you could try and eliminate the incorrect options by seeing whether you can find evidence to support them in the article.

Task 4b

Look at the other options in 4a and say why they are wrong.

Wrong answer option	Reason
A.	
B.	
C.	
D.	

A writer might present a fact or an opinion to suggest something rather than mentioning it directly. You need to think actively about a writer's attitude to understand what they may be suggesting. Some questions in Reading Part C assess your ability to do this.

Let's look at an extract for a Reading Part C question that asks you about what a writer is suggesting.

Extract

> It has long been thought that cholesterol is a key cause of the fatty build-up in arteries (atherosclerosis) that causes heart disease. A controversial study now claims that total cholesterol becomes less of a risk factor for all-cause or cardiovascular mortality the older people get. The authors of this study found that as LDL cholesterol went down, all-cause mortality went up – higher LDL was apparently linked to lower all-cause mortality. These findings contradict the popular 'cholesterol hypothesis' and some of the authors of this study are members of THINCS – The International Network of Cholesterol Skeptics – a group of scientists who 'oppose [...] that animal fat and high cholesterol play a role [in heart disease].' One could argue that this represents a preconceived view of the authors regarding the role of cholesterol, rather than the open, unbiased mind you would hope for in the spirit of scientific enquiry. That said, many important scientific breakthroughs happened due to the efforts of individuals who challenged a prevailing orthodoxy of thinking.

In this extract, the writer decides to include one very important detail about the authors of the study. The writer says they belong to a group called THINCS and goes on to say:

> One could argue that this represents a **preconceived view** of the authors regarding the role of cholesterol, rather than the **open, unbiased mind you would hope for** in the spirit of scientific enquiry.

The adjectives used here tell us the writer's attitude. Even though the writer mentions later that major scientific breakthroughs were made possible when individuals challenged popularly accepted views, it is significant that THINCS is mentioned along with that comment. Including this detail about THINCS helps the writer make a point, without directly stating their own opinion.

Now, answer a question based on this extract.

Task 4c

Choose the answer (A, B, C or D) that you think fits best according to the text above.

2. By mentioning THINCS, the writer suggests that the authors of the controversial study were likely to have

   (A) poor knowledge of the link between cholesterol and mortality.

   (B) a traditional perspective on the link between cholesterol and mortality.

   (C) a prejudiced outlook on the link between cholesterol and mortality.

   (D) adopted a neutral approach to reviewing the link between cholesterol and mortality.

Questions about a writer's purpose

A writer may also report certain facts or opinions for a specific reason, such as:

- to show agreement between findings
- to present contradictory findings
- to discuss limitations of a study

- to highlight a specific issue or problem
- to support an idea in the text
- to contrast an idea in the text
- to explain impact

This is not a comprehensive list, so you will need to practise the skill of recognising why a writer has chosen to present a view or a fact by reading a variety of articles. While there are phrases that can give you clues about what the writer's purpose is, you must read carefully to fully understand the writer's objective.

Task 5

Given below are some phrases that you may find in a Part C article. Match the phrases with their functions.

Function	Phrase	Answer
1. shows agreement between findings	a. the framework only pertains to …	1 – d
2. presents contradictory findings	b. discussions on this subject have dominated research …	
3. discusses limitations	c. previous studies have proven that …	
4. highlights a specific issue	d. the study corroborates …	
5. supports an idea in the article	e. prior research focused on …	
6. describes the recent focus of a topic	f. the investigation challenges …	

Now, look at this extract from the sample article.

Extract

Dr Alessandro Ble, Senior Research Fellow at the University of Exeter's medical school, described the review as a 'great contribution to clinical practice,' but also called for more studies into the impact of statins in those over 80, noting that 'few very old patients were included in the statin clinical trials. As large numbers of the oldest patients are prescribed statins, I would welcome more evidence for very elderly patients. The oldest patients often have several diseases and can be more susceptible to adverse effects.'

In this extract, we see that the writer quotes Dr Alessandro Ble to tell the reader that although the review had a great impact, there were very few older patients included in it. Dr Ble would like to see more evidence from studies of patients over 80. Therefore, the writer's purpose in referring to Dr Ble's opinion is to highlight a gap in the present research.

Now, answer the following question based on this extract.

Choose the answer (A, B, C or D) that you think fits best according to the text.

3. The writer quotes Dr Alessandro Ble to
    - (A) discredit current research on statins.
    - (B) highlight the great impact of research on statins on medical practice.
    - (C) emphasise the need for more research on the effects of statin treatments in patients.
    - (D) draw attention to an area not addressed by most research on statins.

In review articles like this, writers often highlight any gaps in research. This gives the reader the impression that the article has approached the topic as objectively as possible. Readers aren't only presented with views in favour of statins, they're also shown gaps or contradictions in research so that the article isn't one-sided.

Here is another test question based on opinions in the article on statins. Answer the question, referring to the sample article at the beginning of this section.

Task 6b

Choose the answer (A, B, C or D) that you think fits best according to the text.

4. What is Professor Liam Smeeth's view of media coverage given to the statin debate?
    - (A) He believes it is important for health stories to be reported in the press.
    - (B) He predicts that news stories may cause patients to stop taking medication.
    - (C) He fears that widespread news reporting could lead to negative health outcomes.
    - (D) He feels unhappy about news stories focusing on a small section of scientific opinion.

Main idea questions

As mentioned earlier, a review article or any other article reporting opinions on previously conducted research presents several differing views. By doing this, writers give readers a broad perspective on a topic. Every paragraph has a clear message to communicate to the reader. Since each question in Reading Part C is typically based on a single paragraph, understanding the main idea of each paragraph is important.

Using words or phrases to help you spot answers won't help you in Part C as it did in Part A. This is because the purpose of reading Part A texts is to locate specific information, so locating specific words and phrases is appropriate. Remember that you were able to find the words or phrases to answer Part A questions within a single sentence. In Part C, however, the purpose of reading is to understand the meaning of whole paragraphs rather than using words to find answers within short parts of the text. Summarising ideas will help you focus on understanding the meaning of whole paragraphs.

Let's look at an extract from the sample article at the beginning of this section, and at an example of how it could be summarised.

Statins have been used to lower cholesterol and help reduce the risk of cardiovascular diseases. However, researchers argue that the benefits of statin therapy have been repeatedly underestimated and the harms exaggerated due to misinterpretation of the evidence. A major review of the available evidence on the safety and efficacy of statin therapy, published in *The Lancet,* said there had previously been a failure to acknowledge properly both the wealth of evidence from randomised trials and the limitations of other types of studies. The authors said they hoped their review would help both clinicians and patients to make informed decisions about the use of the drugs. The authors noted that, although further research may identify small additional beneficial or adverse effects, it probably won't materially alter the balance of benefits and harms for patients because of the quantity of evidence generated so far.

Summary

There is a lot of evidence available to suggest that statins have more benefits than harms, and future research is unlikely to change these findings.

As you can see, although the summary is short, it contains all the main ideas. Making a quick mental summary of a paragraph before you look at the answer options can be very helpful. It doesn't need to be perfect – it can be just one or two sentences that capture the main idea.

Task 7

Now use the summary to choose the correct answer to a test question based on this paragraph. Then match the explanations with the multiple-choice answer options.

5.   What do we learn about the benefits and risks of statin therapy in the first paragraph?

Multiple-choice answer options	Explanations	Answers
A. Future studies are unlikely to challenge current findings.	1. There is no mention of new methods of analysis in the extract.	
B. An overview of research to date needs to be conducted.	2. This idea contradicts the one presented in the extract.	
C. A new method of analysing its effectiveness has been developed.	3. The extract does not indicate the need for an overview.	
D. Previous research lacked the data to draw a conclusion.	4. Correct answer based on the summary	

Task 8a

Read the extract below.

Extract

Nonetheless, there appears to be only limited evidence for concerns over the use of statins. Statin use was associated with a heightened risk of a diagnosis of diabetes. Being prescribed statins was associated with a 36% heightened risk of going on to be diagnosed with type 2 diabetes. However, one of the researchers studying this explains, 'The modest increases in weight and diabetes risk could easily be mitigated by adopting healthier diets and lifestyles. Reinforcing the importance of lifestyle changes when discussing these issues with patients would further enhance the benefit of statin treatment in preventing heart attacks and strokes.'

Which one of the following is a good summary of the main idea in this paragraph? _____

1	2	3
People who are prescribed statins have a 36% chance of being diagnosed with type 2 diabetes and should make changes to their lifestyle and diet if they want to avoid heart attacks and strokes.	People who take statins have a 36% chance of developing type 2 diabetes so they should ensure they live healthier lives and discuss their problems with their doctors.	People who get statin prescriptions are 36% more likely to be diagnosed with type 2 diabetes but if they eat better and make lifestyle changes, then this risk is reduced and they can benefit more from statin therapy.

Task 8b

a. Using the summary from Task 8a, answer the test question based on the extract, which is the 5th paragraph of the sample article.

6. What point is made about diabetes and statins in the fifth paragraph?

 Ⓐ Diabetes can be controlled by making simple changes to nutrition and living.

 Ⓑ Statin use is associated with a greater danger of being diagnosed with diabetes.

 Ⓒ Discussing changes in behaviour with patients will help prevent diabetes, heart attacks and strokes.

 Ⓓ Healthy life choices can reduce the danger of diabetes and boost the effectiveness of statins.

b. Look at the other options and say why they are wrong.

Wrong answer option	Reason

Vocabulary and reference questions

Two of the eight questions for each article may test your ability to understand vocabulary in context or reference. Vocabulary questions are concerned with the way a word or phrase is used, while reference questions are about what a word or phrase refers to in the article.

With vocabulary questions, you need to understand the meaning of the surrounding sentences to know why the writer has chosen to use that word or phrase. The words and expressions used to explain the ideas are not medical words. This is a test of your ability to work out the meaning of words, not a test of vocabulary you have learnt prior to Test Day. So even if you do not understand a particular word or phrase, you can still answer the question correctly if you understand how the writer uses it.

For vocabulary and reference questions, it is important to read the surrounding words and sentences that will help you understand the writer's intention.

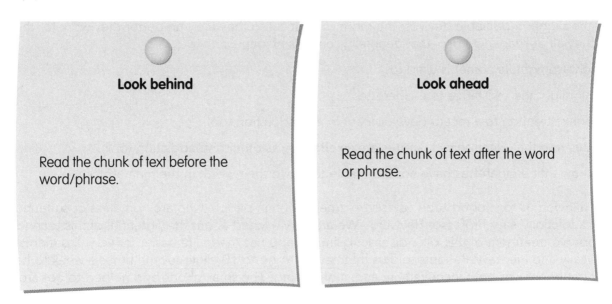

Look behind

Read the chunk of text before the word/phrase.

Look ahead

Read the chunk of text after the word or phrase.

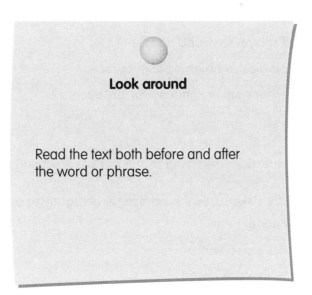

Look around

Read the text both before and after the word or phrase.

Task 9a

Given below are some extracts from articles with a word/phrase in bold. Use the underlined words and phrases to help you answer the following vocabulary and reference questions.

1. <u>E-cigarettes</u> are marketed in England as being <u>at least 95% safer than tobacco</u> and of <u>negligible risk to passive smokers</u> – yet this is a **unique position** and not one that is held worldwide.

   What is the *unique position* referred to in the paragraph?

   Ⓐ the marketing of e-cigarettes across the globe

   Ⓑ the idea that e-cigarettes pose no significant danger

   Ⓒ the fact that smoking e-cigarettes is less harmful than tobacco

   Ⓓ the preference smokers have for e-cigarettes in a particular country

2. It seems counterintuitive that a new technology that promised to see the end of smoking in our lifetime is still having to **fight its corner**, but that is what has happened with e-cigarettes (ECs). The term EC covers all vaping devices, including those that look like cigarettes, pens, the pod systems and the bigger modifiable devices; the more sophisticated they are, the better they work for the user, but they all deliver an aerosol that generally contains nicotine.

The phrase *fight its corner* is used to

Ⓐ highlight the resistance to e-cigarettes.

Ⓑ draw attention to a recent development in anti-addiction tools.

Ⓒ illustrate that electronic cigarettes are as effective as other anti-addiction tools.

Ⓓ show that e-cigarettes have not been able to prove their worth in the marketplace.

3. 'This allowed us to support tuberculosis treatment even in people who are homeless or suffering from drug addiction,' says Professor Hayward. 'We are very excited about the potential of this technology to improve treatment of this killer disease. Using an app has made life easier for very ill patients, both physically and mentally. Patients told us that having to go to TB clinic several times a week to have their treatment was both inconvenient and stigmatising. The smartphone app helped to get around both of **these issues**, allowing patients to fit their treatment around their daily lives. This type of e-health service could have positive implications for all patients, not just those affected by TB.'

The phrase *these issues* refers to

Ⓐ poverty and substance abuse.

Ⓑ disruption to routine and shame surrounding disease.

Ⓒ psychological and physiological problems patients face.

Ⓓ inability to continue follow-ups and to afford new products.

Task 9b

Now, answer the following test questions, referring to the sample article on statins given at the beginning.

7. In the second paragraph, Dr Baker uses the phrase *taken lightly* to emphasise

Ⓐ how bad decisions are made.

Ⓑ how difficult it is to make a decision.

Ⓒ how seriously decisions are considered.

Ⓓ how patients are affected by wrong decisions.

8. In the fourth paragraph, the phrase *These findings* refers to the fact that

Ⓐ LDL cholesterol is the main reason for atherosclerosis.

Ⓑ cardiovascular mortality and atherosclerosis are linked.

Ⓒ lower LDL levels were associated with increased mortality rates.

Ⓓ higher levels of LDL cholesterol had zero effect on mortality rates.

Let's apply all that we have learnt so far in this chapter to a second Reading Part C text.

Read the text below and answer questions 9–16. Do not forget to time yourself.

Caesarean sections

Babies born by caesarean section have an increased risk of becoming heavyweight adults, say researchers. An analysis of data on 38,000 individuals found that those born by caesarean section were 22% more likely to be obese than those who had natural births. They had a 26% greater chance of being overweight, as defined by their body mass index (BMI). Effects of a surgery-assisted birth on a baby's gut bacteria and genes could be two reasons for the trend, they believe. Dr Matthew Hyde, one of the researchers, explains, 'There are plausible mechanisms by which caesarean delivery might influence later body weight. The types of healthy bacteria in the gut differ between babies born by caesarean and those born by vaginal delivery and difference in type and level of gut bacteria in C-section babies can have broad effects on their health.'

The World Health Organisation recommends that there should be no more than between 10% and 15% of caesarean births. However, the rate of such births has been rising steadily in recent years. Now, more than 40% of all babies are delivered by C-section in at least 15 countries globally. A large number of C-section births, especially in Brazil and China, are actually low risk pregnancies that don't require C-sections. Cathy Warwick, chief executive of the Royal College of Midwives in the UK, explains this global trend, 'Some women want a caesarean section for purely social convenience. I am prepared to put my **head above the parapet** and say that I don't think making a choice on this basis is appropriate.' Mervi Jokinen, also from the Royal College of Midwives, reinforces this when she says, 'Whilst some caesarean sections are needed for medical reasons, many are not. We would encourage women to think carefully and weigh up the evidence before they decide to have a non-urgent caesarean. Women should also be aware that this is a major surgical operation that has the potential for increased complications every time a woman has the procedure carried out.'

For many high-risk pregnancies, like in the case of breech presentations, several studies have concluded that planned caesareans are the safest delivery method. However, Professor Yifru Berhan, from Hawassa University College of Medicine and Health Sciences in Ethiopia, explains why C-section may not always be required even in breech cases, 'The relative risk of perinatal mortality and morbidity is between two and five times higher in planned vaginal breech delivery, compared to planned caesarean section birth. However, the absolute risks are very small. Therefore, the practice of individualised decision-making around delivering a breech baby is recommended.'

Previous childbirth experiences impact decision-making about methods of childbirth. Dr Helen White, a midwifery lecturer at the University of Manchester, reviewed the care and outcomes of 405 women who gave birth after previously having a caesarean. She says, 'Where it can be achieved safely, vaginal birth is preferable, but there is a real possibility that women who have already had a caesarean once before may choose to have one again. There aren't many initiatives out there to break this cycle but our research shows that midwives are best-placed to promote vaginal birth. We are not proposing that women should reject caesarean birth when a C-section is medically advised. However, we believe that promoting vaginal birth among women who have previously had C-sections is important and we suggest that midwives are important figures in promoting vaginal birth in suitable women.

There is evidence that C-section rates are also influenced by maternity practices in healthcare institutions. Low C-section rates, consistently below 20%, can be achieved by maternity units applying best practice to pregnancy, labour and birth management. At the maternity unit at Luton and Dunstable Hospital in the UK, the wake-up call came when the unit's C-section rate peaked at 31%. To counteract this, the hospital made a commitment to create more awareness about the benefits of vaginal birth. A Midwife Lead, responsible for promoting normal birth with staff and pregnant women, was appointed. A Birth Options Clinic for women who had previously had a caesarean was set up. As a result, 80% of women who attended the Birth Options Clinic tried a vaginal birth, and around half were successful in bringing down the unit's C-section rate.

The World Health Organisation has published a set of evidence-based recommendations on non-clinical interventions to help reduce C-section rates. A significant part of these guidelines emphasises educational interventions, labour companionship and midwife-led continuity of care. Some of these are childbirth training workshops, relaxation training programmes, psychosocial couple-based prevention programmes and psycho-education for fear of pain or anxiety. The role of midwives in all **these interventions** is central. Cathy Warwick rightly says, 'I really believe that if midwives are able to make sure that women understand what their choices mean for them and their baby – the risks and benefits – then far fewer women will choose elective caesareans. They will be making decisions armed with the necessary knowledge and from a position of trust in maternity services, not one based on a fear of birth and hearsay.'

Questions 9–16

9. What does Dr Matthew Hyde describe in the first paragraph?

   Ⓐ a hypothesis under investigation

   Ⓑ unreliable data that calls for more research

   Ⓒ conclusive evidence offered by several studies

   Ⓓ an explanation of the probable causes of a finding

10. In the second paragraph, Cathy Warwick uses the phrase 'head above the parapet' to suggest her

   Ⓐ willingness to face criticism for a differing view.

   Ⓑ disregard for the comfort sought by expectant mothers.

   Ⓒ concern for a universal problem related to women's health.

   Ⓓ enthusiasm towards a new approach to maternal healthcare.

11. Mervi Jokinen supports Cathy Warwick's views by

   Ⓐ describing how C-sections are performed.

   Ⓑ highlighting the possible risks associated with C-sections.

   Ⓒ drawing attention to the reasons for an increase in C-sections.

   Ⓓ reinforcing the idea that C-sections are permitted in certain situations.

12. What point is being made about breech babies in the third paragraph?

   Ⓐ These babies should always be delivered by C-section.

   Ⓑ C-sections don't guarantee a decreased danger of death or disease.

   Ⓒ Decisions about whether to use C-section should be made on a case-by-case basis.

   Ⓓ C-sections are recommended for women who face any kind of potential birth complication.

13. Dr Helen White believes midwives could promote vaginal birth among women who have

   Ⓐ become pregnant for the first time.

   Ⓑ had a C-section and don't want to have one again.

   Ⓒ have been recommended a C-section, but are reluctant to have one.

   Ⓓ had a C-section and are not at any sort of risk in their present pregnancy.

14. The writer uses the example of the Luton and Dunstable maternity unit to show that

(A) employing a midwife creates a better environment for births.

(B) measures to create awareness have an effect on patient choices.

(C) adhering to tried and tested maternity methods produces improved outcomes.

(D) keeping a record of births helps healthcare institutions maintain a good reputation.

15. In the final paragraph, 'these interventions' refers to

(A) efforts by midwives to reduce the high number of surgical births.

(B) international guidance on encouraging preparation for childbirth.

(C) measures taken by hospitals to highlight benefits of natural birth.

(D) programmes conducted by the World Health Organisation to promote natural birth.

16. In the final paragraph, the writer suggests that fewer women will opt for elective caesareans in the future, because they will

(A) believe what others say about childbirth.

(B) follow suggestions by health professionals.

(C) attend comprehensive sessions on childbirth.

(D) have confidence in the skills of the doctors performing them.

Tips for scoring

- Try to understand the meaning of the paragraphs before you look at the questions so that you don't get confused by the multiple-choice options. Looking for keywords from answer options in the text won't help you.
- Answer the questions in order. They follow the same sequence as the paragraphs presented in the article. Sometimes you're told what paragraph to look at. If you're not, then use an important word or idea mentioned in that part of the text.

- Don't spend too much time on answering a question if you get stuck. Proceed to the next question and come back to it after you've answered other questions. You can still answer the questions that follow even if you haven't understood a previous question.
- Practise using the paragraph summary technique whenever you read articles so that you can use it confidently on Test Day.
- Time yourself doing sample tests and develop methods to use your time effectively.

FAQs

1. How much time should I take to answer Reading Part C?

You have 45 minutes to answer both Reading Part B and Part C together. How long you take really depends on your reading speed and skill. Remember that Part B has only six questions, while Part C has 16; therefore, you will want to reserve the greater part of the 45 minutes to complete Part C. Learn to manage your time for both Parts B and C so you are well prepared for Test Day.

2. What if I do not understand some of the articles, questions or answer options?

Don't worry or become nervous if you read something you don't understand. First, the question will help you locate the paragraph where the answer is in the article. Once you have located the paragraph, do your best to understand the meaning, focusing on the words and ideas that are easier. Try to answer the question again, and if nothing else works, take a good guess, because it's better to try than leaving it blank.

3. What should I do to prepare for Reading Part C?

A good way to prepare for Reading Part C is to begin reading a variety of articles on different healthcare topics online from good medical journals or websites. Part C articles are the kind that report views on research findings to a general medical audience, so reading these kinds of articles is better than reading the original research papers. Remember that you won't be tested on understanding of the medical or scientific facts, so try to find texts that discuss different experts' views on a topic.

You also need to train yourself to read without using a dictionary. Students often have their dictionaries open when reading, and look up difficult words as they read. However, the articles may well contain words you don't know, so you should develop strategies to handle unfamiliar words. For example, if you come across a word you don't understand, underline it and try to guess its meaning by taking into account the context of the whole sentence or paragraph. Then check whether your guess was right by referring to a dictionary only after you finish reading the article.

4. Can I make notes or underline important parts in the article?

You are allowed to make notes or underline certain words/sentences in the text. However, remember that when selecting your final answer, you must shade the appropriate circle next to the answer, in the separate answer booklet that will be given to you. Answers written elsewhere won't be marked.

WRITING IN OET

The Writing sub-test requires you to write a formal letter in response to a typical situation at your workplace. The task materials consist of patient case notes and instructions. The letter is usually a referral letter, but could be a discharge letter, a transfer letter or a letter to inform or advise a caregiver.

Format of the Writing sub-test

There is only one writing task in the sub-test, which is based on a set of case notes. You need to write a letter to a specific recipient using clear and focused language.

Timing

The duration of the Writing sub-test is 45 minutes. Out of the total time allocated, five minutes is allotted to reading the case notes and the task instructions. During these initial five minutes, you are not allowed to write anything on the question paper or your answer sheet. Once your reading time is over, you have 40 minutes to write the letter.

Assessment criteria

You are marked on six criteria which assess different aspects of writing in a healthcare environment. It is important to understand what is expected for each criterion so that you can improve your score.

The first criterion, on Purpose, is marked on a scale of 0–3, while the remaining five criteria are marked on a scale of 0–7. Let's go over the six criteria to determine how writing in OET can best match up to the Assessors' expectations.

Criterion 1: Purpose

Medical professionals need to understand the purpose of written communication quickly, so this criterion assesses whether you are able to make the purpose of the letter clear and immediately apparent to the reader. A clear sense of purpose should also inform the rest of the document. It is not enough to include the word 'referral' or 'transfer' at the beginning of the letter as the only way of showing its purpose, because this does not tell the reader what is expected from him/her with regard to the patient you are referring or transferring. Your letter needs to indicate clearly *why* the patient is being referred or transferred to your reader, so they can act on the information appropriately.

To achieve a higher score in respect of this criterion, you should:

- Read the case notes carefully to get a sense of why you need to refer or transfer the patient to the reader.
- Indicate the purpose of writing at the beginning of your letter so your reader does not need to spend time searching for this information.
- Use relevant case notes to elaborate on and support the purpose of your letter.

Criterion 2: Content

Communicating the necessary information in handover documents is important because it will be used to perform care functions that could impact the patient directly. Therefore, this criterion assesses your ability to include all of the key information, and communicate it accurately. To do this, think carefully about your audience and their role in the patient's continued care. You need to make sure you provide them with all the necessary information from the case notes. This criterion also assesses the accuracy of information in your letter. Try not to change or reinterpret information in a way that changes the meaning, as this will cause you to lose marks.

To achieve a higher score in respect of this criterion, you should:

- Have a good awareness of the reader of the letter. Consider whether your reader is aware of the patient's case, and what is necessary for them to know for continued care on this case.
- Provide the information they need to ensure the recovery and care of the patient. In other words, do not leave out important information that is necessary for the reader to know.
- Be accurate. Convey the information presented in the case notes without changing the meaning in any way. You may paraphrase or summarise as long as this does not affect accuracy of meaning.
- Avoid making interpretations or giving a diagnosis when it is not stated in the case notes.
- Do not add anything extra to the case notes, even if your medical knowledge tells you otherwise.

Criterion 3: Conciseness and clarity

Clear and concise communication is essential to the medical workplace because of the time constraints in a healthcare environment. This criterion assesses your ability to convey information efficiently and recognise irrelevant information. Remember that the OET task case notes contain a lot of information, not all of which may be necessary for your reader to know because it's not relevant to their role in the patient's care, or because they may be aware of it already. For example, you wouldn't write extensively about a patient's medical history if you were writing to the patient's regular GP because they would already know these details.

To achieve a higher score in respect of this criterion, you should:

- Leave out irrelevant information that could distract your reader from the main message.
- Convey the information your reader needs to know in the most efficient way possible.
- Summarise information from the case notes when necessary.
- Avoid explaining key information in a complicated manner.

Criterion 4: Genre and style

Written documents in a healthcare setting are formal, professional and factual. They never contain personal judgements or opinions. Your letter must therefore reflect these features.

To achieve a higher score in this criterion, you should:

- Maintain a polite, formal tone.
- Avoid adding your own judgements and feelings about the case.
- Use medical terms appropriately, always considering how familiar your reader would be with a particular term. We cannot assume that all medical professionals will be familiar with all medical terms and abbreviations. If you are writing to a professional in the same discipline as yours, it is appropriate to use specialist medical terms and abbreviations. However, if your reader is from another discipline entirely, then you may need to explain terms and avoid abbreviations.
- Avoid misuse and overuse of technical jargon and abbreviations.
- Provide simple explanations if writing to a layperson like a caregiver, social worker or parent.

In short, get a clear understanding of the reader and the purpose of your letter. This will simplify your choice of vocabulary and tone.

Criterion 5: Organisation and layout

Organisation helps keep communication clear and easy to read. You need to organise your letter in a way that helps the reader find important information as quickly as possible.

To achieve a higher score in respect of this criterion, you should:

- Divide information logically into paragraphs. However, avoid relying on a template or predeterimed format for this. You need to engage with the case notes on Test Day to decide the best organisation for your letter.
- Order information in a way that is most suitable for your reader. This is not necessarily the same order in which the information is found in the case notes.
- Draw attention to information that you think is important for the reader to know.
- Present your letter in an appropriate layout. There is a variety of accepted letter formats used by healthcare professionals in different local contexts. You do not need to use a particular format in the OET Writing sub-test; just try to ensure that your letter is laid out well and meets the needs of the particular task.

Criterion 6: Language

Using accurate language in workplace communication is important because it prevents misunderstanding and helps the reader to understand your message clearly. The OET Assessor will gauge whether you have used grammar, vocabulary, sentence structure, spelling and punctuation accurately enough to get your point across effectively to your reader.

To achieve a higher score in this criterion, you should:

- Use appropriate vocabulary suited to the context of the task.
- Ensure the language you use serves the purpose of communicating your message, so avoid using complicated sentences, grammar or linking words just to show that you know them. Even if used accurately, unnecessarily complicated language will lead to a reduction in your score. Aim to make it easy for the reader to find the required information.
- Avoid common spelling errors.
- Maintain one spelling convention (US/British English) throughout your letter.
- Punctuate sentences clearly.
- Use the last five minutes to check your work and correct any errors you notice.

If you are preparing for OET, your primary goal is probably to achieve a high score. However, your preparation will also help you perform well in the workplace, where you may be expected to write letters to other medical professionals as well as to laypeople. Therefore, it is useful to learn writing skills that will be helpful even after you pass OET.

In many general-purpose writing tests, your writing is scored according to your range of grammar, vocabulary, sentence structures, etc. As a result, you may feel that 'showing off' your range of writing skills to the Assessor will be to your advantage. In OET, your writing skills will be assessed on how easily the reader is able to understand the information. This doesn't mean that the level of your language is any less important for OET than it is for other tests, however.

Rather than imagining an assessor looking at your writing test and measuring how much language you have, imagine a healthcare professional reading your letter and trying to understand quickly and accurately how they need to care for the patient. Your answers will be marked by a language assessor who is trained to imagine that they are a healthcare professional. Therefore, you should write your letter as though the reader is a healthcare professional.

In this section, you will practise:

- organising ideas
- using sentence variety to convey meaning accurately
- choosing appropriate vocabulary to suit the audience you are writing for
- using grammar to convey meaning in OET contexts
- using punctuation and layout to write clearly
- avoiding common spelling errors

This section will help you acquire some of the basic sub-skills required to meet the marking criteria. However, the focus is on appropriate application of these skills in the context of OET. This section does not attempt to provide an explanation of grammatical concepts or vocabulary. It is designed instead to help you understand how you can use them in your letter. If you feel you need to improve your understanding of grammar or vocabulary, then it would be a good idea to find a resource dedicated to that.

Writing skills: Organising ideas

A well-written letter is all about organising relevant information from the patient case notes into logical paragraphs. As stated earlier, what you choose to include in your letter and how you organise it depends on the reader and the purpose of your letter. Once you select the relevant information from the case notes, you need to organise it into paragraphs.

Here are some likely recipients of an OET letter:

- Head nurse at a community retirement home, inpatient rehabilitation centre or other medical facility
- Physiotherapist
- General practitioner
- Specialist (oncologist, neurologist, gynaecologist, etc.)
- Home health nurse
- Occupational therapist
- Caregiver / parent

You need to understand who your reader is and their role in the patient's recovery so that you know which case notes are most relevant and how you should prioritise information in your letter.

Let's look at an example. Read the patient case notes and the two examples of how they might be used in a task.

Patient case notes

You are Charge Nurse at the hospital where a patient, Ms Shaw, was treated. She is ready for discharge.

Patient details:

Ms Cindy Shaw, 75 years old

Height 5'2", weight 118 lbs.

Admitted on: 23 September 2018

Discharge: 28 September 2018

Diagnosis: Left hip replacement following fracture sustained after fall (referred by her GP)

Medical history:

Diabetes mellitus (diagnosed 20 years)

Precose – 25 mg

No other co-morbid conditions

Social background:

Lives with daughter & son-in-law (30s; no children) in a granny flat

Spouse dead – 10 years

Daughter – leaving overseas next week (4/10) for a year (husband's job)

To move into a self-contained flat. Flat has steps. Okay for walker?

All routine activities – independent

Exercise – regular (walking 30 min/day – 5 days/wk)

Nursing management:

16/9

Pre-operative:

- HbA1c: 6.5
- Fasting: 125 mg/dl
- Post-prandial (PP): 170 mg/dl

(readings = good control)

23/9

Postoperative:

- HbA1c: 7.5
- Fasting: 160 mg/dl PP: 250 mg/dl

(cause: stress hyperglycaemia)

Given 2 units of insulin

Catheter and IV fluids w/pain relief medication

24/9

Decreased mobility

Compression stockings for blood flow

Precose increased to 50 mg postoperatively

25/9

Able to walk to the bathroom with a walker – catheter removed

Vicodin 7.5mg (twice daily) for pain (orally)

27/9

Compression stockings removed

28/9

Readings at discharge:

- 130 mg/dl
- PP: 150 mg/dl

Pain described as 5/10. Increases after walking for 5 mins (7/10)

Moderate mobility – walk approx. 50–60 steps with the aid

Incision site – slow healing

Daily dressing required

Staples removed in two wks (on 09/10)

Monitor blood sugar (2/day)

Discharge plan:

- Physio: ROM and strengthening exercises (weak arms)
- Scar tissue massage (myofascial release technique) – can be considered aft. incision heals
- Balance exercises – decrease risk of falling
- Occupational therapy: Complete a home hazard assessment since she will be living alone
- Discussed with patient: Non-slip mat for bathroom? Rails? Worried, needs help from daughter for cost
- Sock & shoe horn, reacher, dressing stick and raised toilet (purchased by daughter)
- Needs to be shown how to cook meals, i.e. using reacher, no bending, etc. Placement of food items important
- Can resume mild exercise after 12 wks subject to physio review of progress
- Yearly X-rays

Look at examples of two writing tasks that could be based on these case notes. Then read more about which case notes are relevant to each writing task example, and why.

	Example 1	Example 2
Writing task	*Write a letter to home health nurse Mr Minsub Park who will be visiting Ms Shaw every day. Use the information given in the case notes to outline the home care treatment plan and management for Ms Shaw.*	*Write a letter to occupational therapist Claudia Mayhew to outline the home assessment and management for Ms Shaw.*

	Patient details:	Patient details:
Examples of relevant case notes	• Left hip replacement following fracture sustained after fall	• Left hip replacement following fracture sustained after fall
	Social background:	**Social background:**
	• Daughter – leaving overseas next week (4/10)	• Lives with daughter
	• To move into a self-contained flat	• Daughter – leaving overseas next week (4/10)
	Medical history:	• To move into a self-contained flat. Flat has steps. Okay for walker?
	• Diabetes mellitus (20 years)	**Nursing management:**
	• Precose – 25 mg	• Pain described as 5/10. Increases after walking for 5 mins (7/10).
	Nursing management:	• Able to walk to the bathroom with a walker and walk approx. 50–60 steps with the aid
	• Preoperative readings = good control	• Moderate mobility
	• Stress hyperglycaemia; given 2 units of insulin	**Discharge plan:**
	• Incision site – slow healing	• Occupational therapy (complete a home hazard assessment since she will be living alone)
	• Moderate mobility	• Sock & shoe horn, reacher, dressing stick and raised toilet seat (purchased by daughter)
	• Daily dressing required	• Needs to be shown how to cook meals, i.e. using reacher, no bending, etc. Placement of food items important.
	• Staples removed in two wks (on 09/10)	
	• Monitor blood sugar (2/day)	
	Discharge plan:	
	• Physio: ROM, strengthening and balance exercises	
	• Occupational therapy	
	• Review diabetic medication (Precose) aft. 2 weeks (on 09/10)	
	• Ensure hydration	
Why are these case notes relevant?	A home health nurse will visit Ms Shaw at home, provide care and assess her condition regularly. In this task, the home health nurse does not know Ms Shaw, so it is important to keep that in mind while choosing case notes. The nurse will need to know details like her diagnosis, relevant medical history, complications, medication, and follow-up care because he is responsible for managing wound care, administering prescription medicines, monitoring diet and identifying care issues. As he is also generally responsible for sending reports to the patient's physician and coordinating with the physician / other healthcare workers, he needs to know what other aid Ms Shaw will be receiving (like physiotherapy and occupational therapy).	The occupational therapist's job is to help Ms Shaw continue participating in everyday activities by training her to use strategies, techniques and equipment (like the reacher, dressing stick) that can assist her with mobility and everyday living. In this task, the therapist does not already know Ms Shaw, so she needs to know what procedure Ms Shaw underwent. Since the therapist will help adapt Ms Shaw's home environment, she needs to know if Ms Shaw lives alone or not. She also needs to know the level of pain and ability, so she can understand how to help her and teach her techniques for coping with the pain.

(Note: This table does not include all the relevant case notes for these two tasks. Please refer to the answer key to see the sample answer for the letter to the occupational therapist. A sample letter to the home health nurse follows on the next page.)

Once you have decided what case notes are relevant, you will need to organise them into paragraphs by summarising and ordering the information. Each paragraph you write should focus on one main idea. Try not to confuse your reader with a mixture of information all in one paragraph.

You also need to think about the overall organisation of your letter. Always prioritise information that is central to the role the recipient has to play in the patient's recovery. If you are not familiar with the roles of healthcare providers, you may find it useful to read a little about the potential job roles of the reader (physiotherapist, home health nurse, GP, etc.). This will help you make better decisions about which information to prioritise. However, keep in mind that each writing task has its own, specific requirements. You need to think actively about the requirements of the task you are given on Test Day.

Here is a possible way to organise the letter to the home health nurse, Mr Minsub Park. Notice how information from the selected case notes has been reorganised into paragraphs.

Dear Mr Park,

RE: Ms Cindy Shaw, aged 75

I'm writing to detail the home treatment and management you will be responsible for providing for this patient who is being discharged today after a left hip replacement.

> The introductory paragraph states the purpose of the letter.

Ms Shaw had good blood sugar control prior to surgery but it increased suddenly (HbA1c: 7.5; fasting: 160 mg/dl; PP: 250 mg/dl) postoperatively due to stress hyperglycaemia. She was given two units of insulin, and her regular dose of Precose 25 mg, which she had been taking for a 20-year history of diabetes mellitus, was increased to 50 mg. At discharge, her blood sugar readings were 130 mg/dl (fasting) and 150 mg/dl (PP).

> The first body paragraph describes the postoperative complication following the procedure, as it will impact directly on the work of the home health nurse.
>
> Relevant case notes are from **medical history** and **nursing management**.

In addition to this, Vicodin (7.5 mg twice daily) for pain relief has been prescribed. Please change the dressing daily with careful attention to the incision site due to risk of infection. In addition, monitor blood sugar twice daily and ensure she stays hydrated.

> The second body paragraph describes the nursing care required.
>
> Relevant case notes are from **nursing management** and **discharge plan**.

Due to Ms Shaw having moderate mobility, physiotherapy that includes ROM, balance and strengthening exercises has been recommended. She will also receive occupational therapy since she will be living alone in a self-contained flat after her daughter leaves the country shortly.

> The third body paragraph describes what other therapy she is receiving and gives a reason for her need for occupational therapy.
>
> Relevant case notes are from **discharge plan** and **social background**.

Ms Shaw's staples will be removed and medicine reviewed on 09/10.

Please contact me if you have any questions.

Yours sincerely,

Charge Nurse

> The final body paragraph describes details of follow-up appointments/action.
>
> Relevant case notes are from **nursing management** and **discharge plan**.

Choose which of the case notes given below are most relevant to the two recipients – Ms Shaw's general practitioner and the physiotherapist. Think about the recipient's role in the patient's recovery to help you decide, then underline the notes that you think are most relevant.

Write a letter to her general practitioner, who will be responsible for monitoring her progress and providing any intervention if required.	Write a referral letter to physiotherapist Ms Singh, who will be responsible for providing postoperative rehabilitation during her early recovery period.

• Height 5'2", weight 118 lbs
• Diabetes mellitus (diagnosed 20 years)
• To move into a self-contained flat – flat has steps
• Vicodin 7.5 mg (twice daily)
• Postoperative:
   o HbA1c: 7.5
   o Fasting: 160 mg/dl
   o PP: 250 mg/dl
   o (cause: stress hyperglycaemia)
• Given 2 units of insulin
• Incision site – slow healing
• Precose increased to 50 mg postoperatively
	• Lives with daughter & son-in-law (30s; no children)
	• Spouse dead – 10 years
	• Scar tissue massage (myofascial release technique)
	• Exercise – regular (walking 30 min/day – 5 days/wk)
	• Monitor blood sugar (2/day)
	• Can resume mild exercise after 12 wks subject to physio review
	• Vicodin 7.5 mg (twice daily) to manage pain (5/10). Increases after walking for 5 mins (7/10)
	• Moderate mobility – walks approx. 50–60 steps with the aid

Task 1b

Imagine you are writing a letter of discharge to Ms Shaw's general practitioner. Think about how you would reorganise the case notes to write a paragraph about follow-up appointments/action.

What information would you include from the following sections of the case notes?

Nursing management

• _____

Discharge plan

• _____

• _____

• _____

• _____

• _____

• _____

Imagine you are writing a letter of discharge to a physiotherapist for Ms Shaw. Think about how you would reorganise the case notes to write a paragraph about the care Ms Shaw needs to receive under the physiotherapist.

What information would you include from the following sections of the case notes?

Social background

- _____
- _____
- _____
- _____

Discharge plan

- _____
- _____
- _____
- _____

Examples of letters to the occupational therapist, general practitioner and physiotherapist in these tasks are provided in the answer key. Read them to help you understand more about organising case notes in the Writing sub-test.

Writing skills: Summarising

You will need to summarise some parts of the case notes in your letter, especially when the reader needs only the overall idea and not specific details. Here again, the purpose of your letter and the role of the recipient will help you decide which parts of the case notes need to be summarised.

Let's look at a couple of examples.

This example is from a letter of referral to a nutritionist who has to investigate whether there are any diet-related triggers for the patient's atopic dermatitis.

Case notes	Summarised content
Patient: 5-year-old Lily Simons **Medical history** atopic dermatitis 2 yrs – itchy, dry, red skin and small bumps on cheeks and forehead 4 yrs – spread to trunk (bends of elbows and knees) 5 yrs – spread all over body with lichenification	Lily has had atopic dermatitis since age 2 which has progressively spread all over her body.

Since the role of the nutritionist is to prescribe dietary changes, the details of the patient's medical history can be summarised, so that the rest of the letter can focus on providing details of her diet.

The next example is from a letter of discharge to a home healthcare nurse who will be responsible for home care treatment and ongoing management following the patient's treatment for dengue fever in hospital.

Case notes	Summarised content
Patient: Mr Akulo Kent, age 65 years **Medical history** 22.10.2018 Presented with splitting headaches Prescribed acetaminophen (250 mg/once daily) 26.10.2018 Returned to report slight fever with cold Fever – 38°C acetaminophen (250 mg/twice daily) + paracetamol (500 mg/once daily) 28.10.2018 Returned to report developing rash (arms and legs) Fever – 38.2°C Blood test – positive for dengue fever virus Admitted for inpatient treatment	Mr Kent was admitted after a week-long history of dengue fever symptoms.

The role of the home health nurse in the above example is to look after the patient after discharge, so providing details of the medical progression of his dengue fever symptoms is not necessary. It is more effective to summarise this information for the home health nurse, since he/she needs some background to the case but not the exact details.

You can summarise effectively by retaining only the main idea of the information and leaving out details. For example, you could leave out a list of symptoms, details of individual visits, names of medications and readings of specific tests.

Task 2

Given below are case notes for a patient who is being referred to an orthopaedic surgeon for further assessment of his current osteoarthritis.

Decide which part of the case notes given below needs to be summarised. Then write your summary in one sentence, on the next page.

Patient details	Medical history	Medical background
68-year-old Noah Stevens **Social background** Lives with son (40 years old) – engineer Widower – since 2000 Retired teacher	Osteoarthritis (OA) diagnosed 5 years No other conditions **Medication** Year 1 – acetaminophen 250 mg Years 2, 3, 4 – acetaminophen 300 mg Corticosteroid injection in year 4 Year 5 – acetaminophen 350 mg	Stage 3 OA Severe pain in R knee Unable to climb stairs – difficulty while sitting and getting up, using the toilet Slight bowing in of leg

Write your summary here:

_____

Writing skills: Linking words

Using linking words and phrases in the right places in your letter can help you guide your reader through the ideas. Linking words highlight relationships such as contrast, consequence or time. If used appropriately, they can strengthen the logical organisation of your letter and help your reader retrieve information quickly. However, candidates sometimes feel that adding as many linking words as possible will improve their letter. Remember that overuse of linking words or inserting them just for the sake of using them could actually make your letter more difficult to read.

Here are some important kinds of linking words you can use.

Addition	Contrast	Sequence / time order	Consequence	Example
• also	• however	• first/second/third	• as a result	• for example
• furthermore	• in contrast	• prior to	• therefore	
• in addition		• during	• hence	
		• post/following/later		

Let's look at how linking words are used in an example paragraph based on a writing task and case notes.

Writing task: You are a charge nurse at a clinic where a patient has had a persistent cough for the last one month. Using the case notes, write a referral letter to a pulmonologist who needs to carry out an assessment and treat the patient.

Case notes

12.11.2019

Presenting complaint: persistent cough since October – worsens at night – slight fever
Management: Antiviral medication: 75 mg twice daily; Tamiflu for 10 days
Advised to drink plenty of fluids & rest; quit smoking

26.11.2019
Condition worsened: high fever accompanied by pleuritic pain
Physical examination: crackling sound when breathing
Chest X-ray and CBC advised

27.11.2019
X-ray revealed pleural effusion
High WBC count: 11.5

Example paragraph

… On his <u>first</u> visit, Mr Clark complained of a persistent cough that had begun a month ago. He was prescribed a 10-day course of Tamiflu, 75 mg, twice daily, and advised to maintain a high fluid intake. He was <u>also</u> advised to quit smoking. <u>Two weeks later</u>, he presented with a high fever and pleuritic pain. A physical examination of the chest revealed crackling, so a chest X-ray and CBC were performed. The X-ray revealed a pleural effusion and CBC showed a high WBC count of 11.5 …

In this example, the case notes have dates of visits and a progression of the main problem. Hence linking words related to time have been used to help the reader understand the sequence of events clearly.

Task 3a

Read these pairs of sentences from different OET letters and decide which linking words you can use to communicate the relationship between ideas clearly.

Sentences	Connection between ideas	Linking words	Sentences with linking words
1. Mr Hargreaves was admitted for left knee replacement surgery two weeks ago. Mr Hargreaves had been taking NSAIDs up until his surgery to manage his condition.	You want to tell your reader that Mr Hargreaves had been taking NSAIDs up until the time he had surgery.	Prior to	Mr Hargreaves was admitted for left knee replacement surgery two weeks ago. **Prior to surgery**, he was on NSAIDs to manage his condition.
2. Mr Hargreaves has been advised to ambulate regularly and continue with occupational therapy. He requires Tylenol and daily dressing.	You want to give your reader an additional piece of information about medication and dressing.		
3. Ms Lazarus was unable to breathe on her own and was placed on a ventilator for a week. She is able to breathe independently.	You want to highlight the difference in her condition now.		
4. Mr Kumar underwent a series of ROM, stretching and strengthening exercises, and occupational therapy. He has been able to make a full recovery.	You want to tell the reader that he was able to make a full recovery because of this treatment.		
5. Ms Tobias has been asked to eliminate gluten from her diet. She should avoid pasta, noodles, cereal and all processed food.	You want to give examples of what she should avoid.		

Read this extract from an OET referral letter to a physiotherapist. It has two wrongly used linking words and one unnecessary linking word. Replace the wrongly used linking words and identify the extra linking word.

I am writing to refer Ms Taylor, who requires physiotherapy for plantar fasciitis in her right foot.

Ms Taylor has been suffering from plantar fasciitis for the last two months. She sought medical aid when the problem surfaced and was prescribed NSAIDs (Voveran 50 mg). <u>Therefore</u>, she did not complete the course of medication and the problem grew worse. As a result, recent toxicology reports show poor B12 and D3 levels, so she has been prescribed supplements.

In order to compensate for the pain, Ms Taylor developed an antalgic gait. <u>However</u>, she suffers from lower back pain in the lumbar region.

Writing skills: Using sentence variety

In OET, you are tested on how effectively you highlight key information. Using a variety of sentence structures can help you do this.

Read the paragraph below about a patient's current condition, and think about the effect it has on you as a reader.

> Mr Manekshaw's condition has stabilised postoperatively. His chest congestion has been resolved. He does not complain of pain in the arm area. There is still some bruising around the incision.

Although the sentences are short and simple, they do not convey a logical flow of ideas. Moreover, the reader would probably not be able to decide how to prioritise the information presented.

Instead of writing a continuous string of unconnected simple sentences, you can use conjunctions to connect your ideas better. This helps convey information more accurately to your reader.

Now, read the same paragraph with conjunctions.

> Mr Manekshaw's condition has stabilised postoperatively **and** his chest congestion has been resolved. **Although** he does not complain of pain in the arm area, there is still some bruising around the incision.

As you may have noticed, the connections established between ideas in the sentences improve the paragraph. Establishing connections like these helps the reader understand how to prioritise the information in your letter.

Conjunctions

There are two kinds of conjunctions you can use to add variety and prioritise information in sentences: coordinating and subordinating conjunctions.

Coordinating conjunctions	Subordinating conjunctions
⇓	⇓
for and not but or yet so	although while as because since when even though if until after before
⇓	⇓
Use them to join two sentences.	Use them to join two sentences.
⇓	⇓
They appear in the middle of sentences.	They appear at the beginning or in the middle of sentences.
⇓	⇓
The result is a compound sentence with two independent clauses.	The result is a complex sentence with one dependent and one independent clause.

Compound sentences are formed using coordinating conjunctions, while complex sentences are formed using subordinating conjunctions. Both compound and complex sentences have more than one clause, and this can serve to highlight important or new information.

In compound sentences, both clauses in the sentence carry equally important information. However, in complex sentences, the clause that begins with the subordinating conjunction is dependent on the independent clause (or less important than it). Therefore, you can put information you want to draw attention to in the independent clause.

Let's look at an example to see how this works in an OET letter.

Mr Black lives in a retirement home and is returning after a knee replacement operation. The charge nurse, who is writing this letter, wants to tell the resident nurse about the patient's current condition. Here are two pieces of information from the case notes the charge nurse wants to use in the letter:

A. Mr Black can ambulate independently.
B. He needs a walker when outdoors (in the garden).

Which of the two pieces of information deserves greater attention from the resident nurse?

Remember, the resident nurse is responsible for monitoring Mr Black's progress and providing the support and medication required for his recovery as well as for preventing any accidents. While both are important pieces of information, B probably deserves greater attention because if Mr Black goes outside without a walker, he could injure himself.

Now, you have the choice of using either a compound or complex sentence to convey the importance of using a walker outdoors. Which one would you use?

Sentence A: Compound sentence

Mr Black is able to ambulate independently but he still needs a walker when he is outdoors.

Sentence B: Complex sentence

Although Mr Black is able to ambulate independently, he needs a walker when he is outdoors.

Both sentences A and B are grammatically correct. However, what you need to think about is the priority you want to give to information that your reader needs to know. One way to do this is to put the information you want the reader to focus on in the independent clause of a complex sentence. In Sentence A, both clauses are independent and equally important, so both the walker and his ability to ambulate stay in focus. However, in Sentence B, the information about his ability to ambulate appears in the dependent clause, and so the information in the independent clause about using a walker is the focal point of the sentence.

When you want to indicate to your reader that both pieces of information are equally important, you can use a compound sentence. Remember that the focus here is not on grammar, but on the prioritisation of information so that your reader knows what to concentrate on.

Task 4a

Read the information for each letter. Then, using that information, decide which option (A or B) conveys your message most effectively to the reader.

Note that both options are grammatically correct, so focus on how you want your reader to prioritise the information.

Letter 1

Writing task	**Purpose for writing**	**Information about medical history**
• You are a head nurse writing a letter of referral to a chest specialist in another hospital about Mrs Howard, a patient in your care.	• There is a strong possibility she could have cancer, but you want to refer her to a specialist to make a more accurate assessment.	• Regular smoker • Family history of cancer

Which option would be the most effective way to tell your reader that both factors should be considered of equal importance when making an assessment of the patient?

    A. She is a regular smoker. She has a family history of cancer.
    B. She is a regular smoker and has a family history of cancer.

Letter 2

Writing task	**Purpose for writing**	**Information about current condition**	**Information about medication**
• You are a head nurse writing a letter of discharge to a resident community nurse of a retirement home where a patient, Mr Black, lives.	• You want to inform the resident nurse about his current condition following his angioplasty and want to give information about his continued care.	• He has made good progress and is ready for discharge. • He may experience chest soreness for one more week.	• Continue usual hypertension medication • Nurofen Plus, up to a max of 6 tablets/day

i. Which option would be the most effective way to indicate to your reader that he/she should be prepared for a problem the patient may experience as a result of the angioplasty?

    A. He may continue to experience soreness in the chest for another week, although he has made good progress and is ready for discharge.

    B. He has made good progress and is ready for discharge, but may continue to experience soreness in the chest for another week.

ii. Which option would be the most effective way to highlight new medication that the patient needs to be given?

    A. While he needs to continue his usual hypertension medication, he also needs medication to manage pain (Nurofen Plus, up to a max of 6 tablets/day).

    B. He will continue with his usual hypertension medication, and also needs medication to manage pain (Nurofen Plus, up to a max of 6 tablets/day).

Letter 3

Writing task	**Purpose for writing**	**Information about social background**
• You are a charge nurse writing to a social worker about a patient, Ms Diamond.	• You need to give a brief social background of the patient so the social worker can help the patient get the right support.	• Offered counselling help numerous times • Refused counselling

Which option would be the most effective way to highlight the patient's unwillingness to receive help?

    A. Ms Diamond has been offered counselling help several times but has refused.

    B. Ms Diamond has refused counselling help although it has been offered several times.

Letter 4

Writing task	**Purpose for writing**	**Information about medical history**
• You are a head nurse writing a letter of referral to a dietician about a patient, Mr Cole.	• You need to give the dietician the patient's medical history and state why the patient needs a diet plan.	• Bariatric surgery (two weeks ago) • Diabetic for the last ten years

Which option would be the most effective way to highlight two equally important factors to consider when deciding the diet plan?

    A. Mr Cole had bariatric surgery two weeks ago. He has been diabetic for the last ten years.

    B. Mr Cole had bariatric surgery two weeks ago and has been diabetic for the last ten years.

Given below are some sentences based on case notes. Join them together using coordinating and subordinating conjunctions, keeping in mind what you have just learnt. There are two items that do not require any change.

	Case notes	Sentences	Your answer
a.	lives with daughter & son-in-law (30s; no children); spouse deceased	She lives with her daughter and son-in-law. She is a widow.	She is a widow **and** lives with her daughter and son-in-law.
b.	Long history of drug abuse (cocaine); when sad	He has a long history of drug abuse with cocaine. His usage increases when he is depressed.	
c.	Early dementia; is able to do things independently	She has early dementia. She is able to do things independently.	
d.	6 litres of 5% dextrose saline administered postoperatively – hyponatraemia; passed into coma on the second day after surgery	She received 6 litres of 5% dextrose saline postoperatively to manage hyponatraemia. She passed into a coma two days after surgery.	
e.	Angioplasty discharge on 22.5.2018 Restenosis admitted on 24.9.2018	He was discharged following angioplasty on 22.5.2018. He was admitted again with restenosis on 24.9.2018.	
f.	Pain location: deep within the right eye; described as 7/10 Ocular examination – diagnosed as endophthalmitis	She presented with pain deep within the right eye (7/10). An ocular examination was conducted and it revealed endophthalmitis.	

Writing skills: Using appropriate vocabulary

An OET letter is formal because it is written in a professional setting. In most letter-writing tasks you will be required to write to another healthcare professional, but in some cases, the task may require you to write to a layperson. No matter who your audience is, always maintain a formal tone in your letter. This means you should avoid slang, colloquial expressions, and short forms commonly used in SMS or chat communication.

Another way of ensuring that your letter is appropriate for your audience is to use technical or non-technical terms as appropriate for the task. Consider the level of familiarity your reader will have with the subject. If you are writing to another healthcare professional in the same discipline, you can use technical terms – your reader will be able to understand these without difficulty and the purpose of writing the letter will be met. If you are a specialist writing to a GP, on the other hand, you may need to refrain from using highly technical terms and abbreviations. If you are writing to a healthcare professional in a completely different discipline, then use technical terms and abbreviations judiciously.

When writing to a layperson, you need to ensure that you use non-technical terms and explain things in a way they can easily understand. Note that the test does not require you to draw on your medical knowledge – the case notes contain adequate information regarding any technical medical terms used.

Let's take a look at two versions of a part of a discharge letter to the head nurse at a community retirement home. A patient, Mr Blane, has just been discharged from hospital after being admitted for hypertension.

As you read, think about appropriate use of vocabulary and level of formality.

Extract A	Extract B
Mr Blane is taking Novarsc for hypertension, Glucophage for diabetes mellitus and Prozac for obesity-related depression. If morbid obesity persists, these co-morbid conditions will become difficult to manage. Please encourage daily exercise and continue dietary restrictions. If there is no improvement in the next six months, surgical weight reduction may be considered.	Mr Blane is taking Novarsc for high blood pressure, Glucophage for diabetes and Prozac for obesity-related depression. If his weight remains unchanged, these related conditions will be harder to manage. Please encourage daily exercise and stop him from eating food he is not allowed to eat. If he does not improve in the next six months, an operation may be considered.

Extract A uses appropriate technical terms which give the letter a more formal tone; Extract B, however, uses non-technical vocabulary even though the recipient is a medical professional, not only reducing its appropriateness but also decreasing its formal tone. The difference here is subtle, but remember your goal should be to create a formal letter that your reader can understand.

Task 5a

Match the medical words/phrases in Column A with non-medical words/phrases in Column B that have the same meaning. An example has been done for you.

Column A	Column B	Answers
1. hypertension	a. period	1–d
2. erectile dysfunction disorder	b. hay fever	2–h
3. menses	c. having/showing symptoms of a fever	3–g
4. pharyngitis	d. high blood pressure	4–f
5. allergic rhinitis	e. walk	5–f
6. febrile	f. sore throat	5– 6–b
7. ambulate	g. bad breath	7–c
8. halitosis	h. impotence	8–g

Task 5b

The following two tasks are based on the same case. Circle the appropriate reader for each letter below. Then fill in the blanks in the extracts from these letters that follow on the next page, using appropriate vocabulary from the box.

Letter 1

A referral letter to allergist Mr George Engels, 29 Humphreys Road, Newbury, who will need to carry out further assessment and treatment.
Reader: Medical professional / Layperson

Letter 2

A letter of advice to the patient's school teacher, Ms Osler, Newbury Primary School, 56 Queen's Way.
Reader: Medical professional / Layperson

Note that the letter extracts do not have the same content because the purpose of each is different. In Letter Extract 1, the allergist needs to know the details of the hospitalisation and medication to further assess the child, but in Letter Extract 2 the teacher needs to know what happened to the child, and how she must administer the medication during school hours.

acute lower respiratory tract infection		severe chest congestion	

administered	given	fit	stabilised	bronchial steroids	medications

Letter Extract 1

I am writing to refer this patient to you for further assessment and treatment. Miss Rose Jenkins was admitted on 24 November with bronchiolitis following three days of cough and fever.

On admission, she was suffering from (1) _____ (saturation level 93%; pulse rate 72 beats/min). Levolin through nebuliser and oxygen were (2) _____. She has (3) _____ and her vital signs are normal (saturation level 97%; pulse rate 110 beats/min).

(4) _____ – TusQ 5 mg, Kidpred 5 mg, Levolin (50 mcg inhaler) – have been prescribed for three months ....

Letter Extract 2

I am writing to update you regarding Rose Jenkins' recent hospitalisation, and to advise you regarding her care during school hours.

Rose was admitted on 24 November following (5) _____. She has made good progress and is (6) _____ to return to school.

Miss Jenkins has been diagnosed with a common lung infection called bronchiolitis for which she needs medication for the next three months.

One of her (7) _____ (Levolin) needs to be (8) _____ during school hours. Please give her three pumps between 12–12.30 pm. Each pump should be given at an interval of two minutes ....

Writing skills: Grammar

Poor grammar can make any form of communication difficult to understand. It is particularly problematic in writing. Your reader may overlook or misunderstand some important information due to the poor grammar in your letter.

In many general-purpose writing tests, your grammar is scored according to the range of your grammar. Therefore, you may feel that 'showing off' your grammar to the Assessor will be to your advantage. In OET, however, your grammar will be graded according to how effectively it enables the reader to understand the information. This doesn't mean that grammar is any less important for OET than it is for other tests. Being able to accurately and efficiently communicate information from case notes in a formal letter does require a range of grammatical functions. Grammar is no more or less important in OET than it is in other tests. The difference is that OET is not assessing how much grammar you have: it's assessing the way you use that grammar to communicate with the reader. So it is very important that you understand how to use your grammar appropriately. Don't just learn *how* to write a passive sentence, for example. You need to learn *why* the passive is used, *when* you should use it, and *the impact* on the reader that a passive sentence will have. Using an accurately written passive sentence where it is not appropriate will not help your grade. In other tests, you might improve your score because you were able to show the Assessor that you know how to write a passive sentence, but OET is not assessed in this way.

Tenses

In your OET letter, you will not need to use all the tenses in the English language. This is because OET Writing tasks are focused on very specific situations. There are, however, a few particular tenses that you will often use in the letter.

Let's look at an example from an OET letter. A patient named Mr Atkins underwent a left lung lobectomy, and the head nurse at the hospital is writing a discharge letter to a home nurse who will take over care of Mr Atkins. Look at the different types of information the head nurse may need to convey about him, and the most appropriate tense(s) to use for each of them.

Patient information

- Mr Atkins **has** a BMI of 17.9.
- He **is** underweight.

Use the **simple present** to describe patient information.

Medical history

- Mr Atkins **has suffered** from a chronic cough since 2017.
- He **took** OTC antitussives regularly and **started** developing dependence.
- He **had refused** therapy **before** being diagnosed with lung cancer.

Use the **present perfect**, **past simple** or **past perfect** to describe medical history.

Medical background/treatment

- Mr Atkins **underwent** a left lung lobectomy.
- Daily dressing changes **were given**.
- Weak opiods (codeine) **were administered** postoperatively.

Use the **past simple** to describe what happened to the patient in your care.

Current condition

- Mr Atkins **is able to** breathe independently.
- His pain **has subsided**.
- He **has made** a good recovery.

Use the **present simple** and **present perfect** to describe a patient's current condition.

Care

- Mr Atkins **will need** daily dressing.

Use **future time (will)** to say what care will be required.

You will also need to use **modal verbs**. For example:

- He **should** follow dietary restrictions.
- He **must** be monitored closely.

The home care nurse may not need to know a lot about Mr Atkins' social background. However, if the recipient of the letter was a counsellor helping Mr Atkins overcome nicotine addiction, then you may need to add some aspects of his social background.

Social background

- Mr Atkins **smokes** 10 cigarettes a day.
- He **lives** alone.
- He **has been seeing** a therapist to help with his addiction.

Use the **simple present** or **present perfect/perfect continuous** to describe social background.

Remember that this is a guideline for you to follow. While it gives you an idea of the tense you need to use for specific kinds of information, you may still need to think carefully about the timing of an event in the case notes before you decide which tense to use.

Task 6a

Imagine you are writing a discharge letter for a patient, Mrs Baker. You want to communicate information about her condition. For each situation, tick the sentence that uses the right tense to convey the desired information. Then think of a situation when the other sentence would be used.

1. You want to say that this is a regular problem for Mrs Baker with no specific start date.
   a. Mrs Baker suffers from migraines.
   b. Mrs Baker has been suffering from migraines.

2. You want to say that this is a temporary problem for her and is present at the time you are writing the letter.
   a. Mrs Baker has experienced abdominal pain.
   b. Mrs Baker is experiencing abdominal pain.

3. You want to say that she had this surgery at a specific time.
   a. She has undergone left hip replacement surgery.
   b. She underwent left hip replacement surgery two years ago.

4. You want to describe her condition at the time of admission into hospital.
   a. She was experiencing fever and mild chills.
   b. She has been experiencing fever and mild chills.

5. You want to make a prediction about her future condition.
   a. Her recovery is going to take time.
   b. Her recovery has taken time.

Task 6b

Read a discharge letter from the head nurse at Newtown Hospital to the resident nurse at the Garden Community Centre, where the patient will be staying until complete recovery. It has some errors in the use of tenses. Correct these underlined errors. Paying attention to the time references will help you. An example has been done for you.

Mr Harold Barker
Resident Nurse

22 February 2018

Dear Mr Barker,

Re: Mrs Gena Cooper (aged 65)

Mrs Cooper (a) ~~return~~ *is returning* to your care today, and will require your ongoing care as she recovers from tuberculosis.

While in hospital, Mrs Cooper (b) <u>develop</u> drug-induced hepatitis which was treated, but will require your ongoing observation. She is due for a liver function test one month after discharge.

After six weeks of treatment, she (c) <u>stabilise,</u> and her fever and pneumonitis have resolved. Unfortunately, she still (d) <u>experience</u> some chest and abdominal pain. During her hospital stay, she (e) <u>is needing</u> a walker and (f) <u>is requiring</u> assistance with showering. Now, she (g) <u>was able to</u> perform these activities but may need help if her weakness deteriorates. She is on ethambutol for TB, twice weekly. Paracetamol may be administered for her chest pain. Please ensure Mrs Cooper is kept warm and encouraged to ambulate regularly. She needs to remain on the diet suggested by the dietician including no consumption of caffeinated drinks. Mrs Cooper (h) <u>is</u> very weak on admission to hospital, but has made good progress. Her diet (i) <u>needed</u> to be monitored closely for the next three months since she (j) <u>lose</u> a considerable amount of weight.

If you have any questions, please do not hesitate to contact me.

Yours sincerely,

Head Nurse

Modal verbs

When writing an OET letter, you may need to give advice, make requests, or talk about what a patient can or cannot do. Modal verbs are used to perform all of these functions. Let's take a look at some particularly relevant ones in the following task.

Task 7a

Look at these sentences from a discharge letter to a resident nurse at a community home for the elderly. The patient, Ms Loreto, has just undergone cataract surgery on her right eye. The charge nurse writing the letter describes the patient's present condition and treatment plan so the resident nurse can take over care of Ms Loreto.

Match each sentence with the function it performs. An example has been done for you.

Sentence	Function	Answers
1. While she can use the toilet independently during the day, she requires assistance at night.	a. Making a polite request	1 – d
2. Going outdoors and doing any strenuous activity (lifting items and bending) should be avoided for a week.	b. Describing possibility	2 –
3. She may continue to experience redness and blurred vision for another week.	c. Describing a necessity in the past	3 –
4. It would be appreciated if you could make arrangements for someone to accompany her for surgery on her left eye on 23.12.2019.	d. Describing a patient's ability	4 –
5. She should wear her protective eye shield while sleeping and napping.	e. Cautioning	5 –
6. Cataract surgery had to be performed urgently after two minor falls.	f. Giving advice	6 –

Common mistakes with modals

Do not use two modal verbs together. For example:

- She must ~~have to~~ visit a doctor soon.
- She should ~~must~~ avoid rice.
- He can ~~able to~~ walk.

Remember that when the sentence is in the present tense, the verb that follows the modal verb should be in the present tense and not in the past. For example:

- She should **use** a walker. NOT She should used a walker.
- She shouldn't **consume** alcohol. NOT She shouldn't consumed alcohol.
- She can **walk** independently. NOT She can walked independently.

Task 7b

Read these sentences taken from a discharge letter and complete them with appropriate modal verbs.

1. Mrs Bose _____ to undergo an emergency hip replacement following a fracture to the left hip.

2. She has made a good recovery. She ___should___ perform most tasks like showering and using the toilet independently.

3. Mrs Bose ___can___ be encouraged to continue doing contracting and relaxing exercises every hour.

4. She ___should___ need assistance to stand up and get out of bed, and take the first few steps every morning.

5. It ___can___ be appreciated if you ___can___ update her family members on her progress regularly.

Active and passive sentences

You will need to use both active and passive sentences in an OET letter. Let's look at how these sentences work in an OET context.

In an active sentence, the person **who** performs the action is the focus, or subject, of the sentence.

For example:

> Mr Singh accidentally took an overdose of sleeping pills. (*Mr Singh* performed the action, so he is the subject.)

> A paramedic administered CPR. (The *paramedic* performed CPR, so he/she is the subject.)

In the active sentences, the people who performed the actions (*Mr Singh* and the *paramedic*) are important, so they are the subjects of the sentences.

In contrast, the passive voice is used to emphasise what was done or who it was done to. The subject in a passive sentence is unimportant or unknown, and the object is emphasised.

For example:

> On arrival, gastrointestinal decontamination was performed.

> Activated charcoal was administered through a feeding tube.

In these passive sentences, what happened is more important than the person who performed the action.

Task 8a

Look at these sentences from an OET discharge letter. A head nurse is writing to the home care nurse of a patient, Mr Norton, who has just undergone an omental patch closure for treatment of a duodenal ulcer.

For each piece of information the head nurse wants to give, choose the sentence(s) that sound(s) most 'natural' and that highlight(s) the subject/object appropriately. You may choose more than one sentence for each question.

Note that all of these sentences are grammatically correct, so focus on whether the reader needs to know who performs the action.

1. Patient's symptoms or condition
   a. On admission, Mr Norton was experiencing burning abdominal pain accompanied by nausea.
   b. On admission, doctors observed that Mr Norton was experiencing abdominal pain accompanied by nausea.
   c. Mr Norton's vital signs were normal with the exception of a low pulse rate (40 beats/minute).
   d. The nurse recorded Mr Norton's vital signs which were normal with the exception of a low pulse rate (40 beats/minute).

2. Tests / surgery
   a. An endoscopy was conducted, which revealed a 5 mm duodenal ulcer.
   b. Doctors conducted an endoscopy which revealed a 5 mm duodenal ulcer.
   c. Two days later, doctors performed an omental patch closure.
   d. Two days later, an omental patch closure was performed.

3. Patient's post operative progress
   a. Good progress has been made by Mr Norton, and his bowel activity has returned to normal.
   b. Semi-solid food (for example, pureed fruits and vegetables) can be digested by Mr Norton.
   c. Mr Norton has made good progress and his bowel activity has returned to normal.
   d. Mr Norton is able to eat semi-solid food (for example, pureed fruits and vegetables).

4. Medication
   a. The doctor has prescribed oral proton-pump inhibitor (PPI) medication for eight weeks.
   b. Oral proton-pump inhibitor (PPI) medication has been prescribed for eight weeks.

5. Treatment plan / care
   a. Mr Norton's stitches will be removed after a week.
   b. The doctor will remove his stitches after a week.
   c. Alcohol and caffeinated beverages should be avoided.
   d. Mr Norton should not drink caffeinated beverages or alcohol.

Task 8b

Read these sentences from referral and discharge letters. Fill in the blanks by changing the verb in brackets into active or passive form as appropriate.

   a. Mr Abdul Hussain has a history of non-ST-elevation myocardial infarction, and coronary stents _____ (insert) at that time.
   b. Ms Norton _____ (diagnose) with ductal carcinoma five years ago.
   c. Mrs Smith's condition has improved, and knee surgery should _____ (consider) only as a last resort.
   d. Ms Romano should _____ (give) a blood glucose monitoring kit and should _____ (refer) to a dietician.
   e. Since dietary changes did not resolve her uncontrolled hyperglycaemia, Metformin _____ (prescribe).
   f. Strenuous physical activity following a tonsillectomy _____ (discourage). Soft foods such as ice cream, yogurt and jello should _____ (encourage). Liquid Tylenol may _____ (administer) in case of any pain.
   g. Mr Wood _____ (take) NSAIDs for osteoarthritis.
   h. Eye shields and glasses should _____ (wash) with soap and water daily. Cosmetics like mascaras and eyeliners _____ (not / permit).
   i. Ms Devito _____ (suffer) from migraines, which increase in severity when she is at work.
   j. Ms Walker _____ (live) alone with her elderly sister who suffers from dementia.

Articles

The use of articles often requires a lot of practice to master. Consider some OET situations where you need to use them.

a/an and *the*

1. Use *a/an* every time you refer to something for the first time. For example:

   > Ms Thomason underwent **a left hip replacement** operation last year. **The hip replacement** was successful.

   > Use of **a walker and toilet raiser** is recommended. **The toilet raiser** has been arranged by our social worker.

   > Mr Gupta has **a persistent headache**. **The headache** did not subside even after medication, so he was advised to take some more tests.

In these examples, you can see that the first time a reference is made to something, *a/an* is used. When the same thing is mentioned the second time, it becomes specific and both the writer and reader know what is being referred to, so *the* is used. Note that *an* is used before words that start with a vowel sound.

2. Use *the* when a noun is made definite by a qualifying phrase that follows it. For example:

Mr Carter should continue taking **the medication** prescribed by his oncologist. (Medication is specific – the one prescribed by his doctor.)

Ms Goldsmith did not respond well to **the adjuvant treatment** that followed her double mastectomy. (A specific treatment – the one that she received after her surgery.)

3. Use *the* to refer to organs and body systems. For example:

Microcystic oedema was observed throughout **the cornea**.

A VATS procedure was performed on **the right knee**.

She was diagnosed with Non-Hodgkin lymphoma (NHL), a type of cancer that starts in **the lymphatic system**.

MRI tests revealed damage to **the central nervous system**, more specifically the parietal lobe.

4. Use an article with job roles and medical procedures. For example:

Mr Townsend will need to meet **a dietician** next week. (Not a specific dietician in this case.)

The dietician he has been consulting has recommended minor changes. (A specific dietician – the one he has already met several times.)

An ultrasound revealed that he had acute appendicitis. **The ultrasound** also revealed some damage to the liver. (In the first sentence, we are introducing the ultrasound for the first time, so we use *an*, but later since we know which ultrasound we are referring to, we use *the*.)

Task 9a

Read extracts from two letters and put in *a/an* or *the* in the blanks.

Letter A

… Mr D'Souza is (1) _____ widowed pensioner who lives alone. He performs most of his household tasks independently, but (2) _____ neighbour drives him to the local grocery store. (3) _____ neighbour brought him to hospital.

Letter B

… Mr Wright was admitted with (1) _____ persistent dry cough. He had previously been on medication to treat a bout of the flu, but (2) _____ dry cough did not subside. After several tests, including (3) _____ biopsy, it was discovered that (4) _____ cough was a symptom of congestive heart failure.

Zero article

Nouns do not always need to be preceded by an article. *Zero article* is the term used to describe a situation where you do not use an article before a noun.

1. Articles are generally not used with serious medical conditions, names of drugs, and therapies. For example:

The patient was diagnosed with **cancer**.

Mrs Carter suffers from **hypertension**.

She underwent **chemotherapy**.

She requires **occupational therapy**.

Paracetamol may be administered if pain persists.

However, you do need to use articles with minor conditions such as headaches, migraines, the flu and fever. For example:

> On admission, Mr Bora was running **a fever** (BT: 38°C) and reported having **a severe headache**.
>
> He presented with **a dry cough**.

2. Articles are not used with plural countable or uncountable nouns like classes of drugs (painkillers, analgesics, antibiotics, antidepressants) and types of food (proteins, cereals, carbohydrates). For example:

> She should not consume **dairy products** or **baked goods**.
>
> She should consume plenty of **oral fluids**.
>
> She has been on **painkillers** for three years.

3. Articles are not used with states (inflammation, consciousness, depression) and emotions (anger, anxiety). For example:

> Mr Johnston was suffering from severe **inflammation** due to tendonitis.
>
> He has been taking bupropion to manage **depression** and **anxiety**.

Task 9b

Read these sentences and decide which option is correct. Tick the correct option.

a. Ms Brown was prescribed 100 mg of aspirin / the aspirin daily.
b. The skin rash was diagnosed as the eczema / eczema.
c. Ms Brown has a family history of the Parkinson's / Parkinson's disease.
d. Please encourage plenty of vegetables in the diet as well as nuts / the nuts.
e. She had difficulty displaying the emotions / emotions and appeared distant, signalling possible schizoid disorder.

Task 9c

Read this letter extract and put an article (*a/an/the* or *zero article*) in the blanks. If it is a *zero article*, put a dash (–).

Letter C

… Ms Walsh is being referred to your facility so that her progress can be monitored.

While she can shower and use the toilet on her own, she will need (1) _a_ walker when walking outside. In addition, she needs (2) _an_ occupational therapy. Please ensure she stays on (3) _–_ diet recommended by the dietician. If she experiences pain, please administer (4) _–_ ibuprofen (max 3 tablets/day).

Writing skills: Punctuation

You can improve the clarity of your sentences by punctuating them well. Therefore, it is important to know how to use the two most basic punctuation marks well: the full stop and the comma.

Full stops and correcting run-on sentences

Full stops are used to mark the end of a sentence. Each sentence contains an idea, and so full stops help us understand where one idea ends and the next begins. However, many students write 'run-on' sentences: very long sentences with two or more clauses not separated by a full stop or semi-colon, or joined by a conjunction.

Run-on sentences confuse your reader because there is no clear distinction between where one clause ends and another begins. You should know where to break a sentence into parts if it is becoming too long.

A run-on sentence is two, three or more clauses in a single sentence. For example, this run-on sentence contains two clauses:

Ms Dinshaw is on ramipril 5 mg for her hypertension she is compliant with medication.

The two clauses are:

Ms Dinshaw is on ramipril 5 mg for her hypertension | she is compliant with medication.

Therefore, a full stop needs to be used to correct this run-on:

Ms Dinshaw is on ramipril 5 mg for her hypertension. She is compliant with medication.

Note that a comma is not sufficient to separate the sentences above. This is called a comma splice:

Ms Dinshaw is on ramipril 5 mg for her hypertension, she is compliant with medication. **X**

However, you can use a conjunction:

Ms Dinshaw is on ramipril 5 mg for her hypertension **and** she is compliant with medication.

Always read your letter again in the last five minutes of the test, and check if there are any run-on sentences to correct.

Task 10a

Identify the run-on sentences in this short paragraph. Rewrite the paragraph after fixing them.

Note: You can use any of these two correction methods, or a combination of both:

- a full stop
- a comma followed by a conjunction

Mrs Jonas' blood pressure has consistently stayed in the range of 180–190/95–100 a range of investigations, including echocardiogram and renal function tests, has been performed all of them were normal.

Rewrite here:

Commas

A comma is a punctuation mark that separates clauses, phrases and words in a sentence. Commas are used in the following ways in OET:

1. To separate words in a series or list:

Mr Gill is taking ramipril, Glucophage and Prozac.

He is to undergo a series of ROM and stretching exercises, occupational therapy and water therapy to ensure recovery.

2. When a sentence starts with a dependent clause:

> **Although** he has made good progress with occupational therapy, he is not ready to live on his own.

> **Since** there are no signs of scar tissue that could cause restenosis, he may be discharged.

3. To separate an interrupting thought in a sentence (this is called a bracketing comma):

> Mr Hagee, a widower, has been on Prozac for three years since his wife died. (*A widower* is extra information in this sentence and interrupts the flow, so it is placed within commas.)

4. After introductory phrases at the beginning of sentences:

> On 4 February, Mr Gonzales was admitted for pneumonia.

> After a week, he has made good progress.

Task 10b

Add a comma in the right place in the following sentences.

1. Ten months ago Mr Harding was admitted for two days following an asthma attack.
2. Mrs Cooper suffers from hypertension diabetes mellitus and depression.
3. Mr Robert Brown a 25-year-old bachelor was admitted after a drug overdose.
4. While she may never gain complete control of her legs she can use a mobile wheelchair to move around without much assistance.
5. Although her breathing problems have been resolved she complains of frequent headaches.

Writing skills: Spelling

Students generally make a few common errors when it comes to spelling in OET. You need to:

1. Be consistent with spelling conventions. It's your choice whether to use British English or American English, but you must maintain the same spelling conventions throughout your letter. For example, if you use the spelling *litre* in your first paragraph, do not switch to *liter* a few sentences later. Here are some areas of difference to be aware of:

Difference	British English	American English
Words ending in -*re*	-*re* litre, fibre	-*er* liter, fiber
Words ending in -*our*	-*our* neighbour	-*or* neighbor
Words ending in -*ise/ize*	-*ise* or -*ize* acceptable recognise / recognize	-*ize* recognize
Double vowels	*ae* or *oe* leukaemia, oestrogen, paediatric, orthopaedic, anaesthetic	Only *e* leukemia, estrogen, pediatric, orthopedic, anesthetic

This list is by no means a complete one. You will need to refer to additional resources if you want more information.

2. Use the same spelling given in the case notes. There may be names of medicines, treatments or tests that have been spelled in a particular way in the case notes. Ensure that you use the same spellings throughout your letter. Another common error candidates make is to spell the name of the patient incorrectly. For example, if it is *Rachel* in the case notes, do not spell it *Rachael* in your letter.

3. Avoid using symbols to spell words. SMS and chat abbreviations are common in everyday written communication, but these must be avoided in OET. Do not use symbols for words like *and* (&), *at* (@) and *to* (2). Avoid shortening the spelling of words like *department* (dept) and *November* (Nov). Using these compromises the formality of the letter.

4. Be aware of commonly misspelled words. Make a list of words that are generally misspelled. A few examples:
   - advice (noun) and advise (verb)
   - necessary (only one 'c')
   - occurrence (two 'c's and two 'r's – ends with -*ence*)
   - referred/referring (two 'r's) but refer
   - until (one 'l' at the end)
   - lose (to fail to maintain) and *loose* (too big) – *lose weight* but a *loose knot*
   - planning/planned/stopped (two 'n's and two 'p's)

You can also create a list of words that you find yourself misspelling often.

Task 11

Below are some patient case notes, and an extract from a letter based on them. The letter contains <u>eight</u> misspelled words. Correct each one by putting a line through it and writing the correct word above. An example has been done for you.

Case notes

Patient name: Jakob Moore; 68 years
Diagnosis: Severe end-stage knee arthritis – Stage 4 OA (Osteoarthritis)
Treatment: Total knee arthroplasty (TKA) (Right knee)
Discharge plan:
- Move to Transitional Care Unit (TCU)
- Medications – ramipril 5 mg/day (reduced from 10 mg post-op) + naproxen (Aleve) 220 mg/daily for 3 weeks
- Occupational therapy and continue with range of movement (ROM) exercises
- High fibre diet recommended
- Target weight – 60 kgs
- Removal of staples – 2 wks + review by his orthopaedic surgeon

Letter Extract

Jakob
Mr ~~Jacob~~ Moore is being referred to your care until he makes a full recovery following a total knee arthroplasty in his right knee for sever end-stage knee arthritis (Stage 4 OA). This letter provides details of his care plan.

Mr Moore's hypertension is usually treated with ramipril 10 mg daily, but it was reduced to 5 mg post-operatively. Napoxen 220 mg daily has also been prescribed for three weeks. He needs 2 have his staples removed after two wks when he will be reviewed by his orthopedic surgeon.

Mr More has made a good recovery and can ambulate with a walker and assistance. However, he requires occupational therapy and should continue with his usual ROM exercises. He has been adviced to loose weight (target weight is 60 kgs). A high fibre diet has been recommended.

Writing skills: Layout

The layout of your letter can help your reader visually separate information in your letter. While there is no prescribed letter format for OET, you can make sure your letter has the essential parts given below, to help your reader understand its message.

Task 12

Look at the letter below and label its parts using options from the box.

Body paragraph giving instructions for care of the patient	Body paragraph describing medical background	Body paragraph explaining her current condition
Referral subject	Date	Addressee information
Closing remarks	Sign-off	Salutation
	Introductory paragraph explaining purpose for writing	

Ms Jennifer Goldman
Nurse-in-Charge
Grant Transitional Care Home } 1.
42 Greenwell Avenue
Leeds

23 January 2018 } 2.

Dear Ms Goldman, } 3.

Re: Mrs Evelyn Burt, a 79-year-old patient } 4.

Mrs Burt was admitted on 21/1 with severe osteoarthritic pain in her right knee. She is being discharged into your care until she makes a full recovery following viscosupplementation. This letter } 5. outlines her treatment and ongoing management.

On admission, Mrs Burt was experiencing painful ambulation and used a 4-leg walking stick. Since previous treatment consisted of NSAIDs and steroids, viscosupplementation was performed. However, she experienced bruising and fluid accumulation, and was placed under observation for } 6. 48 hours, as well as commenced on tramadol for pain relief.

In addition to acetaminophen (325 mg) thrice daily, Mrs Burt should take one or two 50 mg tablets of tramadol every six hours as required. Please ensure she uses a raised toilet seat and does not squat or climb stairs. Physiotherapy for ROM should be reviewed fortnightly. Water aerobics and } 7. isokinetic exercises can be added gradually. She has been advised to lose weight (target weight of 77 kgs) to ease the load on her knees. Her GP will need to review this after a month. The next injections are due on 28/1 and 4/2.

Mrs Burt has no bruising or fluid accumulation, and can use a walking stick to ambulate. } 8.

Please contact me if you have any questions. } 9.

Yours sincerely, } 10.
Charge Nurse

With the help of this example letter, consider the following points.

1. **Addressee information:** Begin with an address. Copy the address from the writing task. The address will not be considered in the word count of 180–200 words.

2. **Date:** The date should be the same as the date of the test.

3. **Salutation:** Use the correct title (Ms/Miss/Mr/Dr) in your salutation. You will be able to find it in the case notes. Do not use the person's first name with their title. In the example letter, it would have been incorrect to say, 'Dear Ms Jennifer'.

4. **Referral subject:** Specify the patient's name, and age or date of birth.

5. **Introductory paragraph:** Explain the purpose for writing and the main medical condition of the patient so that the reader immediately understands the main idea of the letter. Read the case notes and task instructions carefully, in order to understand the purpose of the letter.

6. **Body paragraphs:** Have one main idea in each paragraph. In this example, the first body paragraph contains the medical background of the patient, and only a brief mention of medical history (NSAIDs and steroid injections). This is because the reader (the nurse-in-charge at the nursing home) needs to focus on caring for her postoperatively rather than investigating or assessing the patient's condition further. In respect to the medical background, this letter describes:
   - the condition of the patient on arrival
   - the treatment given
   - the immediate result of the treatment

7. **Body paragraph 1:** The details you provide here will depend on the purpose for writing the letter. In this example, the writer, a charge nurse at a hospital, needs to convey the details of the care plan for the patient because that is what the recipient is responsible for doing. However, if the letter was a referral letter to a specialist, for example, it would not include instructions for care. Instead, the patient's focus would be on his/her medical history, how his/her problem was managed on admission, and the effect of the treatment on his/her condition.

8. **Body paragraph 2:** This example states the condition of the patient at the time of writing the letter. You can mention if the patient looks stable or has improved. In this example, the condition is described at the end because it is not an urgent letter. However, if you are writing an urgent letter, the condition of the patient needs to appear at the beginning.

9. **Closing remarks:** Avoid closing the letter abruptly. Write a general sentence such as 'Please contact me if you have any questions' as a natural transition to the sign off. This is included in the total word count.

10. **Sign off:** End the letter with 'Yours sincerely' and your designation. You will be able to get this information from the case notes and task instructions.

There is no fixed structure for a letter in OET, so do not memorise one particular structure and reproduce it on Test Day. Always bear in mind that your letter should be readable – the ideas should flow logically from one to the other. Refrain from adding extra information from your own knowledge and experience, even if you know the medical issue being described very well. Finally, it is important to remember that this is a test of your language skills and not your medical knowledge.

CHAPTER 3

WRITING
THE LETTER

As mentioned previously, the OET letter is usually a referral letter, but other possible types include a discharge letter, a transfer letter, or a letter to inform or advise a caregiver. To begin this chapter, let's look at examples of each letter type.

Before you begin writing

At the start of the test, you are given five minutes to read the set of patient case notes (your stimulus material) and the writing task instructions. During this time, you are not permitted to write on the question paper. Instead, you should use these five minutes to think about what the task requires.

It is helpful to read the task instructions first, because these will provide you with an insight into

- *who* you are writing to
- *why* you are writing

With this information in mind, you will be able to read the case notes purposefully, and choose the most relevant details to include in your letter.

Who am I writing to?

When thinking about your reader, ask yourself some questions:

Ask yourself	Understand what the answer means
Is it a medical professional or a layperson?	If you are writing to a medical professional, you can use medical terminology. Consider the discipline of the medical professional to determine your choice of technical terms. However, when writing to someone who is not a healthcare professional, it is better to use simple, non-medical terminology.
What do they already know?	If the person you are writing to already knows about a patient's medical history, then there is no need to go into detail. However, you need to read the task instructions and case notes carefully to understand more about what your reader knows or does not know.
What information do they need to know?	Think about the kind of care your reader needs to provide to the patient. For example, if the person is a physiotherapist, you will need to provide details like condition of bones/muscles, areas of the body that need work and so on.

Task 1

Given below are examples of potential readers of your letter. Match the reader with your approach to writing the letter.

Your reader	Your approach	Answers
1. Admitting doctor in an emergency department	a. Layperson – use limited medical terminology	1 –
2. Nutritionist	b. Medical professional – can use medical terminology	2 –
3. General practitioner (family doctor) who is already aware of the background of the case	c. Focus on treatment plan, not detailed medical history, because the patient is known to them	3 –
4. Community home social worker	d. Focus on dietary restrictions and allergies	4 –

Why am I writing?

The purpose of your letter determines the kind of information you need to include in it.

Ask yourself	Understand what the answer means
Is it to advise about care after discharge?	If the purpose is to advise a medical professional on the medication and care required, you need to focus on those details rather than on the social background or medical history of the patient.
Is it to refer the patient to a specialist?	If your patient has two or three kinds of problems, you may need to give the specialist information about only those problems related to the specialisation.

Task 2

Read the example of a writing task and decide what you would include in your letter, based on your assessment of who you are writing to and why you are writing.

Writing task: Example

Write a discharge letter to Ms Jennifer Goldman, Nurse-in-Charge at Grant Nursing Home, 42 Greenwell Avenue, Leeds, who will be responsible for Mrs Burt's continued care at the Nursing Home.

Tick the items relevant to your letter.

☐ Use simple language
☐ Use medical terms
☐ Give patient's medical history briefly
☐ Explain social background
☐ Provide details of medication
☐ Mention follow-up needed
☐ Provide an assessment of present condition

Once you have understood the requirements of the writing task, you can then go on to reading the case notes.

Reading case notes

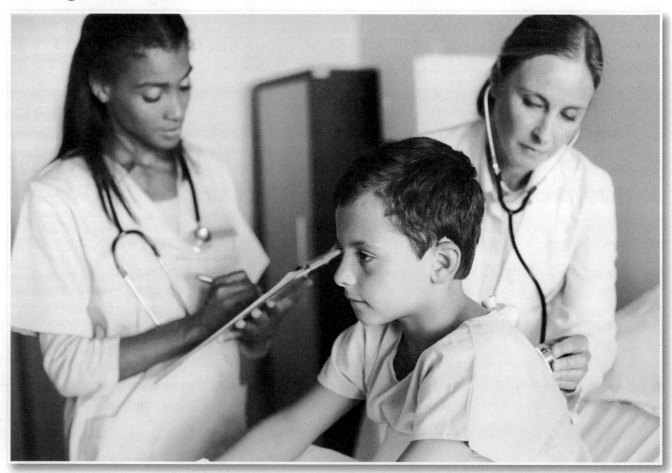

Reading case notes accurately is essential if you want to write a well-structured letter. Once the test begins, don't be in a hurry to start writing your letter. Take time to understand what the case notes tell you about the patient.

Skills focus: Features of case notes

1. **Abbreviations:** Case notes usually contain several medical abbreviations. You can use widely known medical abbreviations in your letter only when the abbreviation is more common than the full form. For example, use *mg* for *milligrams*, and *NSAID* for *nonsteroidal anti-inflammatory drugs*. If the abbreviation is commonly used in your discipline but not in another, then preference the full form. Avoid non-standard abbreviations of the kind used in social media (*L8* for *late*, *Gr8* for *great*, etc.).

2. **Note form:** Case notes are written in note form, not in complete sentences. For example, *be* verbs are usually omitted – *admitted* and not *was admitted*. It is important to remember not to use note form in your letter.

3. **Symbols:** Case notes may use symbols to indicate concepts such as *increase* (↑), *decrease* (↓), *greater than* (>), *less than* (<) and so on. These should not be used in your letter.

4. **Numbers:** Make a note of numbers as you read. For example, the age of the patient, admission date, discharge date, etc. Dates will help you understand how long a patient has been in hospital, the period of sickness, etc. Sometimes the duration of treatment or date of birth may not be stated explicitly, so you will need to look at the other dates provided to draw conclusions.

5. **Shortened words:** Some words may be shortened, because these are notes. For example, *rehab* for *rehabilitation* or *wk* for *week*. Make sure you expand them in your letter. The same applies to contractions (*she's / he's / they're*).

Planning your letter

After you have read the case notes, you will need to plan your letter. You can do this by selecting the case notes that are most relevant to your writing task. How do you choose the most relevant case notes? Remind yourself about the requirements of the task: who you are writing to and why you are writing. Remember that the word length should be 180–200 words, so you do not need to include all the case notes. OET tasks are designed to have enough relevant case notes for you to meet the word count. If you focus on choosing the most relevant case notes, you are more likely to meet the word count.

Discharge letter

Here is a sample writing task based on a discharge letter.

Task 3

Let's look at the case notes about Mrs Evelyn Burt, a patient in the medical ward of the hospital you work in.

Keep track of the time and, using a pencil, put a tick (✓) next to the case notes you think will be most relevant for your letter, a cross (✗) next to the irrelevant ones, and a question mark (?) next to the ones you think could be optional. Try to finish this in five minutes.

NOTE: Remember that you are not allowed to write during the first five minutes of the test, so this is only for practice.

You are a nurse at St. James Hospital attending to this patient, who is ready to be discharged.

Patient details

Name: Evelyn Burt (Mrs)
DOB: 09.08.1939
Residence: 24 Wayford Avenue, Leeds

Social background

Retired in 2000 as school teacher – has good pension
Marital status: Widowed – 3 years
Next of kin: Janet (32 years, married, lives abroad, 2 children <12)
Hobbies: Gardening

Medical history

2013: Diagnosed w/ moderate osteoarthritis in R knee
Mild genu varum w/ palpable crepitus & antalgic gait; slightly obese (BMI 31, 82 kgs)
Knee unloader brace + 325 mg of acetaminophen 3/day + NSAID (naproxen 250 mg) 2/day + physio

2016: Admitted for severe effusion R knee → 3 intra-articular steroid injections taken for 3 months + increased naproxen to 500 mg twice daily

21/01/18

Presenting complaint: severe pain in R knee, painful ambulation, used 4-leg walking stick

Management: Administered R knee viscosupplementation (hyaluronic acid inj. for lubrication)

Admitted for observation and assessment
Observed for 48 hrs post-procedure – bruising & fluid accumulation in R knee, pain rated as 6/10
Pain relief – 1/2 50 mg tramadol every 6 hrs

23/01/18

Review Dr – bruising and fluid reduced – fit to return home with walking stick as backup

Nursing management

Avoid loading on patella-femoral joint (squatting & stairs)
325 mg of acetaminophen 3/day
Breakthrough pain – administer 1–2 50 mg tramadol every 6 hrs p.r.n.
Follow-up injections on 28 January 2018 & 4 February 2018
Raised toilet seat
Review with physio every 2 weeks: ROM exercises
Add water aerobics + isokinetic exercises gradually to increase strength

Counselled on weight loss to ease load on knees, target weight 77 kgs – review with GP in one month

Writing task

Using the information in the case notes, write a letter of discharge to Ms Jennifer Goldman, Nurse-in-Charge at Grant Transitional Care Home, 42 Greenwell Avenue, Leeds, where the patient will be admitted until recovery. Use the case notes to outline ongoing treatment and management following surgery.

Now that you have finished identifying relevant, irrelevant and optional case notes, you can use a simple mind map like the one here to plan your letter, based on the most relevant case notes.

Task 4

Refer to the case notes you ticked (✓) in Task 3 and fill in the gaps in the mind map below.

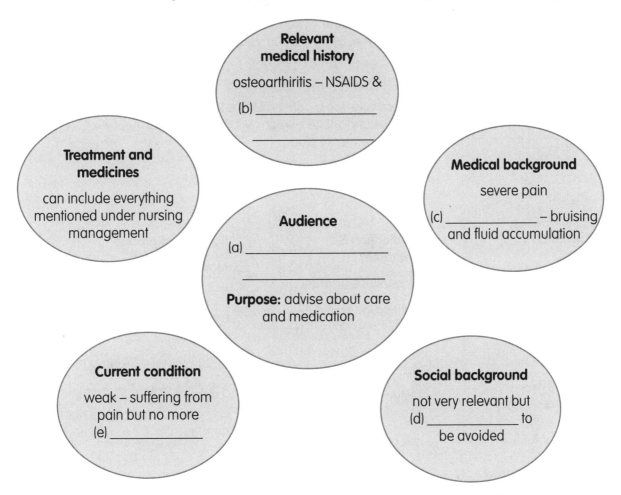

Relevant medical history

osteoarthiritis – NSAIDS &

(b) _____

_____

Treatment and medicines

can include everything mentioned under nursing management

Audience

(a) _____

_____

Purpose: advise about care and medication

Medical background

severe pain

(c) _____ – bruising and fluid accumulation

Current condition

weak – suffering from pain but no more
(e) _____

Social background

not very relevant but
(d) _____ to be avoided

Making a quick plan like this on Test Day will help you structure your letter effectively. Use the five minutes reading time you have to mentally plan the letter. Remember you are not allowed to write during the reading time, so once your writing time begins, do not spend more than five minutes making a plan like this, if you want to. It is essential to practise this skill several times before Test Day. If you practise enough, you may find that you can do it all during reading time and don't need to write down a plan like this at all.

Writing your letter

Once you have planned your letter, it is time to begin writing. After you have read your case notes, remember you have 40 minutes total writing time. How you use this time to plan, write and check your letter is up to you. You could spend about 30–35 minutes writing your letter if you leave time for planning and checking. If you get enough practice and feel confident using the plan you have made in your head during reading time, then you may have a few more minutes to write. It is a good idea to practise writing with a timer before the test, paying attention to speed as well as the legibility of your handwriting, so you know how to plan your writing time.

Let's practise writing the first body paragraph of a letter using all that you have learnt so far.

Look at the writing task and case notes given below, then try the task that follows.

You need to:

- Read the writing task and decide on the purpose of and audience for your letter.
- Select appropriate case notes from the case notes extract given to you. You don't need to use all the case notes given, and you can change the order when you present the information.
- Write the first body paragraph of a referral letter using all that you have learnt so far.

Writing task

You are the charge nurse at a drug therapy centre where a patient, Ms Reddy, has just finished treatment. Write a referral letter to a psychotherapist, Ms Amanda Jones, whom Ms Reddy will now be seeing for individual therapy and the creation of an overall treatment plan.

Patient information

DOB: 20.01.1993

Single – lives alone

Unemployed

Brother married with 2 children

Did not finish Fine Arts degree (due to heavy alcohol consumption)

Medication & treatment

Alcohol use disorder

Naltrexone 50 mg 1/day for 10 days

Thiamine 300 mg for two weeks

Opted for counselling

Social background

Mother – deceased (3 years)

Father – deceased (20 years)

Lost job (sales assistant) age 24 – dependence

Began social drinking age 16

Admitted by brother to rehab age 22

Relapsed after mother's death 6 months later

Here is the introductory paragraph:

Ms Reddy is being referred to you for individual therapy and for the development of an overall treatment plan, following a two-week in-patient drug therapy for alcohol use disorder.

Now, write your first paragraph here:

_____

_____

_____

_____

_____

_____

_____

_____

After you write

Set aside the last couple of minutes of the test to check grammar, punctuation and spelling in your letter. If you find an error, make sure you correct it neatly. Instead of scribbling, strike through the wrong word with one line and write the correction above it. While you practise for OET, use a checklist to help you identify errors.

Task 6

Here is a sample checklist. Match each checklist item (1–13) with the benefit (a–m) of using it in your letter. Use this checklist to check your practice test.

Checklist item	Answers	Benefit
1. Organising ideas	1 – h	a. Allows you to emphasise or indicate importance of certain information in a sentence
2. Using linking words		b. Highlights a procedure that was performed, medication that was prescribed, and who it was for
3. Adding sentence variety		c. Maintains formality and consistency in the letter
4. Using appropriate vocabulary		d. Allows you to indicate which thing or person you are talking about
5. Using tenses accurately		e. Allows you to advise, request politely or indicate possibility
6. Using modals		f. Helps the reader visually segregate information in the letter
7. Using passive sentences		g. Prevents long run-on sentences with too many ideas
8. Using active sentences		h. Increases readability, with one main idea per paragraph
9. Adding relevant articles		i. Puts the patient in focus in the sentence
10. Using full stops		j. Helps indicate the time of an event
11. Adding commas where necessary		k. Helps logical flow of ideas from one sentence to the next or one paragraph to the next
12. Checking spelling		l. Helps separate items in a list or extra information in a sentence
13. Using letter layout		m. Helps the reader understand information in language that is familiar and maintains formality

Transfer letter

Transfer letters are generally written when a patient in one medical facility needs to move to another for treatment and/or assessment. Remember that the medical professional in the facility the patient is being transferred to may not have any idea of the patient's case, so it is important to include as many relevant and important details as possible.

Task 7

Read the writing task and patient case notes. Decide which information needs to be included in the transfer letter, then try the task that follows.

You are Charge Nurse in the oncology ward looking after Mr Jeremy Taylor, a 54-year-old patient.

Hospital: Clare Medical College Hospital, 24 Harley Drive, Brooksbank

Patient details

Name: Jeremy Taylor (Mr)

DOB: 19.10.1964

Admission date: 05.03.2018

Treating doctor: Dr Meena Singh

Moving to: Dr Gerald Jones

Social background

- Works as a banker
- Marital status: Widower (wife died 3 years ago)
- Next of kin: Daughter, Julie (27 years, artist); son, Brad (25 years, dentist) – both single
- Stressful life, works 13-15 hrs/day; lives alone so has takeaway food; no exercise; drinks socially; smokes 10 cigs/day since age 16
- Previously tried nicotine patches + electronic cigarettes unsuccessfully

Medical history

- 2010 – Diagnosed w/ hypertension (was not compliant with medication)
- No family history of cancer

05.03.2018

- Presenting complaint: respiratory infection & rust-coloured sputum
  (Patient was visiting daughter in Brooksbank)
- Temp: 38°C; BP 128/83
- Amoxicillin 500 mg 2/day prescribed for five days

10.03.2018

- Temp: 37°C; BP 125/84
- Cough
- Tests revealed Stage IIA non-small cell lung cancer
- CT scan revealed category T1C, N0, M0 (2.5 cm tumour) in left lung
- Bronchial branches not affected

15.03.2018

- VATS procedure was successful in removing tumour – 4 incisions
- Tubes removed same day – dressing for incision site
- Percocet for breakthrough pain
- Vital signs: BP hypertensive (130/83) – others within normal limits – ramipril 5 mg commenced

17.03.2018

Discharged (under daughter's care)

20.03.2018 – 20.05.2018

- Adjuvant chemotherapy in 4 cycles (once every two weeks) performed to prevent risk of relapse (cisplatin and docetaxel; Zofran administered for side effects of nausea; lost 5 kg (now at 60 kg)
- Borderline leukopenia absolute neutrophil count (ANC) at 1000 (filgrastim 325 mcg daily) – subcutaneous injection

Discharge plan

- Needs referral to a dietician to gain 5 kgs lost during chemo
- Psychotherapist to help quit smoking
- Regular, mild exercise needs to begin in 2 weeks
- Next CT scan after three months; thereafter annually, and chest X-rays three times per year
- Continue ramipril 5 mg for hypertension
- No alcohol
- Daughter and son to take turns living with father in his New Abbey flat
- Monitor complete blood count (CBC) weekly (2 months)

Assessment: Weak from pain, but recovering well from side effects

Writing task

Mr Jeremy Taylor is a 54-year-old patient in the oncology ward of a hospital in which you are Charge Nurse. He is transferring from Brooksbank back to New Abbey. Use the information in the case notes to provide a treatment summary and follow-up care plan. Address your letter to oncologist Dr Gerald Jones, 24 Sophia Avenue, New Abbey.

Now, read a sample transfer letter based on the patient case notes. The letter has been jumbled up and the order is not logical. Reorder it using the letters (A, B, C and D) assigned to the paragraphs.

Dr Gerald Jones
24 Sophia Avenue
New Abbey

21 May 2018

Dear Dr Jones

Re: Mr Jeremy Taylor (DOB: 19.10.1964)

Paragraph A

A successful VATS was performed with a total of four incisions. The tubes were removed the same day and Percocet was administered for breakthrough pain. Over the next two months, adjuvant therapy was performed using cisplatin and docetaxel in four cycles, two weeks apart. Zofran was administered to counter nausea. Since he suffered from borderline leukopenia, with an absolute neutrophil count of 1000, Filgrastim (325 mcg daily) was given by subcutaneous injection.

Paragraph B

Mr Taylor is weak but recovering well. His next CT scan is after three months and then annually. Chest X-rays three times per year are mandatory. He should continue taking ramipril 5 mg commenced post-operatively to manage hypertension. A CBC is required weekly for the next two months.

Paragraph C

This patient, who was in post-treatment recovery following VATS and adjuvant chemotherapy for non-small cell lung cancer, is being transferred to you for follow-up care. This letter provides a treatment summary and care plan.

Paragraph D

Mr Taylor presented with a respiratory infection and productive cough (rust-coloured sputum). Amoxicillin proved ineffective. Further tests revealed Stage IIA non-small cell lung cancer (T1C, N0, M0; tumour 2.5 cms) in the left lung. Bronchial branches remained unaffected.

Please contact me if you need any further information.

Yours sincerely

Charge Nurse

Write the correct order here: _____ _____ _____ _____

Letter of advice to parents/caregivers

Letters of advice to parents or caregivers provide information about the treatment provided to a child, care that needs to be taken, and precautions they need to follow. Generally, technical or medical words and phrases are explained or substituted with simpler words than those provided in the case notes.

Task 8

Read the letter of advice to parents whose son suffered a clavicle fracture and is ready for discharge.

Mr and Mrs Wilson
24 Newton Abbey
Chelmsworth
24 April 2018

Re: 8-year-old Adam Wilson

Dear Mr and Mrs Wilson,

As Adam is being discharged into your care today, we are providing you with further advice to ensure his collar bone fracture heals appropriately.

The fracture Adam suffered is common in children and generally heals well. Adam should continue wearing his arm in a sling, but it can be removed for short periods. You can give him the prescribed painkillers until he stops complaining of pain. Please put a few pillows behind him for support when he sleeps at night.

You can expect the fracture to heal within three to four weeks. Encourage him to move his elbow, hand and fingers while he is healing. While he can resume non-contact sports such as swimming as soon as he feels comfortable doing so, full and limited contact sports such as football and basketball should be avoided for six weeks until after the sling is removed.

A lump at the fracture site is normal and may take up to a year to disappear. You can take Adam to his GP if he feels pain at the fracture site after six weeks.

Please contact me if you need any further information or have any questions.

Yours sincerely

Charge Nurse

What is the order of the information followed in the letter? Think about why this order is a suitable one for letters of advice to parents or caregivers.

1. a. Treatment/care to be given at home
    b. Precautions to take regarding physical activity
    c. Any other additional information caregivers should know

2. a. Precautions to take regarding physical activity
    b. Treatment/care to be given at home
    c. Any other additional information caregivers should know

3. a. Treatment/care to be given at home
    b. Any other additional information caregivers should know
    c. Precautions to take regarding physical activity

Tips for scoring

- Make good use of the reading time given to you at the beginning of the test. The writing task instructions appear after the case notes, but read them first so that you understand the audience and purpose before you read the case notes. Begin planning your letter during the five minutes of reading time.
- Understand the writing task clearly before you go on to read the case notes. Pay attention to who the reader is and why you are writing. Establish whether it is an emergency situation or not. All these factors will influence which case notes you select and how you order the information in your letter.
- Read the case notes with audience and purpose in mind. A good way of doing this is to classify case notes as you read them into 'need to know' (most relevant) information, 'nice to know' (optional) information and 'irrelevant' information.
- Think about how you want to organise your letter before you start writing. Once you decide which information is most relevant, think about where you want to place it in your letter. Decide which information can come at the beginning and which can be placed later. Once you have prioritised the most relevant information, you can then see if there is an opportunity to include any optional information. Include the optional information only if you feel it could help your reader fulfil what he/she needs to do concerning the patient.
- Remember, preparation and practice is the key to improvement. Always time yourself when you practise sample writing tasks during your preparation. This will help you improve your speed at the task.
- While preparing, create a checklist of areas where you struggle (whether it is selecting case notes or an aspect of grammar) so you can work consistently towards improving in those areas.

FAQs

Here are some frequently asked questions about the meaning of the instructions in the writing tasks.

1. What does 'Read the case notes and complete the writing task which follows' mean?

In OET Writing, there are two components you need to pay attention to:

- Case notes
- Writing task

In the question paper, the case notes appear before the writing task, but it is a good idea to read the writing task first so that you can make sense of the case notes. After reading the writing task, you will be able to understand the audience and the purpose for writing the letter.

2. What does 'expand the relevant notes into complete sentences' mean?

Once you know your audience and your purpose for writing, you will be able to select *relevant* case notes. This instruction tells you that you are not supposed to include *all* the case notes in your letter. You also must not choose case notes randomly. The order you choose for case notes in your letter may not be the same as presented in the question paper.

For example, a writing task may say:

Using the information in the case notes, write a letter to Ms Carol Norton, Charge Nurse at Newtown Nursing Home, 14 Amwell Road, Newtown, who will be responsible for Mr Thomson's continued care at the Nursing Home.

After reading this, you know that the person you are writing to is another medical professional who will need information about how to care for the patient, since she is responsible for his continued care at a nursing home. Using this information, you may decide that the charge nurse needs to know what medication the patient is on, his discharge plan and nursing management.

You also need to remember to write your letter in complete sentences. It's not enough just to select relevant case notes; you need to change those case notes into full sentences. Don't simply copy case notes as they appear in the question paper into your answer.

3.   What does 'do not use note form' mean?

The case notes are in note form, which means that they are not written as full grammatical sentences. There may be short forms or abbreviations which need to be written in full (unless the abbreviation is more common than the expanded forms, for example: mg/ml/Hb/BMI).

For example:

Note form	Full sentence
Daily dressing at surgery incision site	He requires daily dressing at the surgery incision site.
Poor mobility – occupational therapy	He needs to receive occupational therapy to improve his mobility.
Anaprox 5 mg 2/day – 2 wks	Pain relief (Anaprox 5 mg) should be administered twice daily for a duration of two weeks.

4.   What does 'use letter format' mean?

Your letter should look like a letter in its layout or format. While there are a number of different formats used by professionals worldwide, OET does not prescribe a particular one. Your format should include an address, date, salutation, subject, body and sign-off. If you are confused about the recipient, look at the writing task again. It clearly mentions the name and address of the recipient of your letter. Choose a format you are comfortable with, and use it consistently.

5.   What does 'the body of the letter should be approximately 180–200 words' mean?

The writing task is designed in such a way that you do not need to exceed the word range. If you have included all the relevant information from the case notes, then your letter is most likely to fall within the word range. However, there is no penalty or negative marking if you write *slightly* more or less, providing that you have included the relevant case notes.

If you find that you have written a lot more than 200 words (close to 300 or 400 words, for example), then you may have included irrelevant information. If you have written a lot less than 180 words, then you may not have included important information. Regular practice with the task should help you understand how to write within the correct range. Also note that the word range of 180–200 words refers to the *body* of the letter, and not to aspects of layout or format such as the address, date, subject, salutation and sign-off.

Sample Practice Test: Writing

TIME ALLOWED: READING TIME: 5 MINUTES

WRITING TIME: 40 MINUTES

Read the case notes and complete the writing task which follows.

Notes:

You are the Charge Nurse on duty at the Maternity Ward at Women's College Hospital. Your patient is being discharged today.

Patient details

> Name: Riya Ray
> DOB: 21.03.1998

Admission date: 21.02.2018

Discharge date: 27.02.2018

Country of birth: Canada

Social background

> Marital status: Single, lived with boyfriend Anton Campbell August 2017 – until admission
> Current boyfriend (23 years) verbally abusive 3 months – she does not want to live w/him – he is not father of child
> No contact w/father of child (lives in Europe)
> Cashier – currently unemployed
> Next of kin: Sister (26, married and overseas)
> Parents died 1.5 years ago in an accident
> Aunt – mother's side – lives 4 hours away – in phone contact

Medical history

> No reported past illnesses or allergies
> Tonsillectomy at 14
> NIL alcohol/cigarettes – Depression since death of parents – untreated

Obstetric history

> First antenatal visit at 14 weeks
> Total visits – 6
> No complications
> Antenatal supplements – folic acid, vitamin D & calcium

Birth details

Presented in hospital at 18:00 hrs on 21.02.2018
Vaginal delivery
1st stage: 8 hrs – Contractions 1:15 mins
2nd stage: 2 hrs – Contractions 1:3 mins
DOB: 22.02.2018
Time: 12.30 hrs
Female, 3.77 kg

Postnatal progress

Minimal blood loss
Haemoglobin 22/02/18: 135 g/L
Breastfeeding with hesitation – prefers to change to bottle feeding
Baby weight at discharge: 3.95kg
Feeding well & normal

Discharge

Referred to women's refuge shelter (temporary)
Referred to clinical psychologist – emotional support and counselling regarding parents and boyfriend relationship dynamics
Advised to apply for single mother benefits – given brochures
Liaise with local Maternal Health Service for ongoing postnatal monitoring

Writing task:

You are the Charge Nurse on duty at the Maternity Ward of Women's College Hospital. Using the information provided in the case notes, write a referral letter to the Director of Refuge Shelter for Women, 105 West Street, Toronto ON M4W 1B7, where the patient needs to be admitted for short term emergency accommodation and support services.

In your answer:

• expand the relevant notes into complete sentences
• do not use note form
• use letter format

The body of the letter should be approximately 180–200 words.

SPEAKING IN OET

CHAPTER 1

INTRODUCTION
TO THE SPEAKING SUB-TEST

The Speaking sub-test takes about 20 minutes. It is a profession-specific test in which you are required to complete two role plays based on typical workplace situations. In each role play, you are expected to demonstrate proficient communication skills in situations that are relevant to nursing. In the role plays, you interact with an interlocutor who takes on the role of a patient or, in some cases, a patient's carer or relative. You always take on the role of a nurse.

The role plays relate to real-life scenarios that you may face in your specific healthcare field, and you are expected to demonstrate a range of communication skills such as:

- eliciting information from a patient using open and closed questions
- seeking clarification when the patient's statement is unclear
- explaining an investigation, diagnosis or treatment using language that the patient can understand
- offering reassurance, warmth, or comfort to anxious or agitated patients or their family members
- providing advice – on lifestyle, health promotion or managing risk factors – that is relevant to the patient's circumstances
- adapting speech when interacting with patients of different age groups, or different patient types (for example, uncommunicative or irritated)

Format of the Speaking sub-test

The breakdown of timings in the Speaking sub-test is as follows:

Section	Actions	Timing
Pre-test introduction (not assessed)	Your identity and profession are checked by the interlocutor and there is a short warm-up conversation about your professional background.	2–3 minutes

First, there is a short warm-up discussion that is designed to make you feel comfortable in the test environment. This discussion is not assessed. The interlocutor asks you questions about your professional background such as:

Where was your last job as a nurse?

How long have you worked as a nurse?

Why did you choose to become a nurse?

What do you like most about your profession?

How would you describe a typical day at work?

Use this time to 'warm up' and get used to speaking to the interlocutor. It is a good idea for you to think of some answers beforehand, so you are at ease when answering these questions.

Role plays (assessed)	Preparation	2–3 minutes each
	Role plays	5 minutes each

For each role play you are given a card and three minutes to prepare. During this time, you can ask the interlocutor any questions about what a word/phrase on the card means, how it is pronounced, or about the context of the role play: for example, 'How do I pronounce this word?', 'What does this word mean?', or 'The cue card suggests that I know the patient already. What should I call you?'. You are also allowed to make notes on the role play card during this time.

Each actual role play is about five minutes long. Around the five-minute mark, the interlocutor signals clearly to you that it's time to conclude the role play.

The interview is recorded, and is marked independently by two trained OET Assessors.

Task 1a

In the left-hand column, you will see steps to manage your three-minute preparation time effectively. Match these to the correct purpose in the right-hand column.

Action	Purpose
1. Think of the opening sentence or question for initiating the conversation, or write down some questions or phrases on the role play card that you intend to use during the role play.	a. To understand what needs to be done, how to structure your conversation in a logical way, and which bullet-point tasks might require more time to be completed
2. Identify key information such as: • What is the setting? • With whom am I speaking?	b. To get the role play started more confidently and have some useful expressions that can quickly be referred to during the role play

• Does the patient have an emotional reaction to the situation? • What details have been mentioned about the patient's visit or admission?	
3. Look at the bullet-point tasks and underline important words such as verbs (find out, persuade, empathise, reassure, explain).	c. To understand what kind of language would be appropriate to the context

Task 1b

Now arrange these steps in the right sequence to use the three-minute preparation time to good effect.

Step 1

_____

_____

Step 2

_____

_____

Step 3

_____

_____

Assessment criteria – an overview

The assessment criteria have been divided into four main linguistic criteria and five main clinical communication criteria. These are further divided into several sub-criteria.

Linguistic criteria (up to 6 marks each)

- Intelligibility
- Fluency
- Appropriateness of language
- Resources of grammar and expression

Clinical communication criteria (up to 3 marks each)

- Relationship building
- Understanding and incorporating the patient's perspective
- Providing structure
- Information gathering
- Information giving

Your performance is marked by two different Assessors. Each Assessor independently scores your performance according to the nine criteria. To understand how best to meet the assessment criteria, refer to the 'Level descriptors' and glossary tables on pages 14 to 20.

Grade B for the Speaking sub-test requires a high performance in all nine criteria. Your performance should share features with the highest level in the descriptors for each criterion. Candidates who secure a grade B achieve predominantly 5 out of 6 on each linguistic criterion, and 2 out of 3 for each communication criterion.

SPEAKING Assessment Criteria and Level Descriptors (from September 2018)

I. Linguistic Criteria

Band	Intelligibility	Fluency	Appropriateness of Language	Resources of Grammar and Expression
6	• Pronunciation is easily understood and prosodic features (stress, intonation, rhythm) are used effectively. • L1 accent has no effect on intelligibility.	• Completely fluent speech at normal speed. • Any hesitation is appropriate and not a sign of searching for words or structures.	• Entirely appropriate register, tone and lexis for the context. • No difficulty in explaining technical matters in lay terms.	• Rich and flexible. • Wide range of grammar and vocabulary used accurately and flexibly. • Confident use of idiomatic speech.
5	• Easily understood. • Communication is not impeded by a few pronunciation or prosodic errors and/or noticeable L1 accent. • Minimal strain for the listener.	• Fluent speech at normal speed, with only occasional repetition or self-correction. • Hesitation may occasionally indicate searching for words or structures, but is generally appropriate.	• Mostly appropriate register, tone and lexis for the context. • Occasional lapses are not intrusive.	• Wide range of grammar and vocabulary generally used accurately and flexibly. • Occasional errors in grammar or vocabulary are not intrusive.
4	• Easily understood most of the time. • Pronunciation or prosodic errors and/or L1 accent at times cause strain for the listener.	• Uneven flow, with some repetition, especially in longer utterances. • Some evidence of searching for words, which does not cause serious strain for the listener. • Delivery may be staccato or too fast/slow.	• Generally appropriate register, tone and lexis for the context, but somewhat restricted and lacking in complexity. • Lapses are noticeable and at times reflect limited resources of grammar and expression.	• Sufficient resources to maintain the interaction. • Inaccuracies in vocabulary and grammar, particularly in more complex sentences, are sometimes intrusive. • Meaning is generally clear.
3	• Produces some acceptable features of spoken English. • Difficult to understand because errors in pronunciation/stress/intonation and/or L1 accent cause serious strain for the listener.	• Very uneven. • Frequent pauses and repetitions indicate searching for words or structures. • Excessive use of fillers and difficulty sustaining longer utterances cause serious strain for the listener.	• Some evidence of appropriate register, tone and lexis, but lapses are frequent and intrusive, reflecting inadequate resources of grammar and expression.	• Limited vocabulary and control of grammatical structures, except very simple sentences. • Persistent inaccuracies are intrusive.
2	• Often unintelligible. • Frequent errors in pronunciation/ stress/intonation and/or L1 accent cause severe strain for the listener.	• Extremely uneven. • Long pauses, numerous repetitions and self-corrections make speech difficult to follow.	• Mostly inappropriate register, tone and lexis for the context.	• Very limited resources of vocabulary and grammar, even in simple sentences. • Numerous errors in word choice.
1	• Almost entirely unintelligible.	• Impossible to follow, consisting of isolated words, phrases and self-corrections, separated by long pauses.	• Entirely inappropriate register, tone and lexis for the context.	• Limited in all respects.
0	• Candidate does not provide any response.			

II. Clinical Communication Criteria

In the role play, there is evidence of the test taker …

A. Indicators of relationship building

A1	initiating the interaction appropriately (greeting, introductions, nature of interview)
A2	demonstrating an attentive and respectful attitude
A3	adopting a non-judgemental approach
A4	showing empathy for feelings/predicament/emotional state

A. Relationship building
- 3 – Adept use
- 2 – Competent use
- 1 – Partially effective use
- 0 – Ineffective use

B. Indicators of understanding & incorporating the patient's perspective

B1	eliciting and exploring the patient's ideas/concerns/expectations
B2	picking up the patient's cues
B3	relating explanations to elicited ideas/concerns/expectations

B. Understanding & incorporating the patient's perspective
- 3 – Adept use
- 2 – Competent use
- 1 – Partially effective use
- 0 – Ineffective use

C. Indicators of providing structure

C1	sequencing the interview purposefully and logically
C2	signposting changes in topic
C3	using organising techniques in explanations

C. Providing structure
- 3 – Adept use
- 2 – Competent use
- 1 – Partially effective use
- 0 – Ineffective use

D. Indicators for information gathering

D1	facilitating the patient's narrative with active listening techniques, minimising interruption
D2	using initially open questions, appropriately moving to closed questions
D3	NOT using compound questions/leading questions
D4	clarifying statements which are vague or need amplification
D5	summarising information to encourage correction/invite further information

D. Information gathering
- 3 – Adept use
- 2 – Competent use
- 1 – Partially effective use
- 0 – Ineffective use

E. Indicators for information giving

E1	establishing initially what the patient already knows
E2	pausing periodically when giving information, using the response to guide next steps
E3	encouraging the patient to contribute reactions/feelings
E4	checking whether the patient has understood information
E5	discovering what further information the patient needs

E. Information giving
- 3 – Adept use
- 2 – Competent use
- 1 – Partially effective use
- 0 – Ineffective use

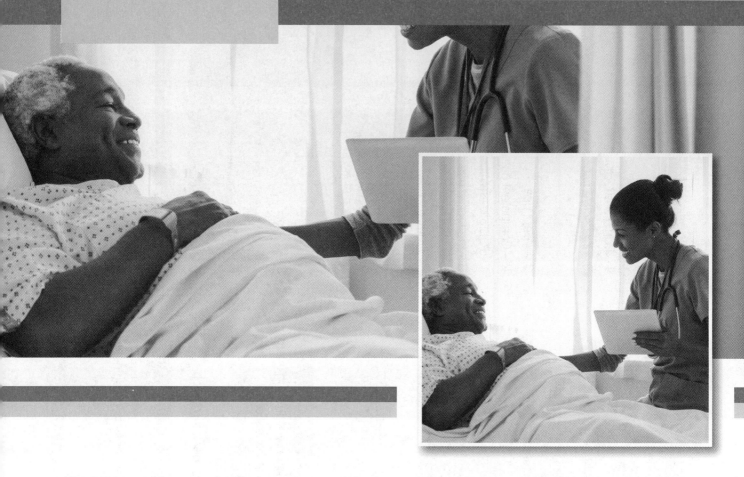

The OET Speaking sub-test focuses not only on the accuracy of the language, but primarily on how effectively you can communicate in a real-life workplace context. It does this through the use of two role plays. In other words, accuracy alone is not enough; as a health professional, you are expected to have the strong communication skills that are necessary to ensure a compassionate and clear understanding of patient needs. You also need to aim for positive health outcomes for patients in diverse healthcare scenarios. Extensive reflective practice, which in essence means consciously assessing yourself and thinking about what you would do differently next time to ensure ongoing improvement, is required to develop good speaking skills. An awareness of the assessment criteria gives you an opportunity to recognise your weak areas and improve on them. The level descriptors table on pages 14 to 15 explains what the desired performance for an A/B grade is.

This chapter focuses on the assessment criteria in detail. The tips, and the exercise under each criterion, help you enhance the quality of your performance. Make use of the audio examples in this chapter, and use the LRRC (Listen, Repeat, Record, Compare) method to improve your speaking.

Let us look at each criterion in detail.

Linguistic criteria

A. Intelligibility

Intelligibility refers to how well and clearly a candidate's speech can be understood. It is affected by aspects of speech like pronunciation, intonation, stress, rhythm, pitch and accent.

Here are some pointers to improve the intelligibility of your speech.

- Pronunciation refers to the way a letter or a word is spoken. Keep in mind that achieving a native-like pronunciation may be unrealistic, and is not necessarily desirable. Aim instead to pronounce words in a way that is easily understandable to native and non-native speakers. Develop an awareness of the 44 unique sounds of English, referred to as phonemes.
- A 'syllable' is a single, unbroken vowel sound, with or without surrounding consonants; for example, the word *anaesthetic* has four syllables (an-aes-thet-ic), while *dressing* has two (dress-ing). Both of these words are examples of polysyllabic words (words with more than one syllable). In polysyllabic words, one syllable is made to stand out more than the other(s). In other words, one syllable is stressed more than the other(s). This is done by saying the stressed syllable slightly louder, holding the vowel a little longer, and pronouncing the consonants clearly to give the stressed syllable prominence. For the examples used above, *dress* is the stressed syllable in **dress**-ing and *thet* is the stressed syllable in an-aes-**thet**-ic.

Task 1

 1. You're going to hear two words that vary only in vowel sounds. As you listen, write down the words and compare the difference in pronunciation. When you practise, ensure that you maintain the difference between the two vowel sounds being compared.

 2. You're going to hear two words that vary only in consonant sounds at the beginning. As you listen, write down the words and compare the difference in pronunciation. When you practise, ensure that you maintain the difference in the two consonant sounds being compared.

 3. You're going to hear three words that vary only in consonant sounds at the end. As you listen, write down the words and compare the difference in pronunciation. When you practise, ensure that you maintain the difference in the three consonant sounds being compared.

 4. Underline the stressed syllables in each of the following words. Then listen to the audio to check your answer, and repeat each word to practise correct word stress.
- comply
- compliance
- vaccinated
- pneumonia
- influenza

In the following questions focusing on pitch awareness, it is important to use the right stress, and avoid speaking in a monotonous tone or with little variation in pitch. Ensure that you vary the high and low frequencies of your voice to draw the listener's attention to important components of your speech.

Pitch awareness exercise

Listen to the syllable *na* said with a high pitch (*^na*) and then with a low pitch (*-na*). Imitate and learn to produce high and low pitch.

 Audio 1 (*^na*) – High Pitch

Audio 2 (*-na*) – Low Pitch

Intonation, in its simplest form, is the melody of speech and refers to the variation in pitch. Intonation can be used for emphasis, or to signal whether you are asking a question or making a statement.

Intonation awareness exercise

Question: What is the difference in the way these two sentences sound?

A. Mrs Johnson has been transferred to the ward from the ICU.

B. Mrs Johnson has been transferred to the ward from the ICU?

Answer:

The intonation or 'melodies' of the two sentences are different. The melody of Sentence A drops at the end, making it a statement. The melody of Sentence B rises at the end, making it a question.

To sound natural and fluent, it is important to understand that English is a stress-timed language. As in music, when English is spoken, it has strong and weak beats. The strong beat tends to fall on nouns, verbs, adjectives and adverbs (words that carry meaning), and the weak beats fall on prepositions, articles and pronouns (words with grammatical function). The unstressed words are said much more quickly than the stressed words, to maintain the rhythm of the language.

Rhythm awareness exercise

Imagine that you receive the following message with just meaning-carrying words. Listen to the audio.

Mr Singh   ready   discharge

It is not a grammatically correct sentence; however, you will probably understand that a patient named Mr Singh is ready for discharge.

Now let's add the structure words and listen to the audio.

Mr Singh is *ready* for *discharge*.

These structure words do not add any new information, but ensure that the sentence is now grammatically correct. The italicised words (carrying meaning) are stressed while the grammatical words are unstressed. A constant beat is maintained between the stressed words. The time gap between each stressed word is approximately the same, and the unstressed words are said quickly to maintain the rhythm.

Within a sentence, the emphasis you place on certain words can change the underlying meaning of the sentence. Let's work on a few examples.

Task 2

You're going to hear four different versions of the same sentence: *I believe she is improving.*

Listen to the accompanying audio snippets and underline the stressed word in each sentence. The stressed word is louder, slightly longer and has a higher pitch.

Then, write below each sentence how the meaning changes based on the stressed word.

1. I believe she is improving.

_____

2. I believe she is improving.

_____

3. I believe she is improving.

_____

4. I believe she is improving.

_____

After you've checked your answers, listen again and repeat the sentences, paying close attention to the differences in stress.

Task 3a

Situation: You are speaking to a diabetic patient to advise him/her on lifestyle changes. You ask him/her: 'What is your attitude towards dietary changes?'.

Answer the following questions on the basis of the above situation.

1. Which intonation pattern would you use for this sentence?

_____

2. What words should be stressed in this sentence?

_____

 Now, read the sentence out loud and compare your response to the accompanying audio.

Task 3b

Write down other phrases/sentences that you might use in the above situation. Applying the above learning, answer the same questions for each of these sentences.

_____

_____

B. Fluency

Fluency refers to the rate of your speech. In other words, it means the ability to speak easily, reasonably quickly, and without having to pause frequently to recall a word to express what you want to say.

Here are a few tips to improve fluency.

- Speak at a natural speed. Don't rush your speech, as it will be difficult for the listener to absorb it. Likewise, if your speech is too slow, the listener might feel frustrated while waiting for you to finish, or may lose the flow of argument.
- Pauses can be used strategically to highlight important parts of your speech as well as to encourage patients' understanding and participation. It is, however, worth noting that if you pause because of a lack of vocabulary, you lose marks for fluency. The goal of fluency is to achieve speech that is smooth and not broken into fragments.
- Pauses can be used in different ways while speaking. For example:
  - Sentence pause: take a short breath at each full stop when moving from one sentence to the next.
  - Comma pause: pause briefly at commas.
  - Pause for effect: place emphasis on a certain word or phrase to allow the listener to reflect on it, or take a tiny pause before it to create an impact.
  - Pause for confirmation from the patient: take a small pause to allow the listener to digest the message you have delivered up to that point and give them an opportunity to clarify doubts, if any.

Although the duration of pauses can be different for different speakers, you should vary your pause length based on the purpose for which you are using it.

Look at the following dialogue and listen to the audio.

Health professional: Now Ralph, I'd like to briefly summarise your history to be sure I have understood everything correctly. You've been suffering from stomach pain since yesterday, and you've experienced some heartburn. You've taken medication from the pharmacy, but it has not relieved your symptoms. Is that right so far?

Now, answer the following question.

Which type of pauses can be used in this dialogue to make it more fluent when spoken?

_____

 Listen to the audio and note the change in impact.

C. Appropriateness of language

This criterion assesses to what degree you can tailor your language to make it appropriate for the context and the patient. In other words, it assesses your ability to explain things in clear language understood by the patient, and to adapt tone and register to deal with different patients and situations.

Here is some helpful advice for you to score well on this criterion:

- Avoid using medical jargon; instead, explain the facts in a manner that the patient understands. Practise explaining medical terms and procedures in appropriate language (without any technical or medical words) to patients. For instance, use standard English when giving general advice for good health, diet control, losing weight, care of wounds, smoking cessation, etc. Simplified instructions in plain language are easier for the patient to follow. For example, rather than asking, 'Do you have amenorrhoea?', a better question would be, 'Are your periods regular?'.

Task 5

Rewrite the following statements/questions to make them suitable for a patient.

1. Do you have rhinorrhoea?

_____

2. Your systolic blood pressure is remarkable.

_____

3. Your brother has had a cerebrovascular accident.

_____

4. Do have a history of hypertension in your family?

_____

5. How long have you been experiencing pharyngitis?

_____

6. We need to take an X-ray of your tibia.

_____

7. Your child has otitis media.

_____

8. Unfortunately, the cancer has metastasised.

_____

9. Getting discharged without the doctor's consent may lead to nephritis.

_____

10. Have you experienced any xerosis?

_____

- When communicating with patients on sensitive matters or topics that they may find uncomfortable, choose language that puts them at ease. The more comfortable a patient feels, the more forthcoming he or she will be when answering questions. Employ indirect language to facilitate the conversation.

What is the difference between direct and indirect language?

Rather than asking questions about sensitive or embarrassing matters directly, soften the questions by prefacing them with appropriate expressions/phrases. This makes your questions sound less intrusive and more polite which, consequently, helps put your patients at ease while answering questions.

How do we form indirect questions?

Indirect questions can be formed by starting your question with a phrase like, 'Can you tell me … ' or 'Can I ask … '. Some other examples of phrases that can be used to turn questions from direct to indirect are:

- Would you mind telling me about …
- Would you please tell me …
- May I ask …
- Please tell me …
- I am wondering if you can tell me something about …

For a _yes/no_ question, add _if_ or _whether_ after the phrase and then follow it up with a normal positive sentence.

For example:

Direct	Indirect
Have you ever been pregnant?	Can you tell me if you have ever been pregnant?
	(Phrase + if + normal positive sentence)
Do you drink alcohol?	Can I ask if you drink alcohol?
	(Phrase + if + normal positive sentence)
Are your periods regular?	May I ask if your periods are regular?
	(Phrase + if + normal positive sentence)

For 'Wh-' questions or those that begin with 'How', add the question word followed by a normal positive sentence. For questions in the Past Simple or Present Simple tense of any verb (except the verb 'be'), do not use _do/does/did_ in the indirect question. For both these tenses, too, form an indirect question by starting it with a phrase, followed by a question word and a normal positive sentence. Here are a few examples:

Direct question	Indirect question
When did you first notice blood in your stool?	Can I ask when you first noticed blood in your stool? (Phrase + question word + normal positive sentence)
How are you coping with your current situation?	Can you please tell me how you are coping with your current situation? (Phrase + question word + normal positive sentence)
What steps have you taken to lose weight in the past?	May I ask what steps you have taken to lose weight in the past? (Phrase + question word + normal positive sentence)
Why do you want to get discharged from the hospital?	May I ask why you want to get discharged from the hospital? (Phrase + question word + normal positive sentence)

Task 6

Intonation is a strong indicator of your attitude when speaking to a patient.

Listen to these two questions. You will hear each question twice. Decide which version uses an appropriate tone of voice. Mimic the intonation pattern.

1.1 Please tell me if you have any children.

1.2 Please tell me if you have any children.

2.1 Would you mind telling me why you want to get discharged from the hospital?

2.2 Would you mind telling me why you want to get discharged from the hospital?

Task 7

Practise forming indirect questions for the following. Use a starting phrase from the list given above.

1. Have you tried losing weight in the past?

    _____

2. Is this your first pregnancy?

    _____

3. Do you have trouble holding your urine?

    _____

4. Are you constipated?

    _____

5. Do you have any pain or burning when you urinate?

    _____

6. How do you feel about incorporating some physical activity into your routine?

    _____

7. How do you feel about cutting some unhealthy foods out of your diet?

    _____

Some very sensitive questions may require you to explain the reason for asking the question. For example, 'I am going to ask you some questions about your sexual health and sexual practices. I can understand that these questions are very personal, but they are important for assessing your overall health, and the information is kept in strict confidence'. This acts as a caution that you are about to ask a difficult question.

Practise forming indirect questions for the following. Add a rationale before each to justify the line of questioning.

1. Have you had unprotected sex in the last month?

   _____

2. Have you ever been sexually active?

   _____

3. Does anyone in your family have a history of depression?

   _____

Task 9

Decide in which of these cases you would use indirect questions.

1. A 30-year-old man complaining of a sore throat. He seems to be in a rush.
2. A 35-year-old, overweight woman referred by her GP for advice on weight loss. She looks shy.
3. A 43-year-old man with poorly controlled diabetes referred by his GP for lifestyle advice. He seems defensive.
4. An 18-year-old schoolgirl for her gynaecological examination.

D. Resources of grammar and expression

This criterion assesses your ability to use a range of grammatical structures accurately in speaking.

Here are some tips:

- Aim for grammatical accuracy, as grammatical mistakes can impede the clarity of your communication and make you sound unprofessional. However, keep in mind that this criterion is not just about accuracy of grammar but how well grammar is used to enhance communication. For example, using advanced grammar accurately in a situation where using simpler grammar would be more appropriate will not result in a better score. You need to consider the communicative impact of grammar on the patient, rather than using a range of grammar for a good score.
- Make sure you can form questions correctly. For example, practise those questions that you often use with patients while investigating the presenting complaint or taking medical history ('How long ... ?', 'When ... ', etc).

Task 10

Read the patient's answers below. Write the nurse's questions.

1. Q. _____

   A. Yes, I drink beer 2–3 times a week.

2. Q. _____

   A. Well, I normally skip breakfast because I have to rush to work. During the day, I eat snacks from the cafeteria or get fast food in my lunch hour.

3. Q. _____

   A. It hurts right here, near the elbow.

4. Q. _____

   A. Yes, I am. I am allergic to peanuts.

5. Q. _____

   A. The symptoms started two days ago.

Task 11

Formulate the nurse's questions by reordering the words.

1. rate / on / pain / one / can / ten / your / scale / you / a /of / to

2. ongoing / any / conditions / have / you / medical / do

3. been / you / hospitalised / have / ever

4. me / mind / bothering / you / telling / would / you / what's

5. family / a / has / had / heart / stroke / anyone / your / attack / in / or

6. taking / long / been / medication / have / this / how / you

7. situation / how / current / do / your / you / manage?

8. of / you / work / do / type / what / do

9. exacerbates / symptoms / is / your / there / that /anything

10. ever / any / had / have / the / past / in / you / surgery

Clinical communication criteria

There are five clinical communication criteria on which candidates are assessed. Each criterion is further divided into sub-criteria. These are the skills that a health professional relies on, in order to have successful interaction with patients.

These skills do not stand alone but rather combine to ensure patient-centred communication.

A. Relationship building

B. Understanding and incorporating the patient's perspective

C. Providing structure

D. Information gathering

E. Information giving

A. Relationship building

Relationship building is divided into four sub-criteria:

A1. initiating the interaction appropriately (greeting, introductions, nature of interview)

A2. demonstrating an attentive and respectful attitude

A3. adopting a non-judgemental approach

A4. showing empathy for feelings/predicament/emotional state.

A1. Initiating the interaction appropriately

Establish a good rapport and create a positive first impression by greeting the patient in a welcoming and friendly manner. Introduce yourself politely and confidently by stating your name and clarifying your role.

For example:

Hello, my name's (your name here) and I'll be your attending nurse today.

Hello, my name's (your name here) and I'm one of the Registered Nurses in this facility.

Good morning, my name's (your name here) and I'll be looking after you today.

Your introduction should be tailored to match the setting mentioned on the role play card.

If the role play card suggests that the setting is in a clinic, you could say:

Hello, my name's (your name here) and I'm one of the Registered Nurses in this clinic. I'll be looking after you today.

The next step would be to ask the patient's name.

Can you give me your name, please?

Then, ask the patient what he/she would prefer to be called (first name or last name) rather than simply addressing the patient as *Sir* or *Ma'am*. Some people prefer to be called by their first name, while others prefer to be addressed as *Mr* or *Mrs* followed by their last name. This helps in building a rapport with the patient.

For example:

How may I address you?

What do you prefer to be called?

In some cases, you may already know the patient (for instance when the patient is returning for a follow-up visit or has been admitted to the hospital ward). In those cases, an introduction may not be necessary, and during the preparation time, you could ask the interlocutor what he/she would prefer to be called and begin the role play.

For example:

Good morning Robbie, how are you feeling today?

Good afternoon Samantha, how are you doing today?

Alternatively, you could say:

Please help me to verify your identity. Could you confirm your first and last name?

Once the patient has answered, you could ask how he/she would like to be addressed during the consultation, for example:

Thank you. What do you prefer to be called?

Each role play card has a unique scenario and requires a different approach. Use the background information to supplement what you already know about the patient's current situation and to formulate the initial question or statement. In other words, the opening statement or question should correspond to the background information on the cue card.

For instance, if you are meeting the patient for the first time, use an open-ended question to start the discussion.

Open-ended questions let the patient answer with something other than *Yes* or *No*, or another one-word response. Such questions open up the discussion and allow the patient to give a more detailed response, so they can express themselves in their own words.

For example:

> What brings you here today?
>
> How may I assist you today?
>
> I see that you rang the buzzer. What can I do for you? (This applies to hospital inpatients.)

Use a closed question when it's a follow-up visit or when the reason for the patient's visit is mentioned in the background information on the role play card.

Closed questions require a one-word answer or a short answer (*yes*, *no*, or specific information) rather than a detailed response.

For example:

> Am I right in thinking that you have been referred by your doctor to discuss ways to manage your diabetes?
>
> Am I right in thinking that you have come here about your arthritis?

You could also use the background information on the role play card to identify clues or elements which can form the basis for your opening question. For instance, if the card states that the patient has an emotional reaction (anxious, upset, angry, frustrated or distressed), address this in your opening question.

For example:

> I can see that you are distressed/anxious/angry/frustrated. Could you tell me what's bothering you?
>
> I can see that you are upset/worried/anxious/angry/frustrated. Would you mind telling me what the problem is?

Task 12a

Practise introducing yourself in the following test scenarios.

1. Setting   Emergency Room

    Nurse   You are speaking to an 83-year-old man/woman who has presented himself/herself to the Emergency Room. He/She looks very concerned.

2. Setting   Hospital Ward

    Nurse   You have been called to a patient's bedside. The patient is a 43-year-old man/woman who was admitted to the hospital yesterday for a total left hip replacement. You notice that he/she looks agitated.

3. Setting   Community Health Centre

    Nurse   You are talking to a 27-year-old man/woman who has been referred by his/her doctor for advice on weight loss. The patient has been experiencing breathlessness on exertion and has been advised to lose weight by his/her GP to improve his/her health status.

Task 12b

How would you initiate the interaction appropriately for each scenario given above?

1. _____

2. _____

3. _____

A2. Demonstrating an attentive and respectful attitude

Throughout the interview, demonstrating attentiveness and respect establishes trust with the patient, lays down the foundation for a collaborative relationship, and ensures that the patient understands your motivation to help. Examples of such behaviour include attending to the patient's comfort, asking permission and consent to proceed, and being sensitive to potentially embarrassing matters. When seeking the patient's consent to ask questions, provide a rationale to clarify the reason for probing into a particular aspect of their life. This helps them to feel comfortable during the interview. The more comfortable the patient feels, the more forthcoming they'll be when responding to your questions.

For example:

> May I sit here? What I would like to do is spend 20 minutes with you now discussing your problems and examining you. Is that okay? Please let me know if you experience discomfort at any time.

> Before proceeding further, I'd like to ask you some questions about your smoking habits. It'll help me get a better understanding of your condition. Is that alright?

> The doctor is worried your weight might put you at risk of complications post-surgery. Is it okay if we discuss your eating habits and lifestyle?

> I'm concerned about your recent sugar levels. Would it be alright if I asked you some questions about how you have been managing your sugar intake?

Using language that reflects common courtesy keeps your interactions with the patient respectful and consequently improves rapport. Let's look at some communicative functions, and examples of them that you can use when speaking with patients.

Communicative function	Example
Expressing gratitude	• Thank you for answering my questions. • I really appreciate your openness.
Reassuring	• You did the right thing coming in. • I will inform the doctor right away so you don't have to wait long.
Sympathising	• I am sorry for the inconvenience that this has caused. • I am sorry that you had to wait for so long.
Acknowledging	• I realise this is difficult. • Now that I understand the situation, I will do my best to resolve it.

Task 13

Rewrite the following statements to make them sound appropriately courteous.

1. You will need to wait to see the doctor.

_____

2. I don't know the answer to that.

_____

3. You need to answer some questions about your medical history.

_____

4. You are not fit to go home. It's a bad idea to even think about it.

_____

5. I don't understand you.

_____

A3. Adopting a non-judgemental approach

Accepting the patient's perspective and views without immediate judgement or rebuttal is a key component of relationship building. A judgemental response to patients' ideas and concerns devalues their contributions. During a health consultation, a patient may reveal personal beliefs with which you do not agree. You should remain impartial to these, as your responsibility is to assist patients in managing their health, not approving or disapproving of their perspective.

A non-judgemental response would include accepting the patient's perspective and acknowledging the legitimacy of their views and feelings.

An effective example would be:

> So what worries you most is that the abdominal pain might be caused by cancer. I can understand that you would want to get that checked out.

Task 14a

🎧 5.15 **Listen to a conversation between a nurse and his patient, Emily, who is a smoker. Write down examples of the nurse's ineffective communication (judging the patient, no reassurance) with Emily.**

_____

_____

Task 14b

🎧 5.16 **Listen to the conversation between the same nurse and his patient, Emily, who is a smoker. Identify ways in which the nurse here avoids passing judgement about Emily's smoking and is able to address her concerns.**

_____

_____

A4. Showing empathy for patients' feelings, predicament or emotional state

Empathy is one of the key skills in relationship building. Empathy involves the understanding and sensitive appreciation of another person's predicament or feelings, and the communication of that understanding back to the patient in a supportive way. It's a vital component of any health professional-patient relationship, and helps in building rapport. It can be achieved through both non-verbal and verbal behaviours. Even with audio alone, some non-verbal behaviours such as the use of silence and appropriate voice tone in response to a patient's expression of feelings can be observed. Verbal empathy makes this non-verbal communication more explicit by specifically referring to the patient's predicament and showing appreciation of their feelings.

An effective example would be:

> I can see that your husband's memory loss has been very difficult for you to cope with.

The concept of empathy can be broken down into three categories, and it is important to understand all three in order to use empathy effectively in OET Speaking.

Cognitive empathy

Also termed 'perspective-taking', this is the process of looking at things from the other person's point of view. It enables a health professional to gain an understanding of how a patient feels, without engaging directly with the patient's emotions.

To build cognitive empathy, try to understand the situation from the other person's perspective.

Emotional empathy

Emotional empathy refers not just to knowing about what's happening to someone else, but being able to feel what the other person is feeling.

In order to build emotional empathy, try to understand how the person feels and why they feel that way; then, connect with the person's emotional state. You can do this by trying to remember a time when you felt similar to how the other person is feeling.

Compassionate empathy

Compassionate empathy is a more intense response than knowing or feeling. It leads a person to either take action, or help the other person take action to resolve the problem. To exercise compassionate empathy, think of how you can provide appropriate support to the other person. Combine the cognitive perspective with emotional understanding, and repeat it back to the patient so that they feel heard.

In OET Speaking, you should employ all three types of empathy to identify and understand a patient's perspective and feelings, and use this understanding judiciously to build a rapport with your patient.

Read the following dialogue. The patient is a 34-year-old woman who has recently been divorced and is experiencing difficulty sleeping. She looks sad. Underline the nurse's words that convey empathy in this conversation.

Nurse: Hello, what can I do for you?

Patient: I am finding it difficult to fall asleep.

Nurse: I am sorry to hear that. Can you tell me when this started?

Patient: I've recently separated from my husband, about 4 weeks ago. Since then, I've had difficulty in sleeping.

Nurse: I can appreciate that this is a difficult time for you. Can you tell me a bit more about what's been going on?

Patient: I've barely slept at all. Even if I do manage to fall asleep, I wake up after a few hours and stare at the clock ticking away. I feel tired all the time, and I am finding it very difficult to cope with everything.

Nurse: I understand it's challenging for you to cope with this situation. It can be distressing.

B. Understanding and incorporating the patient's perspective

This criterion is divided into three sub-criteria:

B1. eliciting and exploring patients' ideas/concerns/expectations

B2. picking up patients' cues

B3. relating explanations to elicited ideas/concerns/expectations.

B1. Eliciting and exploring patients' ideas, concerns or expectations

Understanding the patient's perspective is a key component of patient-centred healthcare. Each patient has a unique experience of sickness that includes feelings, thoughts, concerns and effect on life that any episode of sickness induces. Patients may either volunteer these spontaneously (as direct statements or cues) or in response to questions.

A health professional might need to ask about these directly, as in 'Did you have any thoughts yourself about what might be causing your symptoms?' or 'Was there anything particular you were concerned about?'.

If expressed spontaneously by the patient, the health professional needs to explore this by saying, for instance, 'You mentioned that you were concerned about the effect the illness might have on your work, could you tell me more about that?'.

Task 16

Below are some questions that a health professional could ask a patient to elicit and explore the patient's ideas, concerns or expectations. Write the questions under the appropriate headings.

1. Can I ask what you are thinking at the moment?

2. You seem worried. Would you mind telling me what's bothering you?

3. Could you tell me how this makes you feel?

4. I can see that this has you concerned. What can I do to help you feel less anxious?

5. Can you tell me something about your state of mind right now?

6. It seems you've got something on your mind. Do you mind sharing it with me?

Asking how the patient is feeling

_____

_____

Responding to physical signs

_____

_____

Encouraging a patient to express himself/herself

_____

_____

B2. Picking up patients' cues

Patients are generally eager to tell us about their own thoughts and feelings, but often do so indirectly through verbal hints or changes in non-verbal behaviour (such as vocal cues including hesitation or change in volume). Picking up these cues is essential for exploring both the medical and the patient's perspectives.

Techniques for picking up cues would include:

Mirroring: This means repeating key words or the last few spoken words with rising intonation, which acts as a prompt for him/her to continue. For example, 'Something could be done … ?'.

Echoing or reflecting: This means using your own words to reflect the content and emotion of what the patient has said. For example, 'I sense that you are not happy with the explanations you've been given in the past'.

Questioning and clarifying: This means asking questions about the statements or hints to understand the patient. For example, 'You used the word *worried*; could you tell me more about what you were worried about?'.

'All of the above examples act as verbal encouragement for a patient to talk further if they would like to.

Task 17

How would you respond to these verbal and non-verbal cues by the patient?

Verbal cues

1. It's just that life is a bit hard right now. I hate my job, and I have to find a new accommodation as my lease is expiring soon. I don't know what to do!

   _____

2. It's a shame that I have to come in next week for my results rather than being able to find them out today. I had to take today off work to make this appointment.

   _____

Non-verbal cues

3. I am fine. (worried tone of voice; the tone contradicts spoken words)

_____

4. Um … I guess … okay (rising intonation signalling uncertainty)

_____

B3. Relating explanations to elicited ideas, concerns or expectations

One of the key reasons for discovering the patient's perspective is to incorporate it into explanations in the later parts of the interview. If the explanation does not address the patient's individual ideas, concerns and expectations, understanding and satisfaction suffer as the patient is worrying about their still unaddressed concerns.

An effective example might be: 'You mentioned earlier that you were concerned that you might have angina. I can see why you might have thought that, but in fact I think it's more likely to be a muscular pain because …'.

Task 18

You are speaking to an entrepreneur who feels it is very difficult for them to take time off from their work and make lifestyle changes to manage their hypertension. How can you relate your explanation to their concerns while explaining treatment advice?

_____

_____

C. Providing structure

There are three sub-criteria under the providing structure criterion:

C1. sequencing the interview purposefully and logically

C2. signposting changes in the topic

C3. using organising techniques in explanations

C1. Sequencing the interview purposefully and logically

It is the responsibility of the health professional to maintain a logical sequence apparent to the patient as the interview unfolds. An ordered approach helps both the professional and the patient in efficient and accurate data-gathering and information giving. This needs to be balanced with the need to be patient-centred and follow the patient's needs. Flexibility and logical sequencing have to be thoughtfully combined.

As mentioned earlier in the chapter, during the three-minute preparation time, mentally plan how you can sequence your interview logically and purposefully during the five-minute timeframe.

For example:

Before I review your medications, I'd first like to ask some questions about your past health problems. Would that be alright?

So, here's what I am going to do. First, I'll ask you some questions to get a detailed picture of your situation. Then, I'll take you through some treatment options. Finally, I'd be happy to answer any questions that you might have. May I proceed?

Look at the following role play card and write down a sentence that lets the patient know how the conversation will progress.

Setting	Community Health Centre
Nurse	You are talking to a 35-year-old computer engineer who has been referred by his/her doctor for advice on weight loss. The patient has been experiencing breathlessness on exertion and has been advised by his/her GP to lose weight to improve his/her health status.
Task	Ask questions about the patient's general lifestyle including drinking and eating habits. Provide advice on increasing physical activity and eating a suitable diet (reducing alcohol intake, eating fruit and vegetables).

C2. Signposting changes in topic

Signposting is a key skill in enabling patients to understand the structure of the interview by making its organisation overt: both the health professional and the patient need to understand where the interview is going and why. A signposting statement introduces and draws attention to what we are about to say.

For instance, it is helpful to use a signposting statement to introduce a summary: 'Can I just check that I have understood you, let me know if I've missed something …'.

Signposting can be used to make the progression from one section to another, and explain the rationale behind the next section.

For example:

> You mentioned two areas that are obviously important, first the joint problems and the tiredness, and second how you are going to cope with your kids. Could I start by just asking a few more questions about the joint pains and then we can come back to your difficulties with the children?

> Since we haven't met before, it will help me to learn something about your medical history. Can we do that now?

In OET Speaking, signposting language can be used at different stages of the role play.

Task 20

Given below are signposting phrases that a health professional could use to provide structure to the consultation. Write these under the appropriate stages of the role play, on the next page.

1. If you don't mind, I'd like to ask some questions about your sexual history.

2. Thank you for answering my questions. I have all the information I need, and now I'd like to suggest some lifestyle modifications to improve your health.

3. If you don't mind, I am just going to ask you a few questions about your lifestyle. Would that be okay?

4. What I'd like to do now is to discuss some ways you can manage your present condition.

5. Before we wrap up, is there anything that you would like to ask?

6. OK, before proceeding further, I'd like to ask you some questions about your pain. Is that alright?

7. Now that we've discussed some treatment options, I'd like to know about any questions or concerns that you have.

8. Before I can discuss the treatment options, I'd like to summarise your symptoms to ensure I have accurate information.

9. If you don't mind, I want to ask you some questions about your sexual partners and sexual practices. I understand that these questions are quite personal, but they are crucial for the examination.

To seek the patient's permission before the information-gathering stage

_____

_____

To ask personal questions or questions on sensitive topics

_____

To justify a specific line of questioning

_____

To transition from one topic to another

_____

_____

_____

To wrap up or close the consultation

_____

C3. Using organising techniques in explanations

In OET Speaking, your explanations should be well organised, to make it easier for the patient to follow and stay focused. Some techniques that can be used during the role plays to present and arrange information in a logical order are mentioned below.

Categorisation is a technique in which the health professional forewarns the patient about which categories of information are to be provided. For example, 'There are three important things I want to explain. First, I want to tell you what I think might be wrong; second, what tests we should do; and third, what the treatment might be'.

Labelling means explicitly highlighting certain components of your explanation to emphasise their importance. For example, 'It is particularly important that you remember this …'.

Chunking is a technique in which information is divided into smaller amounts ('chunks') and delivered one bit at a time, with a clear gap between each section. After relaying a chunk of information, you should check that the patient has understood and retained what you have told them by asking a follow-up question such as, 'What is your current understanding of...?'. Proceed to the next chunk only when you are confident that the patient has fully understood the information you have just given them.

Repetition refers to the action of repeating what the patient has said. This enables you to clarify the patient's meaning rather than just focusing on the words they use. For example, 'If I understood you correctly ... you're saying that you've had chest pain for the last three days, which is about a six on a scale of 0 to 10, and it's a burning feeling that causes tightness in the chest. Is there anything else that you would like to add?'.

Summary of important points – for example, 'So just to recap: we have decided to treat the fungal infection with a cream that you use twice a day for two weeks. If the infection is not better by then, you are going to come back and see me'.

When using repetition and summarising skills, always check whether what you have paraphrased is accurate by asking clarifying questions like:

- Is that right?
- Is that correct?
- Would you like to add anything to that?
- Is that an accurate summary?

Remember, the summary statement should not be a word-by-word repetition. You should summarise only the main points.

Task 21

Below are two examples of *Labelling*. Underline the words that highlight the significance of your advice.

1. From what you've told me, the most important thing for you would be to get some more advice on lowering your cholesterol. Is that right?

2. From all the discharge information that I have shared with you, the most crucial is that the medication is to be taken on time. Do you think you will have any trouble with that?

Chunking and checking: 'Chunking' means breaking down longer explanations into small pieces, referred to as 'chunks'. This can aid the patient's understanding because smaller 'chunks' of information are easier to process and retain.

After each piece of information, the patient's understanding must be checked with a follow-up question such as, 'Do you have any questions about what I just explained?'. Proceed to the next 'chunk' only when you are confident that the patient has understood the previous one.

Task 22

Revise this explanation using the organising techniques discussed above. The objective is to aid the patient's understanding.

'Increasing the levels of iron in your body is a slow process due to the amount of iron that your body can absorb from each meal. Some examples of iron-rich foods that can be incorporated into your diet are lean red meat, liver, nuts, seeds, iron-fortified cereals. I'd also like to discuss some things you can do to increase the absorption of iron in the blood. Combine iron-rich foods with foods rich in vitamin C to promote absorption of iron, and reduce your caffeine intake for an hour after eating iron.'

Categorisation

_____

_____

Chunk 1

_____

_____

Chunk 2

_____

_____

Summarising

_____

_____

Task 23

Paraphrase the following statements to repeat back to the patient, summarising only the main points.

1. I haven't been eating well as I've been having back-to-back meetings at my office. I often skip breakfast because I'm running late, and I don't get time for lunch due to work. Dinner is usually a quick bite because I'm busy working on my presentations for the next day.

   (This patient has presented with symptoms consistent with Irritable Bowel Syndrome.)

   _____

   _____

2. The doctor told me to take these antibiotics until the pills ran out, but I felt better the next day, so I stopped.

   (This patient has come for his/her follow-up appointment about a respiratory infection and has recurring symptoms.)

   _____

   _____

3. I don't believe that drinking regularly is bad. I've been drinking whiskey regularly and nothing bad has happened to me.

   (This patient has been referred by his/her GP for advice on improving his/her health status.)

   _____

   _____

4. I'd like to lose some weight, but with my friend's wedding around the corner, I feel it won't be possible.

   (This patient has been advised to lose weight but is reluctant about making changes to his/her lifestyle.)

   _____

   _____

D. Information gathering

Information gathering is divided into five sub-criteria:

D1. Facilitating the patient's narrative with active listening techniques, minimising interruption

D2. Using open questions initially, moving appropriately to closed questions

D3. NOT using compound questions/leading questions

D4. Clarifying statements which are vague or need amplification

D5. Summarising information to encourage correction/invite further information

D1. Facilitating the patient's narrative with active listening techniques, minimising interruption

Listening to the patient's narrative, particularly at the beginning of an interview, enables the health professional to discover the story more efficiently, hear the patient's perspective, appear supportive and interested, and pick up cues to the patient's feelings. Interruption of the narrative has the opposite effect, and in particular, generally leads to a predominantly biomedical history that omits the patient's perspective.

Observable skills of active listening techniques include:

- the use of silence and pausing
- verbal encouragement or 'back-channelling', which is the feedback you give to the patient to show that you understand what he/she is saying. This encourages the patient to continue and contribute more information. It makes the patient feel understood and empathised with. It usually takes the form of utterances such as *uh-huh, mmm, okay, right, I see, go on, OK, really?*
- being aware of your intonation while speaking, as the rise and fall of your tone can indicate different things. Rising intonation indicates that you want the patient to start talking, whereas falling intonation indicates that the patient has finished speaking.
- echoing and repetition such as 'chest pain?' or 'not coping?'
- paraphrasing and interpretation such as 'Are you thinking that when John gets even more ill, you won't be strong enough to nurse him at home by yourself?'

Task 24

Decide whether each of the following is an example of back-channelling, echoing or paraphrasing.

1. Tell me more. _____

2. Patient: I feel scared.

   Doctor: Scared? _____

3. From what I've understood so far, you feel disappointed that your recovery is taking longer than you expected. _____

Task 25

5.17 **Listen to the audio. You will hear a conversation between a nurse and Julie, who has been referred to the Mental Health Clinic by her employer after she missed a few project deadlines and meetings. Note down all examples of back-channelling used by the nurse.**

_____

_____

D2. Using open questions initially, moving appropriately to closed questions

Understanding how to decide between open and closed questioning styles at different points in the interview is of key importance. An effective health professional uses open questioning techniques first to obtain a picture of the problem from the patient's perspective. Later, the approach becomes more focused with increasingly specific, though still open, questions and eventually closed questions to elicit additional details that the patient may have omitted. The use of open questioning techniques is critical at the beginning of the exploration of any problem, and the most common mistake is to move to closed questioning too quickly.

Closed questions are questions for which a specific and often one-word answer, such as *yes* or *no*, is expected. They limit the response to a narrow field set by the questioner.

Open questioning techniques in contrast are designed to introduce an area of enquiry without unduly shaping or focusing the content of the response. They still direct the patient to a specific area but allow the patient more discretion in their answer, suggesting to the patient that elaboration is both appropriate and welcome.

Simple examples of these questioning styles are:

Open: 'Tell me about your headaches.'

More directive but still open: 'What makes your headaches better or worse?'

Closed: 'Do you ever wake up with a headache in the morning?'

Open questioning techniques:

'Start at the beginning and take me through what has been happening ...'

'How have you been feeling since your operation ... ?'

Task 26

Convert the following closed questions to open-ended ones.

1. Is the pain sharp?

    _____

2. Do you have any pain at the moment?

    _____

3. Has this made you worried?

    _____

4. Can you come next week on Tuesday for your follow-up?

    _____

5. Do you exercise regularly?

    _____

D3. Not using compound questions or leading questions

A compound question is when more than one question is asked without allowing time to answer. It confuses the patient about what information is being asked, and introduces uncertainty about which of the questions needs to be answered.

For example:

Have you ever had chest pain or felt short of breath?

A leading question is based on an assumption, which is difficult for the respondent to contradict.

For example:

You've lost weight, haven't you?

You haven't had any ankle swelling?

Note: While leading questions should not be used when gathering information from the patient, they can be helpful in confirming whether the information that you have with you is correct.

For example:

You have recently undergone a knee replacement surgery, isn't that right?

Keep in mind that in the Speaking sub-test you cannot assume anything; you must use only the information mentioned in the background information on the role play card.

Task 27

Transform the following compound and leading questions into open-ended ones.

1. Does the pain always occur in the same place, and how painful is it on a scale of 0–10, where 0 is no pain and 10 is the worst?

   _____

   _____

2. You are not eating too well, are you?

   _____

3. Did stress, travelling or something else cause the problem?

   _____

4. What have you been eating this past month? How much do you eat at one time? How often do you eat?

   _____

   _____

   _____

5. The pain must have been worse after you stopped swimming, right?

   _____

6. You haven't had any heart palpitations, have you?

   _____

D4. Clarifying statements which are vague or need amplification

Clarifying statements which are vague or need further amplification is a vital information-gathering skill. After an initial response to an open-ended question, health professionals may need to prompt patients for more precision, clarity or completeness. Often patients' statements can have two possible meanings: it is important to ascertain which one is intended.

For example:

Could you explain what you mean by light-headed?

When you say dizzy, do you mean that the room seems to actually spin around?

Task 28

How would you clarify what the patient says in the following statements?

1. Patient: I've been feeling so worn out recently.

   Nurse: _____

2. Patient: I exercise almost every other day.

   Nurse: _____

3. Patient: I feel I'm carrying the weight of the world on my shoulders.

   Nurse: _____

4. Patient: It's like I'm seeing everything in a new light.

   Nurse: _____

5. Patient: My stomach never feels right.

   Nurse: _____

D5. Summarising information to encourage correction or invite further information

Summarising is the deliberate step of making an explicit verbal summary to the patient of the information gathered so far. This is one of the most important of all information-gathering skills. Used periodically throughout the interview, it helps with two significant tasks – ensuring accuracy and facilitating the patient's further responses.

For example:

Can I just see if I've got this right – you've had indigestion before, but for the last few weeks you've had increasing problems with a sharp pain at the front of your chest, accompanied by wind and acid. It's stopping you from sleeping. It's made worse by drink, and you were wondering if the painkillers were to blame. Is there anything that I have missed?

From what I have understood so far, you have been experiencing indigestion for the past few weeks, and at times, it is accompanied by headaches which last for a few hours and are only relieved with medication. You feel the indigestion is caused when you eat rice for dinner. Is there anything else that you'd like to add?

Just to recap what you just told me, for the last month you have occasionally experienced an urgent need to urinate. The symptoms have gradually worsened, and you urinate every 2–3 hours and experience an urgent need 2–3 times a day. At times, the urge to urinate is so strong that urine leaks on the way to the bathroom. It's impacting your life negatively by preventing you from exercising and socialising. Is that right?

E. Information giving

Information giving is further divided up into five sub-criteria:

E1. Establishing initially what the patient already knows

E2. Pausing periodically when giving information, using the response to guide next steps

E3. Encouraging the patient to contribute reactions/feelings

E4. Checking whether the patient has understood the information

E5. Discovering what further information the patient needs

E1. Establishing initially what the patient already knows

One key interactive approach to giving information to patients involves assessing their prior knowledge. This means assessing what the patient already knows and giving information accordingly. Ask what the patient already knows, and take note of the discrepancies between the patient's understanding and what is actually true. It helps you to decide on the extent of information and the type of information to be given to the patient.

For example:

It would be helpful for me to understand a little of what you already know about diabetes so that I can try to fill in any gaps for you.

Could you tell me what you know about this condition so far?

What's your current understanding of hypertension?

You said that you've had diabetes before. How was the condition explained to you then?

What do you remember about the treatment of the condition from the last time that you experienced a flare-up?

E2. Pausing periodically when giving information, using the response to guide next steps

This approach, often called 'chunking and checking', is a vital skill throughout the information-giving phase of the interview. As discussed earlier in the chapter, the health professional gives information in small pieces, pausing and checking for understanding before proceeding, and is guided by the patient's reactions to see what information is required next. This technique is a vital component of assessing the patient's overall information needs: if you give information in small chunks and give patients ample opportunity to contribute, they'll respond with clear signals about both the amount and type of information they still require.

For example:

So really, given the symptoms you have described and the way that you wheeze more after exercise and at night, I feel reasonably confident that what you are describing is asthma and that we should consider ways we might treat it. (Pause) How does that sound so far?

Task 29

You are speaking to John, a diabetic patient, who has been referred to you for guidance on how to self-administer insulin injections. Read the communication below. If this information is delivered all at once it can lead to a potential communication breakdown. Divide up the explanation using 'chunking and checking' to ensure that the patient understands the instructions properly.

Choose an area on your skin that you can see and reach. Insulin can be injected into the stomach, backs of the arms, thighs or buttocks, but it gets into the blood more quickly if injected into the abdomen. It is, however, important that you rotate the injection sites to ensure that a particular area is not overused, as this can lead to skin problems like scarring or lumps under the skin. It's equally important to clean the site before injecting by wiping it with alcohol, to reduce the risk of infections. After cleaning the injection site, pinch your skin between your thumb and two fingers, pulling the skin and fat away from the underlying muscle, and keep it in place until the insulin has been injected. Insert the needle at a 90° angle in one quick motion, push the plunger all the way down and count to ten. Finally, release the pinch and remove the needle from your skin. When you remove the needle, do it at the same 90° angle at which the needle was inserted. Also, to ensure that the insulin does not leak out, press the injection site for 5–10 seconds after the needle has been removed.

Chunk 1

_____

_____

_____

Checking the patient's understanding before proceeding further

_____

Chunk 2

_____

_____

_____

Checking the patient's understanding before proceeding further

_____

Chunk 3

_____

_____

_____

Checking the patient's understanding before proceeding further

_____

E3. Encouraging the patient to contribute reactions or feelings

A further element of effective information giving is providing opportunities to the patient to ask questions, seek clarification or express doubts. Health professionals have to be very explicit here: many patients are reluctant to express what is on the tip of their tongues, and are extremely hesitant to ask the doctor questions. Unless positively invited to do so, they may leave the consultation with their questions unanswered and a reduced understanding of and commitment to plans. Therefore, you should encourage active participation from patients, allowing them to ask questions, express doubt, or seek clarification regarding the information.

For example:

What questions does that leave you with – have you any concerns about what I've said?

I'd really like to hear your reaction to this diagnosis.

I can appreciate that this is a lot to take in. Would you like to ask any questions about what I've just explained?

Task 30

In the previous task, after John has been advised about the correct technique of self-administering insulin injections, how would you encourage him to express his doubts or feelings regarding the information given?

_____

_____

E4. Checking whether the patient has understood the information

Checking if the patient has understood the information given is an important step in ensuring accuracy of information transfer. Avoid using statements like 'Does this make sense to you?', as these kinds of statements can make your patients feel pressured to say 'yes'. Instead, use the 'teach-back' method to assess the patient's understanding. In this method, patients are asked to repeat in their own words what they have understood.

For example:

I know I've given you a lot of information today, and I'm concerned that I might not have made it very clear. So it would help me if you repeated what we've discussed so far, so I can make sure we're on the same track.

To ensure that you've understood everything correctly, would you mind reiterating what we've discussed?

Just to be sure I've explained everything clearly, it would be helpful for me to hear your understanding about what you need to do. Can you summarise the treatment plan that you'll be following?

In addition to asking the patient directly, look for non-verbal cues like hesitation or change in tone that convey that the patient has not understood the information or has concerns, and use their responses as a guide to see what information to provide next.

E5. Discovering what further information the patient needs

Deliberately asking the patient what other information would be helpful enables the health professional to directly discover areas to address that have not been considered so far. It is difficult to guess each patient's individual needs, and asking directly is an obvious way to prevent the omission of important information.

For example:

Are there any other questions you'd like me to answer or any points I haven't covered?

Before we wrap up the consultation, is there anything else you'd like to ask?

Task 31

You are speaking to a 71-year-old woman, Hannah, who has just been diagnosed with urinary incontinence. The doctor has asked you to speak to the patient to explain what urinary incontinence is, and to tell her about its treatment. Read the transcript below, then write down examples from it that illustrate the following headings.

Note: You can listen to the conversation as well.

Nurse: Hello Hannah. Since you have been diagnosed with urinary incontinence, it would be a good idea for us to have a discussion about what the condition means and how it can be treated. Before proceeding further, I'd like to know if you have any prior information about this condition?

Patient: Well, yes, I've read about it in a couple of magazines and the doctor has also just explained that it is a common problem for women my age.

Nurse: Yes, that's right. Its prevalence increases as people get older. That being said, let me assure you that it is easily treatable with medication and several treatment options. Would you like me to talk about them now?

Patient: Yes, please.

Nurse: Firstly, the doctor has prescribed some medication for you. In addition to the medication, I'd also suggest using disposable undergarments and continence pads. This would ensure that you're able to participate in social activities without any worry.

Patient: Okay. That sounds good.

Nurse: It would also help if you did some bladder training and pelvic floor muscle exercises. For this, I'd advise seeing a urologist who specialises in treating incontinence of the bladder. Would it be okay if I scheduled an appointment for you tomorrow at the same time?

Patient: Ah, thank you! That would be appreciated.

Nurse: That's alright. Are there any concerns or questions that I've not been able to address? Please feel free to share anything that you have on your mind.

Patient: Oh, you've been quite helpful. I don't think I have any questions.

Nurse: Great. To be sure you've understood everything correctly, could you summarise what we've discussed?

Patient: Yes, I'll be taking the prescribed medication and using disposable undergarments and incontinence pads. Besides this, I'll be seeing a urologist tomorrow who'll guide me regarding pelvic exercises and bladder training.

Nurse: Yes. Is there anything else that you'd like to ask before we end the consultation?

Patient: No, it's clear what I have to do.

Write your answers below.

Establishing initially what the patient already knows

Pausing periodically when giving information, using the response to guide next steps

---

Encouraging the patient to contribute reactions/feelings

Checking whether the patient has understood the information

___

Discovering what further information the patient needs

___

Signposting language that the nurse uses to make it easier for the patient to follow the sequence of the explanation

___

Tips for Scoring

Here are a few tips to increase your score in the Speaking sub-test:

- The best way to improve your English-speaking skills is to immerse yourself in the language. Watch movies in English with subtitles or listen to songs with English lyrics, several times each. Make use of free resources which have extensive content for improving your grammar, vocabulary and pronunciation. Use websites where you'll be able to find videos with transcripts. Doing these types of activities helps you learn passively and become familiar with aspects of language like intonation, pronunciation or rhythm.

- When practising role plays, always record your performance on your mobile/recording device. Recording yourself is an extremely helpful way to improve your speaking. It can help you realise whether you tend to speak quickly, pausing when needed, or whether you are speaking in bursts of language that are impacting on your ability to be understood. You can also evaluate your pronunciation and notice areas where you need to improve. For further work, you can transcribe your own speech from a tape of your talk after you give it. You can then mark the intonation patterns and underline the meaning-carrying words to improve your talk when you re-record it.

- Listen to how you talk in a recording and assess your performance, taking on the role of an observer. Do you sound confident or doubtful? Irritated or pleasant? In the OET Speaking sub-test, you'll need to choose the right tone of voice to suit the patient type and scenario. For example, you should not sound too energetic when speaking to a depressed or withdrawn patient; similarly, you will not want to avoid giving an impression of self-doubt when explaining treatment options. Consider how your tone, pitch, and language vary when you are delivering bad news to a patient, or when speaking to a patient who is depressed or has an emotional response to a situation (anxious, angry, distressed). Practise modulating your voice to meet the needs of a variety of patients (in terms of their ages and emotional reactions), as your language needs to adjust according to the patient type and context.

- Practise the pronunciation of words and phrases in English commonly used in your profession. Use reputable websites to check whether you are pronouncing a word correctly and stressing the right syllable.

- Do not memorise full scripts or sentences, as Assessors are able to identify whether a student speaks freely or uses memorised or formulaic responses. Each role play has a different scenario, and responses need to match the context on the candidate card. Assessors listen for what is appropriate for that particular roleplay, and it is very likely that memorised phrases or sentences may not suit the context of the role play. This lack of suitability can lead the Assessor to figure out that phrases were rehearsed. Therefore, when learning new phrases, do not just memorise them. Remember where such a phrase would be appropriate.

- As in real-life workplace situations, where a patient expects you to begin the consultation, you should take the initiative to start and lead the interview. However, in certain scenarios, it would be appropriate to let the patient take the initiative. For example, if a patient is worried about something and needs to 'get something off their chest', then you can let them take the lead. This will help you understand their concerns or problems.

FAQs

Here are a few frequently asked questions about the OET Speaking sub-test:

1. Will I be penalised for not completing all of the tasks on the cue card?

As with any consultation in a medical setting, the patient is your priority, and the consultation needs to be patient-centred. Even for the same scenario, no two interlocuters give the same responses, and your responses will depend on the answers given by the interlocutor. Although the cue cards are designed in a way that the conversation comes to a natural end at the five-minute mark, it is possible, at times, that you may not be able to complete all elements on the role play card. You do not need to worry about losing marks in this case because Assessors just need to hear an assessable sample of your speech for evaluation. Your focus should be on attending to the patient's needs rather than trying to finish all the tasks on time, as that would lead to a loss of marks. For example, a candidate speaking too fast in an attempt to complete all the tasks would score poorly on fluency. A candidate may frequently interrupt a patient in an effort to get through all of the tasks, thereby causing a communication breakdown and, consequently, scoring poorly on the communication criteria.

2. Do I need to address all sub-criteria outlined under the five communication criteria?

OET has been updated to ensure that the test remains relevant to the continually evolving healthcare industry. Consequently, clinical communication skills have been included in the assessment criteria to ensure that the candidates demonstrate core skills required for effective patient-centred communication. All five communication criteria and their respective sub-criteria should be regarded as a guide/indicator of how a therapeutic and supportive alliance can be established with the patient or a carer during different stages of the consultation, and as a guide to the associated communication skills required. Therefore, your focus should be on the establishment and maintenance of rapport between yourself and the patient, and on sensitively completing the tasks on the role play card, not on whether you have covered all the sub-criteria. It is possible that some role plays might not need you to employ all of the skills outlined in the sub-criteria. For example, there are some role plays where you do not need to use clarifying statements. However, you will always need to use the right questioning technique and employ active listening to gather relevant information. As stated earlier, your focus should remain on maintaining coherence and communicating with the patient compassionately, and not on trying to 'work in' memorised phrases to address the criteria.

3. What if I say something that's medically inaccurate? Will that impact on my score?

It is understandable to have this concern, but OET is a test of your communication skills and not of medical accuracy. The test is designed to include scenarios that an entry-level healthcare professional is expected to encounter in their day-to-day workplace situations. Even so, if you are not confident about the topic in the role play card, you could mention some general health guidelines relevant to the topic; as long as it's done in perfect English. If you demonstrate a range of 'soft' skills corresponding to the communication criteria, you will get a good score on the test.

CHAPTER 3

ROLE PLAYS
FOR PRACTICE

Here are two sets of role plays for practice. Use them to prepare yourself for the sub-test.

Role play   Set 1

ROLEPLAYER CARD NO 1   **NURSING**

Setting: Home visit

Patient: You are a 64-year-old who underwent a total left knee replacement three weeks ago. At the time of discharge, you were advised to use a walker and to adhere to the recommended physiotherapy exercises at home until your follow-up appointment in a month. You stopped using the walker yesterday evening.

Task:
- Tell the nurse why you stopped using the walker (makes you feel disabled/old, can now walk independently, knee healing well).
- Insist that you have been compliant with the recommended exercise regime and you do not want to be dependent on anything for routine activities.
- Admit that it is sometimes painful if you put weight on the knee for extended periods of time.
- Reluctantly agree to use a walker until your follow-up appointment.

CANDIDATE CARD NO 1   **NURSING**

Setting: Home visit

Nurse: You are visiting a 64-year-old patient who underwent a total left knee replacement three weeks ago. This visit is to monitor the patient's progress before his/her follow-up appointment scheduled in a month. The post-discharge instructions included using a walker for mobility and compliance with the recommended physiotherapy. During your visit, you notice that the patient is not using the walker.

Task:
- Find out when and why the patient stopped using the walker.
- Advise the patient on the importance of physiotherapy and using the walker (e.g. physiotherapy increases range of motion/strength. Walker assists with balance, reduces risk of falls, lessens weight/pressure put on weakened muscles of knee, etc.).
- Find out if the patient has been experiencing pain.
- Encourage the patient to use a walker until his/her follow-up appointment (e.g. reduction in pain, shortened recovery time, etc.).

ROLEPLAYER CARD NO 2   **NURSING**

Setting: Hospital Ward

Patient: You are 33 years old and were hospitalised two days ago due to a kidney infection. You feel a little better now, but still find it difficult to consume food or fluids. The doctor feels you are not ready to be discharged. You have two children at home who are being cared for by your husband/wife. You are desperate to go home, and are upset and angry about the situation.

Task:
- When asked by the nurse, explain why you want to be discharged (feeling better, can take medication/care of self at home, wish to be with/assist family).
- Resist the idea of staying in hospital and insist that you can continue the treatment at home with home visits if needed.
- Be difficult to convince, but reluctantly agree to stay if help can be provided for your family.

CANDIDATE CARD NO 2   **NURSING**

Setting: Hospital Ward

Nurse: You are speaking to a 33-year-old patient who was admitted two days ago, and was diagnosed with acute pyelonephritis (kidney inflammation due to bacterial infection). He/she has a fever, has not been able to eat or drink anything, and has been given intravenous therapy. He/she wants to be discharged from the hospital, but the doctor feels they are not fit to go home at present. The patient appears upset and agitated.

Task:
- Find out why the patient wants to be discharged early.
- Explain why staying in the hospital is necessary for their current condition (e.g. intravenous therapy needed because body rejecting food/fluids/oral medication, close monitoring of blood and urine to track infection, etc.).
- Try to persuade the patient to remain in hospital (e.g. potential kidney damage/failure, risk of blood poisoning, unable to provide care at home, etc.).
- Suggest home help be organised by hospital social worker for the family.

ROLEPLAYER CARD NO 1   **NURSING**

Setting: Community Health Centre

Patient: You are a 35-year-old vegetarian who does not cook owing to a hectic lifestyle, and mainly relies on ready meals for convenience. You drink 4–5 cups of coffee a day. Lately, you've been feeling exhausted. Your doctor has explained that you have anaemia (the number of red blood cells in your blood is low). You've now been asked to speak to a nurse for dietary suggestions.

Task:
- Explain to the nurse that you are confused by the diagnosis and how it relates to your diet (you choose vegetarian ready meals because you believe they are healthy).
- Answer the nurse's questions regarding your dietary routine (coffee for breakfast, frozen meals for lunch, coffee and cake for afternoon tea, rarely eat dinner).
- Be resistant to the nurse's suggestions as you dislike tofu and green leafy vegetables, and coffee helps you cope with the stress of work.
- Finally agree to the recommendations, but be adamant that you cannot reduce your coffee consumption.

CANDIDATE CARD NO 1   **NURSING**

Setting: Community Health Centre

Nurse: You are speaking with a 35-year-old who has recently been diagnosed with anaemia (haemoglobin is 8 g/dl). Their doctor has referred him/her to your centre for further advice concerning their condition and necessary dietary adjustments.

Task:
- Find out if the patient has any questions regarding the diagnosis.
- Explain that iron is only sourced from the diet and can be low in vegetarians without planning. Reassure the patient that it is treatable with dietary modification.
- Find out further details about the patient's dietary habits.
- Suggest ways in which the patient can increase his/her iron intake (e.g. beans, leafy green vegetables such as spinach/kale, tofu, iron fortified cereals, reduce consumption of coffee – inhibits absorption of iron). Discuss the importance of food combining as a compromise (allow one hour between consuming iron rich food and coffee to increase absorption; vitamin C at the same time as iron rich food).

ROLEPLAYER CARD NO 2   **NURSING**

Setting: Hospital Ward

Patient: You are a 40-year-old who is scheduled to undergo a colostomy later today. You have never had prior surgery and are frightened about the procedure. You've led a socially active life until now and believe the procedure will have a negative impact. You are also worried about the effects of the surgery on your ability to self-care.

Task:
- Express concern about your ability to return to normal life after having the procedure.
- Emphasise that you are embarrassed about wearing a colostomy pouch and are worried about participating in social activities.
- Ask what additional support is available.

CANDIDATE CARD NO 2   **NURSING**

Setting: Hospital Ward

Nurse: You are speaking to a 40-year-old patient who is scheduled to undergo a colostomy in your hospital later today. You have come to prepare the patient for surgery. This is the patient's first surgery and he/she appears anxious.

Task:
- Ask the patient if he/she has any final questions about the surgery.
- Explain the recovery process to the patient (3–10 days in hospital, education will be given re: care of colostomy pouch, light exercise only, low-fibre diet, sufficient rest, etc.).
- Reassure the patient that the surgery will not prevent his/her participation in any social activities (e.g. pouch can be well hidden, support provided by GP and district nurse for medical care, etc.).
- Explain that the Stoma Care Nurse will meet with the patient after surgery to discuss participating in stoma support groups.
- Outline the management plan to support.

PRACTICE
TESTS

Practice Test 1

Listening Sub-test

Occupational English Test: Listening Test

This test has three parts. In each part, you'll hear a number of different extracts. At the start of each extract, you'll hear this sound: —***—.

You'll have time to read the questions before you hear each extract and you'll hear each extract once only. Complete your answers as you listen.

At the end of the test, you'll have two minutes to check your answers.

Part A

In this part of the test, you'll hear two different extracts. In each extract, a health professional is talking to a patient.

For questions 1–24, complete the notes with the information you hear.

Now look at the notes for extract one.

Extract 1: Questions 1–12

You hear a neurologist talking to a patient called Vincent Cheung. For **questions 1–12**, complete the notes with a word or short phrase.

You now have 30 seconds to look at the notes.

Patient   Vincent Cheung

Initial symptoms

- facial pain – started three months ago
- pain described as **(1)** _____
- affects right side of face (cheek, teeth and **(2)** _____)
- compares the sensation to **(3)** _____

Triggers

- washing face, brushing teeth and **(4)** _____
- anything touching the face (including **(5)** _____)
- eating and drinking
- spontaneous or lengthy **(6)** _____

Development of condition

- attacks becoming more frequent
- whole face now affected
- attacks now last longer
- describes current level of pain as **(7)** _____

Medication

- initially prescribed **(8)** _____
- now on anti-spasmodic
- also taking supplements: vitamin D and **(9)** _____

Impact of medication

- feels constantly **(10)** _____
- easily becomes **(11)** _____ (cause of embarrassment)
- notices uncharacteristic **(12)** _____

Extract 2: Questions 13–24

You hear a pulmonologist talking to a patient called Pam Herbert. For **questions 13–24**, complete the notes with a word or short phrase.

You now have 30 seconds to look at the notes.

Patient   Pam Herbert

Presenting symptoms

- persistent cough – sputum **(13)** _____ in colour
- worse at night – leaves her feeling constantly **(14)** _____
- loss of appetite and weight
- can't **(15)** _____ for longer than ten minutes
- ribs feel painful after **(16)** _____
- sometimes has **(17)** _____ sensation in right arm

Recent illnesses

- flu (nine months ago) – developed into **(18)** _____
- several persistent **(19)** _____ recently

Background

- has smoked for 35 years (several cessation attempts)
- ongoing issues with **(20)** _____
- reports having no **(21)** _____ for at least ten years

Current medication

- **(22)** _____ (ten years)
- Salbutamol inhaler
- **(23)** _____ (one year)

Allergies

- lactose intolerant
- severe **(24)** _____

That is the end of Part A. Now look at Part B.

Part B

🎧 PT 1.2 **In this part of the test, you'll hear six different extracts. In each extract, you'll hear people talking in a different healthcare setting.**

For **questions 25–30**, choose the answer (**A, B or C**) which fits best according to what you hear. You'll have time to read each question before you listen. Complete your answers as you listen.

Now look at question 25.

---

25. You hear a nurse talking to a patient who is about to have a mammogram.
    What is the patient's main concern?

    Ⓐ when the results will be available

    Ⓑ the level of risk involved

    Ⓒ how painful it might be

26. You hear a doctor talking to a patient about a blood pressure monitor.
    What is she explaining to him?

    Ⓐ when to adjust the settings

    Ⓑ what to do when it's taking a reading

    Ⓒ how to check that it's working properly

27. You hear a dentist and her assistant talking about a problem with some sterilising equipment.
    What does she ask her assistant to do?

    Ⓐ inform staff that it isn't working properly

    Ⓑ call the people responsible for maintaining it

    Ⓒ check whether repairs are covered by insurance

28. You hear a GP talking to a patient with hay fever.
    What's making the patient most miserable?

    Ⓐ the intensity of the symptoms

    Ⓑ the attitude of her friends

    Ⓒ the effect on her work

29. You hear two nurses doing a patient handover at the change of shift.
    The incoming nurse needs to

    Ⓐ change the patient's infusion.

    Ⓑ monitor the patient's oxygen levels.

    Ⓒ arrange for the patient to have a special meal.

30. You hear a hospital manager briefing newly recruited staff about patient safety.
    What is he doing?

    Ⓐ explaining how individual incidents should be documented

    Ⓑ comparing the role of record keeping in different contexts

    Ⓒ emphasising the need to identify and deal with potential issues

That is the end of Part B. Now look at Part C.

Part C

In this part of the test, you'll hear two different extracts. In each extract, you'll hear health professionals talking about aspects of their work.

For **questions 31–42**, choose the answer (**A, B or C**) which fits best according to what you hear. Complete your answers as you listen.

Now look at extract one.

Extract 1: Questions 31–36

You will hear an interview with a midwife called Christina Morello, who is talking about the time she spent working as a volunteer in South Sudan.

You now have 90 seconds to read questions 31–36.

31. When she was thinking of applying to go to South Sudan, Christina was most concerned about whether

    (A) her skills would be required.

    (B) she would miss her home and family.

    (C) she would be put in a dangerous situation.

32. What aspect of her role in South Sudan surprised Christina?

    (A) the long working hours

    (B) the impact on the local people

    (C) the number of births she had to deal with

33. Christina suggests that complicated deliveries in South Sudan are related to

    (A) use of poor equipment.

    (B) lack of contraception.

    (C) shortages in funding.

34. Christina talks about a patient called Margaret in order to highlight the

    (A) high risk of infection.

    (B) high infant mortality rates.

    (C) importance of communication skills.

35. Christina says that the hardest thing to adapt to in South Sudan was

    (A) the hygiene facilities.

    (B) the presence of insects.

    (C) having to stay in every night.

36. In Christina's opinion, what is the most valuable skill for a midwife working in South Sudan?

    (A) having a wide range of professional experience

    (B) taking a flexible approach to your work

    (C) being able to speak the local language

Now look at extract two.

You hear a GP called Dr Edward Symes giving a presentation about how the condition called Myalgic Encephalomyelitis (ME) affects young people.

You now have 90 seconds to read questions 37–42.

37. How did Dr Symes feel about the girl called Emma having ME?

   Ⓐ concerned about the effect it was having on her life

   Ⓑ curious about what her actual symptoms were

   Ⓒ upset about how her teachers had reacted

38. Dr Symes decided to specialise in ME because he came to realise that

   Ⓐ no effective treatment existed for it.

   Ⓑ so many families were affected by it.

   Ⓒ there was a lot of ignorance surrounding it.

39. Dr Symes feels that a reliable diagnostic test for ME would be helpful because

   Ⓐ it could lead to the illness being taken more seriously.

   Ⓑ patients could be educated to adjust to the illness.

   Ⓒ the severity of a patient's condition could be determined.

40. Dr Symes thinks that the most challenging aspect of the illness is the way

   Ⓐ it is exacerbated by social and psychological factors.

   Ⓑ its effects on the individual can be difficult to predict.

   Ⓒ it places pressure on close relationships.

41. What does Dr Symes think GPs should do to help patients manage ME?

   Ⓐ encourage them to have a healthy lifestyle

   Ⓑ ensure they understand how the illness develops

   Ⓒ continuously experiment with different approaches

42. What reservations does Dr Symes have about the use of CBT?

   Ⓐ It can cause irreversible damage.

   Ⓑ It's inconsistent with what is known about the illness.

   Ⓒ More research needs to be carried out into its effectiveness.

That is the end of Part C.

You now have two minutes to check your answers.

That is the end of the Listening test.

Reading Sub-test

Part A

Time: 15 minutes

Look at the four texts, **A–D**, in the separate **Text Booklet** that follows.

For each question, 1–20, look through the texts, **A–D**, to find the relevant information.

Write your answers on the spaces provided in the **Question Paper**.

Answer all the questions within the 15-minute time limit.

Your answers should be correctly spelled.

Blood Transfusion: Questions

Questions 1–7

For each question, **1–7**, decide which text (**A, B, C or D**) the information comes from. You may use any letter more than once.

In which text can you find information about

1. the type of IV line to use for a transfusion? _____
2. what to check before administering a transfusion? _____
3. recognising the severity of adverse reactions? _____
4. transfusion rates for different blood products? _____
5. what patient information to record? _____
6. how to respond if a patient becomes unwell during a transfusion? _____
7. storage of blood products? _____

Questions 8–13

Answer each of the questions, **8–13**, with a word or short phrase from one of the texts. Each answer may include words, numbers or both.

8. If a transfusion needs to be stopped, what should you use to maintain the IV?

_____

9. How soon after a transfusion starts should you check a patient?

_____

10. How long does transfusion of one unit of red cells in additive solution usually take?

_____

11. Before a transfusion, what should the patient be warned of?

_____

12. What should be used as an antidote to warfarin?

_____

13. At what rate is Fresh Frozen Plasma usually infused?

_____

Questions 14–20

Complete each of the sentences, **14–20**, with a word or short phrase from one of the texts. Each answer may include words, numbers or both.

14. Circulatory overload is classed as a _____ reaction.

15. For children, an administration set with a _____ should be used.

16. Hb concentration can be increased by _____ if a 4 mL/kg dose of red cells in additive solution is given.

17. The usual administration rate for cryoprecipitate is _____ per hour.

18. A patient showing signs of hypotension requires _____.

19. Blood which has been unrefrigerated for more than _____ should not be used.

20. If a patient develops a rash, they can be given _____ initially.

End of Part A

This question paper will be collected.

Reading Sub-test – Text Booklet: Part A

Blood Transfusion: Texts

Text A Management of Blood Component Transfusion

Technical advice

- Blood **must not** be transfused more than 4 hours after removal from fridge.
- Blood must be returned to blood fridge within 30 minutes if transfusion is not taking place.
- Gravity or infusion pumps may be used.
- Giving sets must be changed every 12 hours **or** at the end of a transfusion (whichever is shorter).

Transfusion reactions

Ensure you are familiar with signs and symptoms of an adverse transfusion reaction and appropriate action to take.

Pre-transfusion procedure

The following checks must be carried out by two qualified staff for each unit at the patient's bedside:

Step 1:	Step 2:
<ul><li>Prescription completed and signed by doctor</li><li>Blood unit number against compatibility form – this form must **never** be used to verify patient ID</li><li>Blood group of bag against compatibility form</li><li>Expiry date of unit</li><li>Prescription for special requirements</li></ul>	<ul><li>Ask patient to state full name and date of birth (where competent).</li><li>Check wristband against details and compatibility label on blood bag.</li><li>Sign and complete all documentation.</li><li>If blood groups of blood unit and patient do not match, **do not transfuse**.</li></ul>

Blood transfusion observations

Vital signs (Blood Pressure, Temperature, Respiratory Rate and Pulse) **must** be recorded on the assessment chart for **all** blood component transfusions:

- Immediately prior to transfusion
- 'Early check' 15 minutes after start of transfusion
- At the end of each unit

Text B Intravenous Access

- Use peripheral or central venous catheters. Flow rate is reduced by narrow lumen catheters and long peripherally inserted central catheters (PICC lines).
- Use administration set with a 170–200 µm integral mesh filter. For paediatric administration, use sets with smaller prime.
- Platelets should not be transfused through a set previously used for other blood components. A new administration set should be used if blood components are followed by another infusion fluid. Change administration sets at least every 12 hours to reduce the risk of bacterial infection.
- Blood and other solutions can be infused through the separate lumens of multi-lumen central venous catheters. Where possible, one lumen should be reserved for the administration of blood components.

Text C Blood component administration to adults

Blood component	Administration notes
Red cells in additive solution	• Safe transfusion rate is typically 90–120 minutes per unit. • A dose of 4 mL/kg raises Hb concentration by 10 g/L. • For major haemorrhage, rapid transfusion (1 unit = 5–10 minutes) may be required.
Platelets	• One adult therapeutic dose (ATD) raises the platelet count by 20–40 x 10^9/L. • Usually transfused over 30–60 minutes per ATD • Should not be transfused through giving-set used for other blood components. • Start transfusion as soon as component arrives in the clinical area.
Fresh Frozen Plasma (FFP)	• Dose typically 12–15 mL/kg • Infusion rate typically 10–20 mL/kg/hour • Patients receiving FFP must have careful haemodynamic monitoring. • Do not use FFP to reverse warfarin (prothrombin complex is an effective antidote).
Cryoprecipitate	• Typical adult dose is two five-donor pools (ten single-donor units). • Will raise fibrinogen concentration by approximately 1 g/L in average adult • Typically administered at 10–20 mL/kg/hour (30–60 min per five-unit pool)

Text D Adverse Transfusion Reactions

- Before transfusion, inform the patient of potential adverse reactions.
- Management for all symptoms: stop transfusion immediately, maintain IV access at 0.9% sodium chloride, go through procedure checklist, record observation, provide patient care.

Category 1: Mild	Signs / symptoms	Management
Allergic	urticaria/rash, pruritis (itching)	1. Evaluate patient. 2. Consider antihistamine. 3. Restart if no other symptoms. 4. If symptoms worsen, treat as Category 2.
Category 2: Moderate / severe		
Allergic (moderately severe) Febrile Non-Haemolytic	facial flushing, urticaria, fever, rigors, pruritis, anxiety, tachycardia, restlessness, headache, (mild) dyspnoea, palpitations, vomiting	1. Contact Medical Officer. 2. Consider antihistamine / paracetamol. 3. Further investigation and management. 4. Return blood pack & document to bank.
Category 3: Life-threatening		
Acute Intravascular Haemolysis Bacterial Contamination and Septic Shock Circulatory Overload Anaphylaxis Transfusion-Related Lung Injury (TRALI) Hypotension	rigors/chills, fever, erythema, tachycardia, edema, restlessness, dark urine, unexplained bleeding (DIC), chest pain, pain at IV site, loin/back pain, headache, vomiting dyspnoea, respiratory distress	1. Contact Medical Officer (use emergency number if necessary). 2. Attend to immediate needs: Fluid for hypotension / Oxygen / Adrenaline for anaphylaxis / Diuretic for overload. 3. Return blood pack and document to bank.

End of Part A

This test booklet will be collected.

In this part of the test, there are six short extracts relating to the work of health professionals. For questions 1–6, choose the answer (A, B or C) which you think fits best according to the text.

1. The email reminds physicians prescribing controlled drugs that they should

    (A) document the reasons for doing so.

    (B) ensure that there is no record of addiction.

    (C) discuss the dangers of sharing medication.

To: Prescribing physicians

Re: Controlled Drug (CD) Prescriptions

This is a polite reminder that when prescribing CDs, the benefits for the patient must be weighed against the risks, which include dependency, overdose and diversion. All medication currently being taken by the patient should be considered and, if necessary, further advice and information from other healthcare professionals should be sought.

A prescription exceeding a 30-day supply should not be given, other than in exceptional circumstances, which must be entered on the patient's notes. The prescriber must note and ensure that the patient (or administering carer) understands how long he or she is expected to take the medication, how long it will take to have an effect and why it has been prescribed. It should also be made clear that the medication is intended solely for the patient.

---

2. The extract from the policy document states that decontamination of equipment

    (A) must be done by official suppliers.

    (B) should occur outside the hospital.

    (C) may not always be necessary.

3.4.2 Decontamination of equipment prior to service or repair

Anyone who inspects, repairs or transports medical equipment has a right to expect that it has been appropriately treated in order to remove or minimise the risk of infection or other hazards. Appropriate documentation must be provided to indicate the contamination status of the item.

If items are dispatched to suppliers or presented for service or inspection on hospital premises without a declaration of status and without prior agreement, they may be rejected until the appropriate paperwork has been provided.

In particular situations, for example when the condition of an item which is the subject of complaint or investigation may be altered or influenced by neutralisation process, the investigator may wish the item not to be decontaminated.

---

3. According to the guidance notes, an assessment should be offered if a patient is

    (A) unsteady on their feet.

    (B) at risk in their home.

    (C) visually impaired.

Preventing falls

Elderly patients should be routinely asked whether they have fallen in the past year, and about the frequency, context and characteristics of any such fall/s. Those responding positively should be observed for balance and gait deficits and considered for their capacity to benefit from interventions to improve strength and balance. If an abnormality is identified, a multifactorial assessment should be offered. This would check a variety of possible contributing factors, including loss of sight, osteoporosis, muscle weakness and urinary incontinence. An evaluation on the safety of the home may also be carried out and, if hazards are identified, intervention may take place.

4. The extract from the guidelines establishes that a personal search can be carried out if a patient has

   Ⓐ a criminal record.

   Ⓑ self-harmed in the past.

   Ⓒ hidden a dangerous item before.

Personal search procedure

We are required to provide an environment which is safe and secure for patients, staff and visitors. Conducting a personal search of a patient and/or their belongings is a delicate and potentially provocative procedure, which should be managed with the utmost integrity and highest professional standards at all times.

A decision to carry out a search can be made if the following indicators apply:

- A patient has threatened to injure another person with an offensive weapon.
- Information has been received that the patient has an offensive weapon in their possession.
- A patient is behaving in a threatening and unpredictable manner and is reluctant to give any information or cooperate with a search.
- A patient has a known recent history of carrying or concealing an offensive weapon.
- There is reason to believe that the patient is concealing an item that is a potential threat to their own health and safety or that of others.

5. The guidance states that young people with recurrent UTIs

   Ⓐ should be involved in any decision-making process.

   Ⓑ sometimes prefer sweet products to antibiotics.

   Ⓒ may need to review their hygiene routines.

Guidance: Treatment for children and young people under 16 with recurrent UTIs

Ensure first that any current UTI has been effectively treated. If behavioural and self-care measures alone are neither appropriate nor effective, then trialling a daily antibiotic prophylaxis should be considered.

After having carried out specialist investigations and assessment, take into account any underlying causes, previous antibiotic use, urine culture and susceptibility results, as well as severity and frequency of previous symptoms. Risks of long-term antibiotic use and developing complications should be discussed with the patient, as well as their preferences.

Some patients may wish to try cranberry products, although evidence of benefit is uncertain. A warning should be given about the sugar content of these products.

6.   The guidelines state that care home residents should

(A)   be given responsibility for their own oral hygiene.

(B)   be consulted about their oral hygiene routine.

(C)   be visited by an oral hygiene specialist.

Oral health care guidelines

An oral health assessment must be given to all residents on arrival at the home, and the results should be recorded in their care plan. The oral health assessment tool should be used, and it may be appropriate to involve family and friends if they are involved in ongoing care. Oral hygiene should be discussed with the patient and the following information collected and recorded:

- how daily mouth care is usually managed and whether support is required
- which dental aids are used
- whether the patient wears dentures (or partial dentures) and whether they are marked or unmarked
- the name and address of their dentist and when they were last seen

Oral healthcare needs should be regularly reviewed and updated. Residents' teeth should be brushed at least twice a day, using a fluoride toothpaste and the patient's own choice of cleaning products for dentures. Dentures should be cleaned (brushed and debris removed) and removed overnight.

In this part of the test, there are two texts about different aspects of healthcare. For **questions 7–22**, choose the answer (**A, B, C** or **D**) which you think fits best according to the text.

Text 1: Egg Freezing

During the last 70 years, global life expectancy has increased from less than 30 years to over 70. This creates new possibilities for many aspects of people's lives, but however long life is, the decision of when to have children often remains a sticking point, not least because the fertility window isn't lengthening in step with lifespans. Egg-freezing is a new technique that could be a game changer. In theory, it allows women to stop their biological clock for a decade or more, and gives them the gift of being able to pick and choose the optimum moment to have a child, for example when it fits in with a career.

The first live human births from previously frozen eggs occurred during the late 1980s. High failure rates and concerns that freezing would damage chromosomes and cause birth defects kept egg freezing on the sidelines for a decade. However, a new and more reliable technique called vitrification has been shown to be more effective than the older method. It involves a very rapid freezing process, which is thought to cause less damage to the eggs and therefore increase the chances of achieving a pregnancy when the eggs are thawed. It has made egg freezing seem a feasible option for women seeking to win time before having a family.

However, egg freezing presents ethical challenges and therefore isn't being widely promoted for healthy women. Questions surrounding access have been raised and fertility experts are in a quandary. Some say that the procedure should be reserved only for women who need to freeze their eggs on medical grounds – for example, those about to have certain types of cancer treatment that will cause irreversible damage to their ovaries. There are also problems related to the ways in which the media portrays egg freezing and the implications for society as a whole if it is normalised or mandated. One thing is for certain, at approximately US$ 7500 for a cycle of hormone treatment, egg harvesting, and freezing, it's likely to become the preserve of a privileged few who can afford it; yet another misgiving to add to the case against it.

The city of Urayasu in Japan has made the controversial decision to pay for women to freeze their eggs in response to a shrinking and ageing population in the context of a very low national birth rate and the problems that ensue. A three-year pilot project has been announced, and it will use public money to cover 80 per cent of the costs for female residents aged between 25 and 34. The aim is to boost fertility rates by facilitating delayed childbearing, and the eggs will be used up to the age of 45. This is the first 'social' egg freezing subsidy programme of its kind, and hopefully the last. Egg freezing offers a short-term, naïve solution to the problem. The practice targets individuals and so fails to address the need for social and structural changes to entice people to become parents when they are younger: paid parental leave, flexible work schedules, affordable housing and childcare to name but a few. These issues are broad, complex and underlie the need for egg freezing in the first place.

When it comes to success rates for the procedure, the deciding factor is the age at which women have their eggs frozen. Egg vitrification is best performed before the age of 36 because the quality of women's eggs deteriorates over time. Whilst some clinics are claiming rates of live births to women using their own frozen eggs of between 40% and 60%, fertility experts have pointed out that there is some confusion over the statistics themselves, with the result that some women are placing too much confidence in this nascent freezing technique. Data on successful births from frozen eggs is limited, variable, and much debated, but most research suggests a success rate of between 5% and 15%.

Those who opt to freeze their eggs will have to resort to IVF, which poses additional risks and costs. Most of the symptoms (restlessness, hot flushes, headaches) are mild, although there is also a very small risk of ovarian hyperstimulation syndrome – a potentially fatal complication that can result from the hormone injections used to obtain eggs for freezing. Meanwhile, there are concerns about the risks of multiple pregnancies that may occur if doctors attempt to compensate for the lower efficiency of IVF with a frozen egg by putting several embryos into a woman's womb at once. These risks are localised, however, and may distract attention from the broader issue of the risk to society. After all, playing with our demography could be a dangerous game.

Text 1: Questions 7–14

7. In the first paragraph, the writer suggests that egg freezing will make it easier for women to

    (A) decide whether to have a baby.

    (B) manage their time efficiently.

    (C) conceive more frequently.

    (D) extend their fertility.

8. In the second paragraph, the writer implies that the introduction of the process called vitrification will lead to

    (A) fewer complications in associated pregnancies.

    (B) egg freezing becoming a viable choice.

    (C) more full-term babies being born.

    (D) healthier eggs being produced.

9. In the third paragraph, the 'quandary' mentioned in relation to egg freezing concerns

    (A) the moral question as to who should have access.

    (B) the high costs associated with the procedure.

    (C) the risk of its becoming an entitlement.

    (D) the people making the final decision.

10. In the third paragraph, the writer criticises the provision of egg freezing because

    (A) expecting taxpayers to fund it is unreasonable.

    (B) it will eventually become a money-making scheme.

    (C) women who are well off will be at a distinct advantage.

    (D) it should be only for those requiring it on medical grounds.

11. What reservation does the writer express about the programme in Urayasu?

    (A) It overlooks the causes of the current demographic problems.

    (B) Public money is better spent on assisting childless couples.

    (C) It is likely to exacerbate the problem in years to come.

    (D) The time scales involved are inadequate.

12. In the fourth paragraph, what does the phrase 'these issues' refer to?

    (A) declining birth rates

    (B) a lack of support for parents

    (C) a reluctance to have children

    (D) the financial burden of raising a family

13. In the fifth paragraph, the writer suggests that success rates in egg freezing

(A) are anticipated to rise.

(B) are open to misinterpretation.

(C) could be impossible to measure.

(D) might vary according to the clinic.

14. In the sixth paragraph, the writer suggests that the risks associated with egg freezing

(A) are relatively small compared to other fertility treatments.

(B) depend on the expertise of the particular clinician.

(C) remain the responsibility of the individual patient.

(D) are more fundamental than people realise.

Text 2: Circadian rhythms

In this era of global travel, 24-hour shift patterns and insomnia-inducing gadgets, the awarding of the Nobel Prize for work on the mechanisms controlling circadian rhythms was entirely appropriate. Circadian rhythms are the internal clocks that living organisms use to track the day-night cycle and they are synchronised with solar time. All life on Earth has evolved on a planet that spins on its axis once every 24 hours, and as different parts of its surface face the sun, bringing warmth and light, conditions can change dramatically. Virtually every living organism anticipates these fluctuations and adapts to optimise its behaviour and physiology. The existence of this internal clock was first discovered in 1729 when the French scientist Jean-Jaques d'Ortous de Mairan found that mimosa plants opened their leaves during the day and closed them again at night, even when kept in cold, dark conditions around the clock.

Because circadian rhythms control so many of our biological processes, they have profound implications for our understanding of disease and all-round well-being. Many metabolic pathways, including hunger, pain thresholds and productivity, peak and ebb in specific patterns and they are regulated by peripheral clocks and interactions with other organs. Circadian health has been linked to the risk of diabetes, cardiovascular disease and neuro-degeneration. It is also known that the timing of meals and drugs rounds can influence metabolisation, meaning that the delivery of chemotherapy and blood-pressure drugs can be timed to achieve optimum effect at lower doses, minimising the risk of side effects.

The internal body clock can fall out of sync or weaken as we grow older or due to a range of disorders, but it can also be disrupted as a result of lifestyle. One study has suggested that normal reproductive cycles can be disturbed by having irregular sleep patterns, for example using the weekend to catch up on a sleep debt accumulated during the working week. Whilst we are still somewhat in the dark and haven't yet fully understood the mechanisms behind it, it appears that unsettling a woman's circadian rhythms may impact reproductive hormone secretion. Changing sleep and wake times leads to mistiming when the body is expecting to sleep and be exposed to light. We already know that female shift-workers are more prone to irregular menstrual cycles, difficulties falling pregnant and miscarriages, and evidence is now pointing to circadian rhythms as the culprit. These cycles also regulate inflammation, which could explain the link discovered by irregular sleep patterns and menstrual pain.

More recent research has raised the question of whether disturbances to the circadian rhythm could influence cancer survival rates. Breast cancer has a survival rate of up to 99% when detected in the early stages. However, if it is metastatic, meaning that it is spreading to other parts of the body, the rate plummets to just 26%. This points to an urgent need for a greater understanding of how it travels. The answer could lie in a circadian rhythm gene, known as ArnH2. Ken Hunter from the National Cancer Institute, in Maryland USA, discovered that active variants of this gene appear to be associated with the advancement of cancer. He claims that this raises the possibility that disruption to our circadian rhythms might affect metastasis in cancer cells, therefore lowering chances of survival.

Many critically ill patients suffer from circadian disrhythmia, a sleep disturbance that negatively impacts cellular and organ function, and this often exacerbates a condition. It is now looking increasingly likely that this vicious circle can be addressed using a cheap and effective remedy: light. Recent research by Klaus Martiny of the Psychiatric Centre in Copenhagen has shown that people being treated in hospital for severe depression were discharged almost twice as quickly if their rooms were south-west facing and therefore 17 to 20 times brighter. Although the precise mechanism is not known, it is believed to be connected to exposure to the morning light, which advances and stabilises their sleep-wake cycles.

Other experiments have had equally positive outcomes, including one which was carried out in an attempt to strengthen the sluggish circadian clock in sufferers of Parkinson's. This discovery could change the shape of medicine to come. Most hospitals have small windows and 24-hour lighting, both of which could exacerbate health problems, so several hospitals in Europe and the USA are installing dynamic 'solid-state' lighting, which emulates the 24-hour cycle of daylight. Such lights can, for example, shine whitish-blue in the morning, grow warmer and dimmer throughout the day, and turn orange or switch off at night. They have been shown to assist with depression and fatigue, creating an effect comparable to prescribing antidepressants.

These developments in our understanding of how our body clock operates and how it can be manipulated positively to impact on many aspects of our health open up a wide range of possibilities for integrating time into bespoke, individualised medicine. Medical researchers envision circadian health tests becoming part of routine health checks and rhythms becoming a consideration when scheduling surgery, vaccinations and medication. All this is happening at the same time as technological advances, which allow us to exploit the full potential of our knowledge.

Text 2: Questions 15–22

15. What is suggested about circadian rhythms in the first paragraph?
    (A) People's lifestyles still tend to follow them.
    (B) An award has brought them to public attention.
    (C) They are particularly affected by global location.
    (D) Studying them has proved to be very worthwhile.

16. In the second paragraph, the writer explains that greater insight into circadian rhythms leads to
    (A) better management of public health.
    (B) cures being found for certain diseases.
    (C) medications being used more efficiently.
    (D) people being able to regulate their weight.

17. In the third paragraph, the writer says that disruption to circadian rhythms may
    (A) make it harder for women to conceive.
    (B) cause the body to age prematurely.
    (C) lead to more frequent infections.
    (D) affect females more than males.

18. In the fourth paragraph, what point does the writer make about cancer?
    (A) The speed at which it moves in the body is determined by DNA.
    (B) Patients will be able to play a greater role in limiting its progression.
    (C) Fluctuating sleep patterns could lead to a higher risk of mortality.
    (D) It will soon be possible to predict its level of advancement.

19. In the fifth paragraph, the expression 'vicious circle' is used to stress the fact that
    (A) sleep deprivation is a heavy financial burden for health services to carry.
    (B) sleeping disorders associated with certain illnesses can worsen them.
    (C) patients with mental illnesses often suffer from disrupted sleep.
    (D) poor sleep leads to a sharp deterioration in overall health.

20. In the sixth paragraph, the writer suggests that solid-state lighting
    - (A) can be used in an impressive range of healthcare settings.
    - (B) gives patients a more positive experience in hospital.
    - (C) could change the way certain conditions are treated.
    - (D) is more effective than prescribing medication.

21. The phrase 'This discovery' in the sixth paragraph refers to the idea that
    - (A) there is a link between well-lit hospitals and high-quality care.
    - (B) consistent exposure to brightness can lead to faster recovery.
    - (C) colour treatments may be the next important breakthrough.
    - (D) illumination can be used in the treatment of certain illnesses.

22. What does the writer highlight in the final paragraph?
    - (A) New findings will influence the care we offer patients.
    - (B) Treatment programmes require radical transformation.
    - (C) Patients will be offered personalised treatment options.
    - (D) Up-to-date equipment is needed to keep pace with expertise.

End of Reading test

This booklet will be collected.

Writing Sub-test

Read the case notes and complete the writing task which follows.

Notes

Mr Bob Warren is a 73-year-old patient in your ward. You are the charge nurse.

Patient Details

Name: Bob Warren

Date of birth: 02/09/1945

Admission date: 12 June 2017

Discharge date: 16 June 2017

Reason for admission:

   Right Total Knee Replacement (TKR)

Marital status:

   Married (to Angela Warren, 64-year-old ex-school teacher)

Social background:

   Lives with wife and 2 dogs in three-storey house
   4 adult children, 2 daughters live nearby, other daughter visits regularly, rarely sees son – resides Hong Kong
   Wife (supportive) does all cooking and housework
   Car mechanic for 53 years – retired 1 year ago
   Enjoys walking dogs, watching football, travelling, spending time with wife and daughters
   Enjoys red wine and Indian take-aways
   Feeling depressed recently – feels stuck in house. On waiting list for physio and surgery for total 3 years.
   Frustrated – gained weight (8 kg) as result.

Medical background:

   Feb–Nov 2016 – IM steroid every 3 months (osteoarthritis)
   October 2010 – coronary angioplasty
   September 2010 – mild myocardial infarction
   March 2001 – right knee injury playing football (knee occasionally giving way)

Medications

   Rivaroxaban 10 mg orally once per day (anticoagulant)
   Atorvastatin 40 mg orally at night (statin)
   Aspirin 75 mg orally once per day (analgesic)
   Tylenol 3 360 mg four times per day (analgesic)
   Fludrocortisone 0.1 mg once per day (for hypotension)

Nursing management and progress:

Dry dressing changed daily

Post-op complicated by significant postural hypotension (88/60 mmHg)

Compression stockings issued

Exercises set by physiotherapist – needs encouragement with compliance due to pain

Attend clinic in 2 weeks (1/7/17 10 am) for full review and removal of stitches

Assessment:

Mobility limited – uses stairs with considerable difficulty

Mobility on flat ground good with frame

Very low BP post-op (90/59)

Patient depressed before surgery – now in high spirits

High cholesterol

Approximately 15 kg overweight

Discharge plan:

- Community nurse to visit home and change dry dressing daily until removal of stitches
- Monitor compliance with exercise programme
- Use pain medication when necessary (patient reluctant – please monitor)
- Keep BP diary for full medication review in 2 weeks
- Compression stockings to be worn until review
- Medical equipment provided: frame, crutches and toilet raiser
- Patient instructed on wound care (must be kept dry until stitches removed) and no driving for six weeks

Writing task

Using the information in the case notes, write a referral letter to Mrs Gillian Dorey, Community Nurse, Sandhurst Medical Centre, Albion Road, Sandhurst, outlining relevant information for the continued care of Mr Warren.

In your answer:

- expand the relevant notes into complete sentences
- do not use note form
- use letter format

The body of the letter should be approximately 180–200 words.

Speaking Sub-test

ROLEPLAYER CARD NO 1   **NURSING**

Setting: Hospital Ward

Carer: You are the son/daughter of an 82-year-old woman, who had bunion surgery two weeks ago. Your mother is coming to live with you for six months, so you can care for her while she recovers.

Task:
- Respond to the nurse's question by saying you are not sure what level of care will be required.
- Respond in surprise and concern at the amount of care required (worried you will make a mistake or won't be able to manage physically or emotionally).
- Find out why your mother needs to wear a surgical boot.
- Ask the nurse to explain the medicine and how it should be taken.

CANDIDATE CARD NO 1   **NURSING**

Setting: Hospital Ward

Nurse: You are speaking to the son/daughter of an 82-year-old female patient who had bunion surgery two weeks ago. The patient will be in the son/daughter's care for the six-month recovery period.

Task:
- Find out how prepared the son/daughter feels for their mother's discharge to their home.
- Explain the mother's needs for the first eight weeks (NSAIDs/painkillers, dressing changes, mobility, personal hygiene, meal preparation).
- Reassure the son/daughter that it is manageable, and give advice on strategies which will make caring for their mother easier (set up a routine, get a medicine organiser, ensure she has everything she needs nearby and wears a surgical boot).
- Explain the role of the surgical boot (protects the foot).
- Explain the painkillers and anti-inflammatory drugs x 1 naproxen (painkiller & anti-inflammatory) every 12 hours, ibuprofen (painkiller and anti-inflammatory) x 2 every 4 hours, not to exceed 8/day.

ROLEPLAYER CARD NO 2   NURSING

Setting: General Practice

Parent: You are the parent of a four-year-old boy, who has just put a rusty nail through his hand whilst playing at the local park. Your child is very upset and does not want to receive the necessary tetanus injection.

Task:
- Explain that it happened about 25 minutes ago at the local park, when he picked up a plank of wood to play with. You removed his hand from the nail.
- Say that you don't want your son to receive the tetanus injection now because it's too stressful.
- Explain that you forgot to bring him for his childhood vaccination and tell the nurse that you would prefer your partner to come after work to support you.
- Reluctantly agree to your son having the injection.

CANDIDATE CARD NO 2   NURSING

Setting: General Practice

Nurse: You are the Nurse at a General Practice. A parent comes to see you with their four-year-old son, who has just put a rusty nail through his hand whilst playing at the local park. He needs to have a tetanus injection immediately but is distressed and refusing to have it.

Task:
- Find out the details of the incident.
- Explain that you need to clean and dress the wound and that he will need a tetanus injection.
- Explain why the child needs the injection immediately (did not receive it as part of childhood vaccination programme, deep wound, foreign bodies present).
- Persuade the parent to allow their child to have it now and warn about the potential risks of tetanus (fatal disease, causes seizures, muscle stiffness, lockjaw, difficulty breathing). Offer your support and reassurance.
- After giving the injection, explain the rare and mild side-effects (feeling achy/tired, mild nausea / light-headedness).

Listening Sub-test

PT
2.1

Occupational English Test: Listening Test

This test has three parts. In each part you'll hear a number of different extracts. At the start of each extract, you'll hear this sound: ---***---.

You'll have time to read the questions before you hear each extract and you'll hear each extract **once only**. Complete your answers as you listen.

At the end of the test, you'll have two minutes to check your answers.

Part A

In this part of the test, you'll hear two different extracts. In each extract, a health professional is talking to a patient.

For questions 1–24, complete the notes with the information you hear.

Now look at the notes for extract one.

Extract 1: Questions 1–12

You hear a gastroenterologist talking to a patient called Martin Rush. For **questions 1–12**, complete the notes with a word or short phrase.

You now have 30 seconds to look at the notes.

Patient   Martin Rush

Symptoms

- troubled by severe **(1)** _____ (especially after meals)
- brings up **(2)** _____
- frequent belching and burping
- constantly feels **(3)** _____
- pain on **(4)** _____
- discomfort when lying down (especially at night)
- no sickness or diarrhoea

Management of condition

- taking **(5)** _____ (over the counter)
- dietary changes
- reduced **(6)** _____ intake
- having a **(7)** _____ after dinner

Patient's concerns

- worried that he may have **(8)** _____
- doesn't want to lose weight and fitness
- effect on his job **(9)** _____ (in the construction industry)
- anxious about the possible need for surgery

Medical history

- childhood **(10)** _____
- food poisoning when travelling four years ago (Central Asia)
- **(11)** _____ last year (whilst moving furniture)

Medication

- On ramipril for three years
- Regular ibuprofen for **(12)** _____ pain

Extract 2: Questions 13–24

You hear a physiotherapist talking to a patient called Sally Winter. For **questions 13–24**, complete the notes with a word or short phrase.

You now have 30 seconds to look at the notes.

Patient   Sally Winter

Symptoms

- tingling pain in right arm below **(13)** _____
  - commenced five years ago
- pain sometimes extends to **(14)** _____
- pain severe when cycling (braking and turning corners)
- unable to perform everyday tasks, e.g. **(15)** _____
- **(16)** _____ described as weak

Pain management

- ice packs and resting the arm (no longer effective)
- **(17)** _____ advised by a friend (most effective)
- over-the-counter pain relief (for work)

Treatment by chiropractor

- ball squeezes
- stretches with **(18)** _____ on hand
- lifting a weight up and down slowly

Medical history

- **(19)** _____ as a child
- **(20)** _____ – two years ago (climbing holiday in Spain)
- episodes of **(21)** _____ over past five years linked to
  - relationship break-up
  - bereavement (brother died from **(22)** _____)

Patient's concerns

- unconvinced that physiotherapy will help
- would like treatment via **(23)** _____
- keen to discuss **(24)** _____ as a further option

That is the end of Part A. Now look at Part B.

Part B

In this part of the test, you'll hear six different extracts. In each extract, you'll hear people talking in a different healthcare setting.

For **questions 25–30**, choose the answer (**A, B or C**) which fits best according to what you hear. You'll have time to read each question before you listen. Complete your answers as you listen.

Now look at question 25.

---

25. You hear a nurse talking to a patient whose six-month-old baby is having childhood immunisations.

    What is the nurse emphasising?

    Ⓐ the fact that it's a safe procedure

    Ⓑ which adverse reactions could be dangerous

    Ⓒ the importance of the booster immunisations

26. You hear a pharmacist talking to a customer about an emergency contraceptive.

    What is the patient's main concern?

    Ⓐ feeling ill at work

    Ⓑ vomiting after taking the pill

    Ⓒ obtaining a second prescription

27. You hear a practice manager talking to a physiotherapist who is about to carry out a home visit.

    What should the physiotherapist do before he leaves the practice?

    Ⓐ find out why the patient hasn't attended treatment sessions

    Ⓑ ensure that the patient's paperwork is up to date

    Ⓒ inform a family member of his intended visit

28. You hear an occupational therapist talking to a patient who has recently suffered a stroke.

    The patient is worried that the spasms in his hand will

    Ⓐ affect his mobility.

    Ⓑ worsen over time.

    Ⓒ lead to an injury.

29. You hear a GP talking to a patient at a community practice.

    The patient wants to establish whether

    Ⓐ she can accompany her daughter on future visits.

    Ⓑ she's entitled to information about her daughter.

    Ⓒ her daughter was informed about her rights.

30. You hear a senior nurse talking to the staff at a care home about the use of hoists.

    What is she highlighting?

    Ⓐ the importance of documenting a procedure

    Ⓑ the difficulty in maintaining patient safety

    Ⓒ the complexity of the training required

This is the end of Part B. Now look at Part C.

Part C

PT 2.3 In this part of the test, you'll hear two different extracts. In each extract, you'll hear health professionals talking about aspects of their work.

For **questions 31–42**, choose the answer (**A, B or C**) which fits best according to what you hear. Complete your answers as you listen.

Now look at extract one.

Extract 1: Questions 31–36

You hear an interview with a bio-engineer called Mark Kendall, who's developed a new method of administering vaccinations called a 'nanopatch'.

You now have 90 seconds to read questions 31–36.

31. Mark says that the needle and syringe vaccination method needs to be updated because
   Ⓐ patients are complaining that it's too painful.
   Ⓑ it's becoming less effective in protecting against new diseases.
   Ⓒ people who are frightened of needles are not being immunised.

32. Mark says the nanopatch is particularly successful at delivering vaccines due to
   Ⓐ the size of the equipment that's needed.
   Ⓑ the way the substance is delivered.
   Ⓒ the material from which it's made.

33. What does Mark see as a key advantage of the nanopatch?
   Ⓐ It requires a lower dose.
   Ⓑ It triggers a faster reaction.
   Ⓒ It offers complete protection.

34. Mark thinks that the low cost of the nanopatch means that
   Ⓐ the range of diseases targeted could be expanded.
   Ⓑ more funding will be made available for research.
   Ⓒ lethal viruses will become a thing of the past.

35. What challenges in transporting needles and syringes does Mark identify?
   Ⓐ liquid evaporating in high temperatures
   Ⓑ maintaining constant temperatures
   Ⓒ the need for specialised vehicles

36. Papua New Guinea was chosen for the nanopatch trials mainly because
   Ⓐ its healthcare system required support.
   Ⓑ it has unreliable power supplies.
   Ⓒ it has a high rate of HPV.

Now look at extract two.

You hear a practice nurse called Bruce Wilkins giving a presentation about a project aimed at delaying the onset of dementia amongst older patients.

You now have 90 seconds to read questions 37–42.

37. Bruce's team decided to set up the project because they wanted
     (A) to contribute to research on dementia.
     (B) to influence public attitudes towards dementia.
     (C) to find ways of managing dementia more efficiently.

38. Why did Bruce encourage his patients to see an audiologist?
     (A) to enable more people to use their equipment properly
     (B) so that they could access a wider range of entertainment
     (C) because auditory impairment is linked to intellectual decline

39. Bruce says that learning a new language can benefit patients by
     (A) forming strong connections in the brain.
     (B) building confidence in acquiring expertise.
     (C) providing opportunities for social interaction.

40. What does Bruce say is the best thing about the activity groups his team have set up?
     (A) They reduce the risk of cardiovascular disease.
     (B) They encourage people to spend time outdoors.
     (C) They address many of the risk factors simultaneously.

41. In the immediate future, Bruce's team aims to
     (A) promote the project beyond the local area.
     (B) increase the scope of their own local project.
     (C) invite neighbouring practices to join their project.

42. How does Bruce feel about the outcomes of the project?
     (A) optimistic regarding its wider relevance
     (B) disappointed that it hasn't been taken more seriously
     (C) cautious about drawing any specific conclusions from it

That is the end of Part C.

You now have two minutes to check your answers.

That is the end of the Listening test.

Reading Sub-test

Part A

Time: 15 minutes

Look at the four texts, **A–D**, in the separate **Text Booklet** that follows.
For each question, **1–20**, look through the texts, **A–D**, to find the relevant information.
Write your answers on the spaces provided in the **Question Paper**.
Answer all the questions within the 15-minute time limit.
Your answers should be correctly spelled.

MRSA: Questions

Questions 1–7

For each question, **1–7**, decide which text (**A, B, C or D**) the information comes from. You may use any letter more than once.

In which text can you find information about

1. what to wear during the decontamination process? _____

2. the first signs of MRSA? _____

3. the people most likely to be affected by MRSA? _____

4. parts of the body in which MRSA infections may prove fatal? _____

5. settings and contexts where MRSA is likely to spread? _____

6. how much medication to administer? _____

7. how to ensure that equipment is not contaminated? _____

Questions 8–13

Answer each of the questions, **8–13**, with a word or short phrase from one of the texts. Each answer may include words, numbers or both.

8. Which type of MRSA is most responsive to antibiotics?

    _____

9. Which parts of the body carry the bacterium without producing symptoms?

    _____

10. What should take place before equipment is chemically disinfected or sterilised?

    _____

11. What can be used as an alternative to hot water and detergent for cleaning equipment?

    _____

12. Which type of MRSA is associated with hospitalisation?

    _____

13. What is highest dosage of clindamycin you can give a child?

    _____

Questions 14–20

Complete each of the sentences, **14–20**, with a word or short phrase from one of the texts. Each answer may include words, numbers or both.

14. You can administer _____ without needing to set up another IV.
15. MRSA is particularly dangerous when it spreads beyond the _____.
16. It is unacceptable to use _____ as a cleaning method before decontamination.
17. For more severe cases of MRSA, a minocycline dosage of _____ is necessary.
18. Linezoid should be administered at _____ intervals.
19. Gowns worn by staff performing an endoscopy should be of _____ material.
20. CA-MRSA has a tendency to result in abscesses and _____ at the area of infection.

End of Part A

This paper will be collected.

Reading Sub-test – Text Booklet: Part A

MRSA: Texts

Text A **What is MRSA?**

Methicillin-Resistant Staphylococcus Aureus (MRSA) is a bacterium that causes infections in different parts of the body. Although these are usually mild, superficial and can be treated successfully with proper skin care and antibiotics, they can be lethal.

Infections generally start as swollen, painful red bumps that might resemble pimples or spider bites, which can quickly turn into deep, painful abscesses that require surgical draining. Sometimes the bacteria remain confined to the skin, but they can also burrow deep into the body, causing potentially life-threatening infections in bones, joints, surgical wounds, the bloodstream, heart valves and lungs.

Associated issues:

- Resistant to most commonly used antibiotics – more difficult to treat than most strains of staphylococcus aureus, or staph
- Highly contagious
- Predominantly spread by direct physical contact
- Mostly carried on the skin or in the nose without causing any disease, a process known as colonisation

Text B **HA-MRSA versus CA-MRSA**

Parameter	HA-MRSA (Healthcare Associated)	CA-MRSA (Community Associated)
Typical patient	elderly, debilitated and/or critically or chronically ill	young/healthy, e.g. students, professional athletes, military
Infection site	often bacteraemia with no obvious infection focus. Surgical wounds, open ulcers, IV lines and catheter urines. May cause ventilator-associated pneumonia	predilection for skin and soft tissue, producing cellulitis and abscesses. May cause necrotising community-acquired pneumonia, septic shock or bone/joint infections
Transmission	within healthcare settings; little spread among household contact	community-acquired; may spread in families and sports teams
Clinical setting of diagnosis	inpatient setting, but increasingly infections in soft tissue and urine are occurring in primary care	in an outpatient or community setting
Medical history	MRSA colonisation; infection; recent surgery; admission to a hospital or nursing home; antibiotic use; dialysis; permanent indwelling catheter	no significant medical history or healthcare contact
Virulence of infecting strain	community spread is limited, PVL genes usually absent	community spread occurs easily. PVL genes often present, predisposing to necrotising soft tissue or lung infection
Antibiotic susceptibility	often multi-resistant resulting in limited choice of agents	generally susceptible to more antibiotics than HA-MRSA

Text C Antibiotic treatment

Administration	Antibiotic	Dosage
IV	Vancomycin	30 mg/kg (max 2 gm/24 hours)
	*Daptomycin (Cubicin)	4–6 mg/kg
	Linezolid (Zyvox)	600 mg 12-hourly
	Tigecycline (Tygacil)	100 mg x 1 then 50 mg 12-hourly
Oral	Trimethoprim-sulfamethoxazole (TMP-SMX)	160 mg/800 mg x 2 per day
		**320 mg/1600 mg x 2 per day
	Clindamycin (Cleocin)	150–300 mg 6-hourly; increase to 450 mg 6-hourly if severe infection
		Paediatrics: 3–6 mg/kg x 4 per day (max dose 450 mg)
	Tetracycline **or** doxycycline/minocycline (Dynacin/Minocin)	250 mg x 4 per day, increase to 500 mg 3–4 per day in severe infection

* administrated via existing IV (piggyback)

** patients weighing >100 kg / trauma-induced SSTI / immunosuppressed

Text D Procedures for decontamination of equipment

Protective clothing required:

Ward Areas: Aprons, disposable nitrile gloves, eye protection

SSD/Endoscopy/Urology: Waterproof gowns with long sleeves, disposable Nitrile or Nitrile & rubber gloves, protective footwear, eye protection, e.g. visors/goggles

Cleaning principles and methods:

Physical cleaning (i.e. not simple immersion) is an essential pre-requisite of chemical disinfection or sterilisation and should be undertaken when necessary, prior to any of the decontamination processes.

Detergents: Hot water, detergent and drying is the preferred method of decontamination for the vast majority of items. Detergent wipes may also be used.

The physical removal of all visible contamination reduces the number of relevant micro-organisms present but does not necessarily eradicate all micro-organisms. When cleaning equipment, check for signs of damage, e.g. to mattresses, pillows, cushions. If there are signs of damage report them to the nurse-in-charge who can initiate repair or disposal.

End of Part A

This test booklet will be collected.

In this part of the test, there are six short extracts relating to the work of health professionals. For questions 1–6, choose the answer (A, B or C) which you think fits best according to the text.

1. According to the memo, staff requiring a free flu vaccination must

    (A) have it done on site.

    (B) respond electronically.

    (C) be above a certain age.

Memo: To all hospital staff

Re: Staff flu vaccination programme

The staff influenza vaccination programme enables the hospital to keep running effectively during a flu outbreak when we are particularly busy. The offer of a free of charge quadrivalent flu vaccine to all staff has been extended. The following arrangements have been put in place in order to maximise uptake:

- Mass vaccination clinics have now ended. Please contact Occupational Health to arrange an appointment.
- An online form, which has been sent to your email inbox, must be completed and submitted beforehand. This will generate a reference number, which must be noted and brought to your appointment.
- Staff working in community settings or who are unable to attend an appointment due to shift rotations should contact Peer Immunisation.
- The above information applies to staff aged 18 and over only. Those who are 17 or younger may only receive their vaccine from Occupational Health, and will be granted time off shift to do so.
- Staff may also attend a community / high street pharmacy to get the flu vaccine privately. There will however be a charge, which cannot be reimbursed by the hospital.

2. The guidance for administering medication in care homes states that

    (A) timings should be strictly observed.

    (B) highly qualified staff should be employed.

    (C) disturbances should be kept to a minimum.

Medication in the care home

Staff should ensure that 'when-required' medicines are kept in their original packaging. The carer, prescriber and pharmacist should agree with the resident the most suitable time for administration, avoiding busy periods where possible. In order to avoid disruption during the medication round, planned staff breaks should not be scheduled, and more trained and skilled employees could be put on duty. The administration times could also be reviewed (for example, administering once-daily medicines at lunchtime rather than in the morning, if clinically appropriate).

Health professionals visiting the home to give residents medicine should make their record of administration available to care home staff, if requested.

3. The purpose of the email is to

    (A) update details given in an earlier message.

    (B) inform physicians about a new form of assessment.

    (C) explain when a new clinical procedure will be available.

Email

To: All Primary Care staff

Topic: Diabetic Eye Screening

This recently introduced service is designed to detect retinopathy at an early stage, thereby ensuring early treatment and preventing a deterioration in vision in 70–90% of sufferers. Primary carers should refer all patients who have a confirmed diagnosis of diabetes mellitus for screening. Those meeting the criteria will be invited for retinopathy screening within three months of registration. To ensure equity of service, clinics are arranged as close to the patient's primary care practice as possible.

The screening is straightforward and takes approximately 40 minutes. Following mydriasis, photographs of the retina are obtained using a specialist camera. Images are then assessed for the presence and severity of diabetic retinopathy. If sufficient levels are present, the patient will be referred to Ophthamology for further assessment.

4. The notice says that if the medicine refrigerator is not working,

    (A) there is a need to establish whether the contents may still be used.

    (B) relevant paperwork must be given to a senior member of staff.

    (C) potentially unsafe medicines should be destroyed.

Notice

In the event of this refrigerator breaking down, prompt arrangements for its repair should be made. Medicines should be placed in a bag marked **'Do not use'** and transferred to another medicine refrigerator, if available. Ensure the quarantined medicines are kept separate from the rest of the contents. If no alternative refrigerator is available, quarantine the medicines as above and leave the medicines in the malfunctioning refrigerator with the door closed. Note the maximum and minimum temperatures displayed on the refrigerator and check the monitoring form for when the refrigerator was last working properly.

Try to ascertain how long the medicines have been stored outside of the required temperatures. Record the names of the drugs and manufacturer and attempt to find out if the medicines are still safe to administer. Contact the medicines management team for further advice.

5. The extract from the guidelines tells us that as soon as a patient is confirmed missing,

   Ⓐ the entire site should be checked.

   Ⓑ the incident should be recorded in the log.

   Ⓒ a senior member of staff should be informed.

Missing patient procedure – initial search

If a patient is thought to be missing from an area, staff must initially and quickly ascertain whether the patient is attending another area of the hospital for treatment, or whether they are with a relative, carer or friend. The care plan should be consulted in order to establish factors likely to increase the patient's vulnerability, and known risks for the patient.

The search log should be consulted in order to ensure that all areas are formally investigated. A thorough search of the ward and department must then be undertaken to ascertain whether they have inadvertently been detained in a different room or area.

Once a patient is believed to be missing, the 'worst case' scenario must be assumed and the Missing Patient Procedure initiated, and the ward/department manager on duty must be alerted immediately.

6. The policy extract states that

   Ⓐ chaperones are usually the same gender as the patient.

   Ⓑ a note should be made of why a chaperone was necessary.

   Ⓒ urgent treatment must go ahead even if a chaperone is declined.

Offering a chaperone

If a patient requires an examination involving close proximity, physical contact, dim lighting or if the patient is vulnerable or at risk, a clear offer of a chaperone should be made. Whether the patient and doctor are the same sex is irrelevant; in this case the risk may be reduced but is by no means absent. If the patient does not accept, explain why a chaperone is necessary and re-offer. Although you may prefer not to proceed if you feel uncomfortable, in all emergency scenarios, patient safety should override the clinician's assessment of his or her own safety.

Presence or absence of a chaperone should be recorded in the patient's medical records. It is also advisable to document any doubts or reservations expressed by the patient and any reassurance offered. The records should make clear why the examination was required.

In this part of the test, there are two texts about different aspects of healthcare. For **questions 7–22**, choose the answer (**A, B, C** or **D**) which you think fits best according to the text.

Text 1: Medical Cannabis

The medicinal properties of the cannabis plant have been used by many cultures for thousands of years to treat a host of disorders. It is thought to have been used as early as 10,000 years ago in Taiwan as a source of fibre and later in China as food. This led to the discovery of its medicinal properties approximately 3,000 years ago, when it was mixed with rice wine to produce an anaesthetic. It was used for centuries in India as a remedy for dysentery, sunstroke and insomnia and the ancient Greeks used it to dress wounds and soothe inflammation. This impressive history would lead one to assume that we would be using it to its full potential today, yet cannabis has struggled to gain acceptance in modern medicine.

It was not until the mid-nineteenth century that interest in medical cannabis began to grow in the West. The Irish physician William Brooke O'Shaughnessy returned from India and introduced it to Western medicine in the 1830s and conducted experiments to treat muscle spasms, stomach cramps and general pain. This marked a short-lived period of scientific inquiry, although cannabis did become a mainstream medicine between 1850 and 1915, when it was widely used and easily obtained throughout the USA. However, what could have been the start of a golden period of scientific breakthroughs was about to be nipped in the bud by a period of prohibition.

The 1910s saw a surge in prohibition sentiments in the USA, as concerns rose regarding the social consequences of alcohol and narcotics abuse. In the decades that followed, states started passing prohibition laws. Eventually, the 1937 Marijuana Tax Act criminalised use of cannabis, despite protests from the American Medical Association, who argued that there was no evidence that it was dangerous and that it held potential for substantial medical use. This was quickly followed by the release of the film *Reefer Madness*, which warned against the dangers of smoking cannabis for recreational use, an entirely different matter. This shaped and misled mainstream attitudes for decades to come.

Further investigation effectively ground to a halt in 1970 when federal law in the USA classed cannabis as a schedule one substance, meaning it had high potential for abuse, no accepted medical use, and was unsafe. This led to a ludicrous 'catch 22' situation and introduced all kinds of obstacles to research. Apart from it being impossible to obtain a research license, the cannabis itself could not legally be acquired for studies into its potential benefits. However, several landmark events led to increased acceptance, including a US court case in 1976, which ruled that a man could legally be prescribed cannabis for treatment of glaucoma. Increasing pressure from lobbyists, the medical profession and patient groups eventually led to a relaxation of the laws. In 1995, California became the first individual US state to enact legislation permitting exemption, and today cannabis is legal for medicinal purposes in most American states.

Cannabis is now used in licensed products across the world to treat pain, spasticity, nausea, vomiting and appetite loss. However, the range of other conditions for which it has been claimed to be effective reads like a medical encyclopedia. One recent study analysed the data of 188 children with Autistic Spectrum Disorder (ASD), who had been treated with medical cannabis between 2015 and 2017. Over 30 percent reported a significant improvement and over 53 percent a moderate improvement. Compliance was 80 percent, which is in itself good evidence of satisfaction and indicates that cannabis is a well tolerated, safe and effective option for relieving symptoms and improving sufferers' quality of life. However, it was an observational study and parents of patients were self-selecting, so didn't necessarily constitute a representative patient sample. Although encouraging, outcomes may also have been biased by parents' opinions of the treatment. This indicates that more double-blind, placebo-controlled trials are crucial to enhance understanding of the effects on ASD patients.

Further case studies in my own clinic add to the increasing amount of supporting evidence. One 52-year-old male patient had been suffering from fibromyalgia for five years and spinal stenosis for over 20. He had tried numerous methods to control his pain, including physiotherapy, chiropractic, osteopathy and corticosteroid injections, yet none had been successful. He also had a diagnosis of irritable bowel syndrome (IBS) and anxiety. After 60 days of being prescribed 1g per day of medical cannabis administered via a vaporiser, the pain had reduced to a manageable 3/10, whereas during his initial in-clinic assessment he rated his pain score at 9/10. Another unexpected benefit was that he also reported his IBS practically going into remission and he had significantly reduced his use of painkillers. More research into the efficacy and side effects would mean that we could produce cannabis-based drugs tailored to particular conditions, taking into account the most beneficial method of ingestion.

Text 1: Questions 7–14

7.   In the first paragraph, it is suggested that the cannabis plant
   (A) is more important now than ever before.
   (B) wasn't initially cultivated for nutritional purposes.
   (C) has been used to treat a wide range of conditions.
   (D) has long been considered an unreliable form of medicine.

8.   What do we learn about cannabis in the West in the period 1830–1915?
   (A) It remained relatively unknown.
   (B) Its use wasn't officially sanctioned.
   (C) Its medicinal benefits were investigated.
   (D) It was treated with suspicion by doctors.

9.   In the second paragraph, the phrase 'nipped in the bud' is used to express the idea that
   (A) a therapeutic trial was largely unsuccessful.
   (B) an opportunity for further study was lost.
   (C) a new discovery changed attitudes.
   (D) a particular theory was disproved.

10. In the third paragraph, the writer suggests that prohibition of cannabis in the USA was due to
   (A) concern regarding increasing tobacco consumption.
   (B) an attempt to control a rise in anti-social activity.
   (C) fear caused by widespread misunderstanding.
   (D) a lack of financial resources to fund research.

11. The writer points out that legislation passed in the USA in 1970
   (A) made further studies practically impossible to carry out.
   (B) was a protective measure widely welcomed by doctors.
   (C) was a response to more harmful strains of the plant.
   (D) required scientists to use new study methods.

12. In the fifth paragraph, it is suggested that the study of children with ASD
    (A) didn't need to follow standard clinical procedures.
    (B) was limited by the participants' expectations.
    (C) was a particularly valid piece of research.
    (D) produced some surprising results.

13. The word 'This' in the fifth paragraph refers to
    (A) a widespread prejudice.
    (B) some compromised data.
    (C) some overestimated risks.
    (D) a lack of concrete evidence.

14. In the final paragraph, the case of the patient in the writer's clinic illustrates
    (A) that cannabis may be the only effective analgesia for fibromyalgia.
    (B) that the method of ingesting cannabis determines how effective it is.
    (C) how cannabis is most effective when taken over an extended period of time.
    (D) how cannabis can provide relief for several medical conditions simultaneously.

Text 2: Effective teamwork

Most healthcare professionals probably consider themselves good communicators, but the number of complaints and cases involving patient safety indicate that they could be overestimating themselves. Many assume that individual clinical excellence is enough to keep patients safe, but it is estimated that up to 98,000 deaths per year in the USA alone are caused by medical error. If embedded into practice, techniques and tools such as those included in the Team STEPPS (Team Strategies and Tools to Enhance Performance and Patient Safety) programme can help to lower this figure. The programme works on key competences, namely leadership, mutual support, situation awareness and communication.

Breakdowns in communication often occur in workplace cultures where there is a strong hierarchy and some team members are hesitant to raise concerns, share observations or ask for explanations. The most common reason for this is fear of being seen as incompetent or as a trouble-maker. A positive work culture is a key element of the STEPPS programme. Members of staff should be instructed to raise any concerns, however trivial. At handovers, proper introductions should be made and everyone should be made aware of what everyone else is doing. This is particularly important as nowadays many healthcare settings in western countries rely on temporary staff, which means teams are becoming increasingly fluid and can vary from day to day. Teams no longer know each other well and members may make incorrect assumptions about each other's expertise, knowledge and abilities, based on age, or other social markers. It also means that staff may feel unable to approach each other should a problem arise and mistakes could occur, such as tasks being repeated or overlooked.

Another key element of a positive culture is mutual support. Patient care should be prioritised at all times, and that means staff being able to ask for help without fear of being wrongly perceived. Effective teamwork means collaborating with each other, watching for signs of work overload in colleagues and offering help without resentment or judgement. This ethic is more likely to lead to a more rewarding work life and sparks a virtuous circle, as evidence shows that it also leads to higher quality healthcare.

Introducing a new approach to communication is core to the programme. Ironically, it is standard practice in many other professions for receivers of information to repeat it back to givers, yet this is not the case in healthcare. Implementing checklists and standard procedures has been proven to help avoid potentially harmful misunderstandings, as well as increasing staff awareness of their own vulnerability and potential for making errors. Oversights can also occur when staff have different perceptions of how the team is functioning and situations are developing. For example, if a highly-skilled nurse correctly makes a diagnosis of sepsis, but fails to escalate the case in time, the patient is put at risk. Losing awareness in key situations can easily happen on particularly busy wards and departments, as staff are often distracted from the wider picture. But systems such as 'huddles' can be put in place to address this issue. These briefings are popular as they're short, impromptu and address current concerns in specific areas, such as falls or pressure ulcers, as well as allowing staff to share their workload when they are feeling overwhelmed.

So, how effective is the approach in practice? Alice McCarthy manages a busy orthopaedic ward in an urban hospital. She found that six months after implementing Team STEPPS, although certain aspects of the programme had become embedded in staff communication and operation, others were no longer being used, mainly due to time constraints. It had also become clear that new behaviours and routines require constant reinforcement, a job that falls to the leader, says McCarthy, who believes sustainability to be as important as the initial roll out. 'Closed loop communication' or 'readback' – systems which involve ensuring the receiver has correctly understood information – were not used routinely, but rather when there was a perceived risk of misunderstanding.

However, a noticeable shift in culture had taken place. Certain methods had become firmly ingrained and support for the new approach was unanimous as it made staff feel more valued, supported and included. Furthermore, they felt they had been 'given permission' to act in the interest of those in their care. This had led to situations such as student nurses interrupting doctors and speaking up in meetings, rather than keeping quiet. Huddles were considered the most valuable tool, as they were a highly effective use of time. Another firm favourite was the SBAR (situation, background, assessment, recommendation), a communication structure which generates information that may otherwise be overlooked and enables the receiver to voice concerns, ask questions and make observations. Staff were committed to implementing Team STEPPS as they feel that the changes are genuinely making their day simpler and safer for all concerned.

Text 2: Questions 15–22

15. In the first paragraph, the writer says that rates of medical error can be reduced by
    - (A) increasing technical skills and knowledge.
    - (B) using rewards to build staff confidence.
    - (C) improving incident reporting procedure.
    - (D) adopting a systematic approach.

16. In the second paragraph, the writer suggests that a positive work culture results from encouraging staff to
    - (A) understand each other's roles and responsibilities.
    - (B) carry out tasks best suited to their expertise.
    - (C) ask senior colleagues to provide feedback.
    - (D) work for the same team regularly.

17. In the second paragraph, the word 'It' refers to
    - (A) a frequent tendency to cover up errors.
    - (B) a worryingly inflexible approach to workload.
    - (C) an increasing risk of prejudice amongst colleagues.
    - (D) a recent development which changes the way teams work.

18. The phrase 'virtuous circle' in the third paragraph is used to show
    - (A) how a helpful attitude towards colleagues improves standards of patient care.
    - (B) the importance of supporting colleagues when mistakes are made.
    - (C) that accepting help from colleagues leads to higher morale.
    - (D) how confiding in colleagues increases job satisfaction.

19. In the fourth paragraph, the writer uses the example of a diagnosis of sepsis to demonstrate
    - (A) the importance of individuals understanding the role of the whole team.
    - (B) that conflicts of interest are common when working under pressure.
    - (C) how reminding colleagues to stay on task can save lives.
    - (D) how a stable condition can quickly become critical.

20. In the fourth paragraph, the writer suggests that 'huddles' might be beneficial as they
    - (A) give staff the opportunity to share their feelings.
    - (B) are effective in more pressured environments.
    - (C) help to convey complex messages correctly.
    - (D) can be used in any healthcare setting.

21. Alice McCarthy's experience of the Team STEPPS approach was that

(A) some members of staff required further clarification.

(B) it was regarded with a degree of suspicion by the staff.

(C) it was impossible to maintain because managers were busy.

(D) some parts of the project were more successful than others.

22. In the final paragraph, it is suggested that the Team STEPPS approach gives junior staff more confidence to

(A) evaluate colleagues' performance.

(B) oversee aspects of ward management.

(C) make decisions regarding patient care.

(D) give advice to senior members of staff.

Writing Sub-test

Read the case notes and complete the writing task which follows.

Notes

You are a registered nurse in the hospital where Mrs Charlotte Price has been staying. She is now ready to be discharged with home visits from a community nurse.

Patient: Mrs Charlotte Price

Date of birth: 04/08/1932

Age: 86

Admission date: 2 December 2018

Discharge date: 4 December 2018

Diagnosis: Mild concussion (following fall at home)

Infected right toe (discovered during hospital stay)

Social background:

Lives alone – reluctant to receive visitors
Retired 19 years (postal worker)
2 children, both medical doctors; one lives overseas
Husband deceased – lung cancer 14 years ago
Owns dog – neighbour walks it occasionally
Lives in 3-bedroom house (owned by daughter)
Wants to live independently / refuses meal delivery service
Reluctant to visit GP
At risk of falls (walking stick, scoliosis, infected toe)

Medical history:

Severely infected right toe since approximately 9/18 (result of untreated ingrown toenail)
Conjunctivitis (02/02/18, 18/03/18 & 08/08/18) & Gastroenteritis (13/05/18) – both possibly associated with poor hygiene
Skin cancerous moles (x3) removed 2000
Knee replacement 1998
Whiplash injury in 1987

Medical background:

Hypertension (25 years)
Occasional drinker (whisky)
Heavy smoker (cigarettes x 40 /day)
Urinary incontinence
Mild scoliosis
Walks with stick

Medication:

Ramipril 10 mg (hypertension)
Ibuprofen (as required for scoliosis)
Amoxicillin 500 mg x 3 daily x 2 weeks (for toe infection)
(concerns re. compliance)

Nursing management and progress:

Concussion tests: Initial questioning (satisfactory), Finger-Nose-Finger test (satisfactory), CT scan (satisfactory)
48 hours precautionary admission, monitoring and rest – now ready to be discharged home
Right toe cleaned and dressed, antibiotics prescribed

Discharge plan:

- Home visits by community nurse twice a week
- Provide assistance with showering, dressing
- Provide advice re. hand and food hygiene
- Oversee treatment of right toe (clean, change dressings twice a week, encourage adequate rest)
- Monitor medication compliance (amoxicillin and ramipril)

Writing task

Using the information in the case notes, write a referral letter to Ms Leyla Ward, Community Nurse, Ashton Health Centre, Somerville, outlining the patient's current condition and needs for ongoing care.

In your answer:

- expand the relevant notes into complete sentences
- do not use note form
- use letter format

The body of the letter should be approximately 180–200 words.

Speaking Sub-test

ROLEPLAYER CARD NO 1   **NURSING**

Setting: Community Health Centre

Patient: You have recently become a parent and had your 40th birthday. You are thinking of giving up smoking and have come to talk to the Nurse Practitioner who is in charge of a support group to find out how it can help you. You are not sure whether to give up, and need help deciding.

Task:
- Explain that you smoke 'roll your own' cigarettes every evening, but only a few during the day. You love smoking and look forward to it all day, but it is expensive and you know it is bad for your and your baby's health.
- Express concern that the activities suggested often act as triggers for smoking.
- Show enthusiasm and say that the extra help may prevent you from returning to the habit as you have done in the past. Find out what the next step is.
- Agree to make an attempt and request a non-judgemental approach from the nurse and a weekly consultation.

CANDIDATE CARD NO 1   **NURSING**

Setting: Community Health Centre

Nurse: You are the Nurse Practitioner at a Community Health Centre and run a support group for patients who wish to give up smoking. Your patient is a 40-year-old, who is a new parent and has been smoking 20 cigarettes a day for 25 years.

Task:
- Find out as much as possible about the patient's smoking habit (quantity, products smoked, reasons for wanting to quit, etc.).
- Reassure the patient that you will be able to help and offer suggestions of other pleasant things that could be introduced and looked forward to in the evening (calling a friend, good movies, delicious meals).
- Suggest products to support giving up smoking (Champix tablets – reduce cravings, block rewarding effects of cigarettes; electronic cigarettes – satisfy cravings without the damaging effects of smoking).
- Recommend that you make a plan together. Help the patient identify triggers, rewards and benefits (e.g. more money, fewer health problems, better for baby, smell nicer). Help fix a date to give up, prescribe the Champix and suggest the patient buys and prepares an electronic cigarette before the agreed quit date.
- Agree to offer ongoing help and support.

ROLEPLAYER CARD NO 2   **NURSING**

Setting: Hospital Accident & Emergency Department

Patient: You have just fallen down the stairs at home and think you have broken one of your toes. It is black, swollen and at a strange angle. You cannot put weight on it or wear a shoe. You have come to the hospital for treatment. The Emergency department is very busy.

Task:
- Tell the nurse that you fell down the stairs and heard and felt your toe crack. You cannot bear weight or stand on it and are unable to wear a shoe. Ask whether it is broken.
- Ask for an X-ray as you have been waiting a long time.
- Reluctantly agree to the standard treatment and ask how quickly it will heal.
- Ask what to do if you are still in pain after a few weeks.

CANDIDATE CARD NO 2   **NURSING**

Setting: Hospital Accident & Emergency Department

Nurse: Your patient has come to the Emergency Department because he/she thinks he/she has broken a toe. It is a very busy weekend night and the patient has been waiting for some time.

Task:
- Find out what happened to the patient's foot and about their mobility/pain.
- Explain that you do not know whether it is broken but the procedure is the same for a badly hurt or broken toe (dress and tape it to the next toe).
- Explain that an X-ray would mean a very long wait and have no bearing on the treatment. The hospital is busy with emergencies tonight.
- Tell the patient that it usually takes about 6 weeks to heal if cared for properly. Provide information about caring for the toe (ice pack every 20 minutes for the first few days, elevate the foot above heart level to reduce swelling and pain, try to rest it).
- Reassure the patient that painkillers (ibuprofen and paracetamol) usually work, but to contact his/her GP if there is no improvement after 2–3 weeks.

Notes

Notes